D0789083

Heavenly Necromancers

Francesco Petrarca, *Das Glückbuch Beydes des Guten und Bösen*, 1539 (courtesy the Newberry Library).

Heavenly Necromancers
The Magician
in English Renaissance Drama

Barbara Howard Traister

University of Missouri Press
Columbia, 1984

Copyright © 1984 by The Curators of the University of Missouri
University of Missouri Press, Columbia, Missouri 65211
Printed and bound in the United States of America

Library of Congress Cataloging in Publication Data

Traister, Barbara H.
Heavenly necromancers.

1. English drama—17th century—History and criticism.
2. English drama—Early modern and Elizabethan, 1500–1600
—History and criticism. 3. Magicians in literature.
4. Magic—Europe—History—16th century. I. Title
PR658.M27T7   1984   822'.3'0935213   83–27433
ISBN 0–8262–0442–2

For Daniel, Rebecca, and Aaron

Acknowledgments

From my original observation that it was "passing strange" that Faustus, Friar Bacon, and Prospero, central characters in important Renaissance plays, were all magicians, this study has developed over a number of years. During those years I have accumulated a number of debts. R. Mark Benbow introduced me to the English Renaissance; had he not also introduced me to the excitement of involved teaching this book would have been finished sooner. Eugene M. Waith patiently encouraged and oversaw my studies of magic and drama from their beginnings. Albert Hartung read my discussion of medieval backgrounds and helped me negotiate not so familiar territory. Edna de Angeli, C. Robert Phillips, and Kathryn Reichard smoothed my translations. Maurice Charney and Barbara Mowat read the manuscript at various stages and offered invaluable advice. Maurice Shapiro gave me many helpful suggestions about sources for illustrations. James Baker, Steven Crow, Frank Hook, Jean Howard, Rosemary Mundhenk, John Vickrey, and Diane Willen provided good conversation and encouragement. Linda Allen—typist, babysitter, and friend—prodded me, not so gently, through the book's final revisions.

For help with the illustrations, I owe thanks to Jeannette Boothby of the Davison Art Center, Wesleyan University; Karen Chittenden of the Folger Shakespeare Library; Charles McNamara of Cornell University's Olin Library; Tobin Sparling of the Prints Room, The New York Public Library; Lucille Wehner of the Newberry Library; and Neda Westlake of the Van Pelt Library, University of Pennsylvania.

Lehigh University generously provided me a research leave and supported preparation of the manuscript.

Two people who were in many ways responsible for my completion of this study are no longer alive to read it. Rosalie L. Colie showed me how truly satisfying it is to follow an idea home. Aaron Traister, model of patient determination, assured me that even loiterers may eventually reach their destinations.

My children, Rebecca and Aaron, have lived around this study with patience and good humor. My husband did not type a single page. Nevertheless, my greatest debts are to him for bibliographical expertise, a pitiless editorial hand, and his steady confidence that, after all, this was a game worth the candle.

B. H. T.
June 1984

Contents

Contents

Heavenly Necromancers

Heinrich Khunrath, *Amphitheatrum sapientiae aeternae*, 1609 (courtesy University of Pennsylvania, Van Pelt Library).

I

Literary and Philosophical Background

Doctor Faustus, The Tempest, Friar Bacon and Friar Bungay—these very different plays have in common a major character who is, or claims to be, a magician. Scores of less well known plays from the Tudor and early Stuart period also have in their casts of characters a magician. Indeed, for some thirty years, the magician was a familiar stage figure; then, quite suddenly, he vanished from the stage, reappearing only in a few court masques or as a parody of himself, as a pseudo-magus. Exploration of this abrupt rise and fall of the stage magician forms part of the subject of this study.

The magician filled a symbolic role in many plays. He functioned as a man whose horizons were both limitless and limited, a self-contained paradox. The convergence of two views of the magician—one, popular and literary, perhaps most clearly expressed in the medieval romances,[1] the other, elitist and philosophical, best studied in the writings of the Italian

1. Other literary forms in addition to narrative romances undoubtedly influenced Renaissance dramatic portrayals of the magician. Barbara A. Mowat, "Prospero, Agrippa, and Hocus Pocus," suggests that commedia dell'arte scenarios, wizard legends, and classical portraits of witches and enchanters—as well as the nonliterary carnival juggler and illusionist—are background for Shakespeare's Prospero. Evelyn Bess Fieberling, in her detailed study of Italian pastoral and comic drama, "The Magician in Italian and English Renaissance Drama," discusses many characteristics of the magician that are echoed, or perhaps borrowed, by English dramatists. For my purposes, however, the medieval narrative romances provide the best examples of what the magician was like in literature before the Renaissance and supply a fairly thorough catalog of the main characteristics of the literary character.

neoplatonists—led to an ambivalence that made the magician
a potentially fascinating stage character. Brief exploration of
these traditions of magic leads to an understanding of how
the magician functions in individual plays and provides some
background for examining his association with magical com-
petitions, sensual delights of all sorts, and a master-of-
ceremonies image.

Interest in magic ran high during the Tudor and early Stuart
period. It is important to understand both the preconceptions
the audience was likely to have had about magicians and what
the playwrights themselves might have known and felt about
magic and the men who practiced it. The subject was seriously discussed in the court circles of Elizabeth and James, in
the English law courts, in church, and in philosophical works
imported from the Continent. Thanks largely to pioneering
studies of neoplatonic and hermetic magic emanating from
the Warburg Institute, since the 1950s literary scholars have
become increasingly aware of the influence of magic on Renaissance thought.[2] A somewhat different line of inquiry, not
yet as well explored, concerns how—if at all—that influence
was translated into literary, fictive creations.

In this spirit of inquiry, then, I examine both the historical
and literary climate of Renaissance magic in preparation for
close analysis of several important stage magicians. It is impossible to claim direct influence, except in a few unusual
cases, of the literary and historical materials on specific plays
or specific dramatists. However, the conflux of magical traditions in the early Renaissance helps explain how, for a few
playwrights, the magician figure focuses issues of human potential and limitation and raises the question of how much
man is permitted to know.

I.

Religious and philosophical attitudes toward magic were
varied and complex. Until the thirteenth century—and, officially, much later than that—the medieval church's position
was simple and straightforward: magic was to be avoided by

2. Among the most important contributions are D. P. Walker, *Spiritual
and Demonic Magic from Ficino to Campanella;* Frances A. Yates, *Giordano
Bruno and the Hermetic Tradition;* and I. R. F. Calder, "John Dee Studied as
an English Neoplatonist" (a microfilm copy is on deposit at Harvard University).

God-fearing men. God permitted magic partly to demonstrate, by its overthrow, his own miraculous powers,[3] and
partly as one of the pitfalls that appeared in the world as a
result of original sin.

But difficulties arose from such a sweeping condemnation
of magic, and uneasy perceptions of problems produced by the
complete rejection of magic appear in the writings of men
such as Albertus Magnus and Roger Bacon.[4] Of primary concern was the impossibility of drawing any clear line between
magic and science. To experiment, to inquire into the secrets
of the universe, was to come very close to involvement with
magic. Medicine and astronomy, for example, were frequently
associated with magic. Was the doctor practicing magic when
he prescribed herbs to be taken at the full moon? Was the man
who predicted the stars' influence on one's life or one's har-
vest a magician? Already uncomfortable questions in the thirteenth century, they grew increasingly vexing in ensuing centuries as the demand for scientific experiment increased.

> Physician, alchemist, professor all then wore the same long robe,
> which might mark either the scholar or the magician. And when
> so much of what was new in science was concerned with the very
> frontiers of knowledge, and dealt with almost unimaginable prob-
> lems of the organisation, complexity and harmony of Nature,
> scientists themselves were puzzled to know certainly where nat-
> ural philosophy stopped and mystic science began.[5]

Some philosophers attempted to clarify the issues by distinguishing demonic magic from what became increasingly well
known as natural magic (*magia naturalis*). Writers as early as
Roger Bacon distinguished between demonic ("not human")
magic and natural wonders, though most did not yet call the
natural wonders "magic":

> Nam licet naturae potens sit et mirabilis, tamen ars utens natura
> pro instrumento potentior est virtute naturali, sicut videmus in

3. See Saint Augustine, *The City of God*, trans. Marcus Dods, pp. 311–12
(10.8), for the explanation of the contest between Pharaoh's magi and Moses.
See also the contest between Saint Peter and Simon Magus in "The Acts of
Peter," *The Apocryphal New Testament*, trans. Montague Rhodes James, pp.
300–336.
    4. See Lynn Thorndike's *A History of Magic and Experimental Science*,
vols. 2 and 3, for discussions of the magical positions of these writers and
their peers.
    5. Marie Boas, *The Scientific Renaissance 1450–1630*, p. 166.

multis. Quicquid autem est praeter operationem naturae vel artis, aut non est humanum, aut est fictum et fraudibus occupatum.[6]

Granted that nature is powerful and wondrous, nevertheless, by using nature as its instrument, art is stronger than natural power, as we see in many things. Moreover, whatever is beyond the operation of nature or of art is either not human, or is invented and usurped by fraud.

Gradually the linguistic distinction between natural and demonic magic became familiar (though the church never officially accepted it), and when, in the mid-sixteenth century, Giambattista della Porta used the phrase *magia naturalis* to title his collection of remedies and superstitions, it was a well-known phrase.

But the verbal distinction between natural and demonic magic created new difficulties: how was the natural magician to be regarded? A familiar example of the problem arises from the biblical account of the three magi visiting the Christ child. The magi foretell the birth and then confirm its occurrence by reading the heavens; yet they are clearly positive figures. Writers against magic were always rather embarrassed about this passage and developed numerous ingenious ways of getting around the problem. Albertus Magnus turned to etymology to solve the difficulty and at the same time worked in his distinction between good and evil magicians:

Magi enim grammatice magni sunt. . . . Nec sunt Magi malefici sicut quidam male opinantur. Magus enim et Mathematicus et Incantator et Maleficus sive Necromanticus et Ariolus et Aruspex et Divinator differunt. Quia Magus proprie nisi magnus est, qui scientiam habens de omnibus necessariis et effectibus naturarum coniecturans aliquando mirabilia naturae praeostendit et educit.[7]

For Magi are, grammatically speaking, great men. . . . Nor are Magi evildoers, although they are often thought ill of in this way. For a Magus and a Mathematician and a Charmer and an Evil-doer, or a Necromancer and Seer and Haruspex and Diviner all differ. Since a Magus is surely nothing unless a great man, knowledgeable and making guesses about nature from all its requirements and effects, he often demonstrates and teaches nature's wonders.

But such distinctions had to be repeated by each writer who dealt with magic. Interestingly, no one seems to have doubted

---

6. Roger Bacon, "Epistola Fratris Rogerii Baconis de secretis operibus artis et naturae et de nullitate magiae," p. 523.
7. Quoted in Thorndike, *History of Magic*, 2:554.

that there was demonic magic. Rather, all efforts were directed at proving that "good" or natural magic did, or did not, exist.

As late as the mid-seventeenth century some writers were still trying to define *magic* and *magus* and distinguishing between acceptable and unacceptable types. But many Renaissance commentators seemed confident in the treatment of natural magic:

> Magick is taken amongst all men for Wisdom, and the perfect knowledge of natural things: and those are called Magicians, whom the Latines call Wise-men, the Greeks call Philosophers. . . . There are two sorts of Magick: the one is infamous, and unhappie, because it hath to do with foul spirits, and consists of Inchantments and wicked Curiosity; and this is called Sorcery . . .[which] stands meerly upon fancies and imaginations, such as vanish presently away, and leave nothing behinde them. . . . The other Magick is natural; which all excellent wise men do admit and embrace, and worship with great applause; neither is there any thing more highly esteemed, or better thought of, by men of learning.[8]

Words like *worship* as Porta's anonymous translator used it in the statement above (Porta himself used the phrase *excipit, colit, & veneratur*) had the potential to get their author into a good deal of trouble with the church, but such effusions demonstrate to what heights admiration for natural magic rose in some circles.

In theory, demonic and natural magic were distinguished by a single incontrovertible difference—demonic magic was performed with the aid of spirits; natural magic was not. But in time, *natural magic* became a more general term, covering more territory than had originally been permitted it. The people most responsible for the alterations in the meaning of *natural magic* were a group of Italian philosophers who revived neoplatonism during the latter half of the fifteenth century. The magical theories of this group had some influence on the way magic is portrayed in English Renaissance literature.

The revival of neoplatonism provided its adherents with a belief in a general animating spirit (*spiritus* or *anima mundi*) operative in the universe. This spirit in turn infused souls or spirits into other parts of the creation, usually the planets and

---

8. Giambattista della Porta, *Natural Magick in XX Bookes*, pp. 1–2.

other heavenly bodies. This belief probably originated from Plato's *Timaeus*:

> [And when he framed the universe he distributed] souls equal in number to the stars, and assigned each soul to a star; and having there placed them as in a chariot, he showed them the nature of the universe, and declared to them the laws of destiny, according to which their first birth would be one and the same for all.[9]

As this doctrine of world soul emerged, having been filtered through Plotinus and influenced by hermetic writings, it was seen as a source of tremendous cosmic energy and wisdom that man, under very special conditions, might be permitted to tap. Neoplatonists had individual theories about how one might tap into this suprarational wisdom and power, but most subscribed to the general idea that, by purifying himself of earthly ties and steadily pursuing wisdom and knowledge, man could lift himself above the concerns of the sublunar world and participate in knowledge of cosmic affairs. One of the most famous expressions of belief in man's ability to ascend to a semidivine state is Pico della Mirandola's *Oration on the Dignity of Man*: "It will be within your power to rise, through your own choice, to the superior orders of divine life."[10] And Giordano Bruno, often far less restrained than Pico, sang in the poem that introduces *On the Infinite Universe and Worlds*:

> Henceforth I spread confident wings to space;
> I feel no barrier of crystal or of glass;
> I cleave the heavens and soar to the infinite
> And while I rise from my own globe to others
> And penetrate ever further through the eternal field
> That which others saw from afar I leave far behind me.[11]

Not only is this an expression of Bruno's cosmography; it also suggests the potential that Bruno believed man had to transcend his own globe and mentally explore "far other worlds and other seas."

But, of course, it was not granted to every man to gain such wisdom. Like other writers on magic, the neoplatonists jeal-

9. In *The Dialogues of Plato*, trans. B. Jowett, 3:728.
10. *Renaissance Philosophy I: The Italian Philosophers*, ed. and trans. Arturo B. Fallico and Herman Shapiro, p. 144.
11. In *Giordano Bruno: His Life and Thought*, ed. and trans. Dorothea Waley Singer, p. 249.

ously guarded their magical secrets, carefully limiting those who could be expected to attain communication with the heavens to a select group of initiates. Certainly not all neoplatonists subscribed to Pico's ideas about magic or even to Marsilio Ficino's milder views. But those who did concern themselves with magic usually believed that only the magus, the rare wise man, could accomplish contact with the infinite: "As the farmer weds his elms to the vines, so the *magus* weds earth to heaven—the lower orders, that is, to the endowments and powers of the higher," stated Pico in the *Oration*.[12]

Neoplatonists called magic that performs the synthesis of the earthly with the heavenly *natural magic* but gave the term a significance at odds with its original meaning. If man's ascent to divine wisdom was purely the result of his goodness and intense study, then the meaning of the term remained essentially unchanged. But most neoplatonists, not content to have man do all the work, felt the need for means to attract (or even to compel) the planetary spirits to visit the magician. Ficino, for example, developed theories of how to attract planetary daemons (to be carefully distinguished from "demons," evil spirits) by the use of music, particular words similar to incantations, special colors, and perfumes. These sensual lures were designed to draw spirits that a recent commentator on Ficino's magic, D. P. Walker, described as "like men without earthly bodies who live in the heavenly spheres; they perform the function of transmitting celestial influences; they can, being both soul and spirit, act both on man's spirit and his soul."[13] The major difference between such "spiritual magic"[14] and truly demonic or devilish magic seems to be that Ficino intended to attract benign angelic spirits to influence his own disposition rather than evil spirits who would perform malevolent feats or interfere with the lives of other people.

Of the writers who shared Ficino's belief in planetary daemons or held more extreme beliefs, a few admitted to something more in their art than natural magic. Agrippa distinguished between natural and "ceremonial" magic, the latter

12. *Renaissance Philosophy I*, p. 166.
13. Walker, *Spiritual and Demonic Magic*, p. 47.
14. Walker labels Ficino's magic "spiritual magic" (ibid., p. 53) but seems to identify it with natural magic, an example of the confusing nomenclature of the subject.

involving rituals and special ceremonies for getting in touch with spirits.[15] All ceremonial magic is dangerous, he warned, but he went on to distinguish two kinds—"goetic" and "theurgic." Goetic magic, the calling up of evil spirits, is, he admitted, truly commerce with the devil and is as reprehensible as the opponents of magic claim. Theurgy, on the other hand, is the calling of angelic or planetary spirits and, though dangerous, is very attractive.[16] Tommaso Campanella, writing in the seventeenth century and thus possessed of a latecomer's perspective on the changes in theories about magic, distinguished three kinds: diabolic, natural, and "divine," the last a kind of heavenly gift to those who have practiced natural magic in a spirit of reverence and piety.

> Now I affirm that there is divine magic: magic that man can neither understand nor employ without the grace of God.... There is natural magic, as that of the stars, and that of medicine and physics, with religion added to give faith to those who hope for favors from these sciences; and there is diabolical magic for those who, by the art of the devil, seem, to those who do not understand, to do marvelous things.... Natural magic, then, stands between: and those who exercise it with piety and reverence for the Creator, frequently come to be elevated to the supernatural kind of magic, thus participating in magic of a higher form.[17]

As must be evident, the study of Renaissance magical theory is enormously complicated by the imprecision of terminology and by variations in kinds of magic, many of which seem to overlap or duplicate one another. Discussions of magic are further obfuscated by a deliberate vagueness on the part of philosophers about their specific beliefs. Contemporary examples of the church's power over heretics warned writers against being too outspoken about their magical ideas. So magicians denied or apologized for their magical theories, shrouding their ideas in seemingly innocuous contexts. D. P. Walker has commented on the difficulty of deciphering what Ficino actually believed about magic from the extremely cautious and often ambiguous way in which he wrote of it;[18]

15. For a discussion of ceremonial magic and its relationship to the Christian mysteries, see ibid., pp. 153–56.

16. Henry Cornelius Agrippa, *Of the Vanitie and Vncertaintie of Artes and Sciences*, trans. Ja[mes] Sa[nford], fols. 57^r–59^v.

17. Campanella, "On the Sense and Feeling in All Things and on Magic," in *Renaissance Philosophy I*, p. 374.

18. Walker, *Spiritual and Demonic Magic*, pp. 45–53.

Agrippa apologized for and virtually retracted his most outspoken book on magic, De occulta philosophia, even before
he published it. The book was completed in 1510, the year
Agrippa visited England, but circulated in manuscript until
published in 1533. In 1526, evidently as a precaution against
charges that might be made against the positive comments
about magic in De occulta, Agrippa published De incertitudine et vanitate scientiarum declamatio inuectiua, which re-
pudiated many of the views on magic contained in the yet-to-
be-published De occulta.[19] Bruno's allegorical obscurity is undoubtedly also due in part to his fear of being too outspoken.
To some degree, of course, magical theorists used deliberate
obscurity as a tactic to keep from the uninitiated wisdom that
they neither deserved nor could handle. These philosophers
were not disposed to cast their magical pearls before swine.

Adding to the confusion surrounding magic is the adoption
by leading neoplatonists of much theory that was not neoplatonic in origin. Ficino, one of the earliest and perhaps the
most influential of the philosophers who espoused neoplatonism, was deeply influenced by hermetic material that he
translated and published at the behest of Cosimo de Medici.
Thought to be ancient Egyptian writings antedating Moses,
the assorted occult treatises ascribed to Hermes Trismegistus
influenced theories abut magic, medicine, and astronomy for
nearly two centuries until Casaubon revealed their spurious
nature in the mid-seventeenth century. Thus, even in Ficino's
best-known work, De triplici vita (1489), his neoplatonism
was adulterated by occult material from other sources.[20] Similarly, Pico della Mirandola added to the neoplatonic elements
of his magical theory a good deal of cabalistic belief in the
importance of words and language for contacting spirits. This
cabalistic element was passed to later writers mixed with Pico's neoplatonic beliefs.[21] Clearly, to talk of neoplatonic
magic is to talk of a general magical theory—philosophically

19. For further information on the complex publishing history of Agrippa's
works and on Agrippa's astonishing career, see Charles G. Nauert, Agrippa
and the Crisis of Renaissance Thought.
20. Yates, Giordano Bruno, pp. 1–61, presents a clear explanation of how
hermetic writings, through the translations of Ficino, influenced Italian philosophers. For more detail on the hermetic texts, see R. P. Festugière, La Révélation D'Hermès Trismégiste, vol. 1.
21. Yates, Giordano Bruno, pp. 94–102.

based, seeking wisdom and knowledge, recognizing the existence of extraterrestrial spirits whose influences may be felt
and, to an extent, controlled by man—not of a rigid set of
beliefs conforming strictly to the tenets of neoplatonism.

With his discussions of how to attract planetary spirits, Ficino was at first the most important theorist of neoplatonic
magic. But he did not go far enough with his magic to qualify
even as a theurgic magician. Ficino's theory involved no compulsion. He merely wanted, through various ceremonies, to
prepare the operator to be receptive to planetary spirits and
perhaps to attract—never to compel—the spirits to visit the
anxiously waiting operator. It was the revision of Ficino's
ideas by such men as Agrippa and Paracelsus, who added cabalistic and expanded already present hermetic elements, that
gave the magician not only attraction for but also power over
both good and evil spirits and produced the strong and notorious kinds of magic. Ficino's reputation in his own time does
not seem to have been that of a magician, and he was not
persecuted by the church for heretical practices. Agrippa and
Paracelsus, on the other hand, were known primarily as magicians and only secondarily as philosophers. What is so attractive and so dangerous about the strong magic of someone
like Agrippa is the power it grants to man, who is able, if he
is a properly initiated magus, to compel spirits to obey him.
Agrippa would have quickly emended the preceding sentence
to read: "the good, angelic spirits to obey him," but clearly
the emendation was often forgotten by Agrippa's contemporaries. The line between goetic and theurgic magic was often
blurred or omitted. Campanella, commenting on Agrippa,
said that he rejected magic that subjects man to the devil but
kept the magic by which man subjects the devil and con-
strains him to do his will.[22] And Pico, making the distinction
between magicians who are controlled (having made a pact
with or a promise to evil spirits) and those who control, made
a similar claim for the magician's power over evil spirits: "For
just as that first form of magic makes man a slave and a pawn
of evil powers, so the second form makes him their ruler and
lord."[23] This promise of rule over spirits, whether angelic or
demonic, tantalized philosophers and dramatists alike, and

22. Ibid., p. 384, n. 1.
23. "Oration," *Renaissance Philosophy I*, p. 165.

much of the magic discussed in the Renaissance involved the compulsion of spirits, a far cry from Ficino's original, mild theories of daemonic attraction.

What is important in all this is to recognize the very real philosophical concern with magic in the fifteenth and sixteenth centuries. Philosophers who were, at least to some degree, known and respected were writing seriously about magic and, under the label *natural magic*, were talking positively about a magic that involved communication with spirits. The magus, in some circles, was regarded as a man of great wisdom, to be respected as a superior man among men. Indeed, the magus became in some writers' minds a symbol for the infinite possibilities that then seemed open to man. Through magic, some felt, man could climb to God (granted divine grace, of course) rather than simply mark time waiting out a weary life on earth. Eugenio Garin summarized this view of the magician as possessor of tremendous potential:

> True magic was defended because it was work which made use of the given forms in order to construct an ascending chain of Being. Ceremonial magic, on the other hand, was attacked because it was work which led into the abyss of sin and chaos. In both cases, however, the ambiguous reality of man consisted in the fact that he was a possibility, an opening through which one could rejoice in the inexhaustible richness of Being. He was not a being, defined once and for all, immobile and secure, but was always precariously balanced upon the margin of an absolute risk.[24]

The magician could damn himself, as Faustus does, but there was also a possibility that he could lift himself into the sphere of immortal spirits or at least call some of those spirits down to him. A character with such potential might well prove attractive to a dramatist.

Nonetheless, little evidence has been offered that this philosophical view of magic, based primarily in Italy, had any effect on the writers of sixteenth-century England. Though England was not in the mainstream of the neoplatonic revival, the movement clearly had some influence on English letters. Many of the seminal magical texts had been translated into English by the end of the sixteenth century, and others were

24. *Science and Civic Life in the Italian Renaissance,* trans. Peter Munz, p. 153.

available to English readers in their original languages.[25] In addition to the written word, England had other contacts with philosophic magicians. As evidence of this, I would like to look briefly at three men—Agrippa, Giordano Bruno, and John Dee—all three magicians or magical theorists, all deeply influenced by neoplatonism, and all well known or active for a while in England.

The earliest of the three is Henry Cornelius Agrippa (1486–1535), a German physician, a correspondent of Erasmus, and contemporary with the Englishmen Thomas More and John Colet (who was for a short time Agrippa's teacher). The question of Agrippa's contribution to the history of magic and science is much debated—Thorndike, for example, labeled him a "wayward genius" and "intellectual vagabond,"[26] whereas Charles Nauert maintained that he was a vital and influential figure in the history of magic.[27] What seems agreed upon, however, is the breadth of his reputation and the popularity of his works, attested to in part by numerous editions of his *De occulta philosophia* in the sixteenth and seventeenth centuries.

While Agrippa was not wholly a neoplatonist and, indeed, leaned rather more toward Aristotelianism in his later years, he did base much of his magical theory upon the neoplatonic magic set forth by Ficino (passages from *De Triplici Vita* are

25. *A Short-Title Catalogue of Books Printed in England, Scotland, & Ireland and of English Books Printed Abroad 1475–1640*, ed. A. W. Pollard and G. R. Redgrave, records extensive publication by English presses of Bruno's works (six were in print by 1585). Agrippa's *De incertitudine* received an English translation in 1569; some of Paracelsus had been translated by the 1580s; and minor, nonmagical works by both Pico and Porta had been published by 1585. The catalogs of two of the greatest English libraries of the late sixteenth century indicate, moreover, that most of the principal neoplatonic magical texts were present in England, though in Continental editions. The library of John Dee, for example, possessed the complete works of Ficino; Pico's works, including the *Conclusiones*; over one hundred items by Paracelsus; Agrippa's *De occulta* and *De incertitudine*; and much else related to magic (see Peter J. French, *John Dee: The World of an Elizabethan Magus*, p. 50, for a summary of the library's magical texts). Though Dee's holdings may be explained as exceptional because of Dee's own concern for magic, the library of Lord Lumley, who showed no particular interest in magic, records nearly the same magical holdings: Ficino's hermetic translations as well as his *De triplici vita*; several works by Pico; items by Paracelsus; and both the 1533 and 1550 editions of Agrippa's *De occulta* as well as copies of *De incertitudine* and of its 1569 English translation (see *The Lumley Library: The Catalogue of 1609*, ed. Sears Jayne and Francis R. Johnson).

26. Thorndike, *History of Magic*, 5:127.

27. Nauert, *Agrippa*, p. 230.

sometimes quoted verbatim by Agrippa, though with no acknowledgment given to Ficino) and also borrowed much, including some cabalistic elements, from Pico.[28] He believed
that the magus was able to gain contact with angelic spirits
through the construction of images, but he added that such
images were useless "unless they be so brought to life that
either a natural, or celestial, or heroic, or animistic, or demonic, or angelic power is present in them or with them."[29]
Nauert explained, "The soul of the magician who employs
these images draws its ability to use them not from reason but
from a mystical ascent aided by ceremonial preparation and
dependent for its consummation on divine illumination."[30]

Despite numerous denials that he advocated theurgic
magic, Agrippa could not hide his interest in it. In the middle
of a stern warning about the dangers of ceremonial magic,
Agrippa gives himself away by breaking into the first person
as he speaks of the power of theurgy:

> Many thinke that *Theurgie* is not prohibited, as who saithe it were
> gouerned by good Angels, and by the diuine power, whereas yet
> oftentimes vnder the name of God, & the Angels it is bounde with
> wicked deceites of the Diuels, for not onely with naturall forces,
> but with certaine solemnities & ceremonies also, we winne and
> drawe vnto vs heauenly thinges, and thorowe them the diuine ver-
> tues.[31]

Perhaps it is not surprising that, despite his attempts to dis-
approve of all ceremonial magic, Agrippa's reputation as a
black magician grew.

Agrippa's influence was perhaps felt more in the worlds of
art and literature than in the work of his fellow philosophers
(which may in part account for Thorndike's scorn). For example, Erwin Panofsky has suggested that Agrippa's brand of
neoplatonism in *De occulta* is the primary literary source for
Albrecht Dürer's famous *Melancholia I*.[32] In England, Agrippa's name was well known to men of letters. In 1510, the year
in which he completed the manuscript of *De occulta*, Agrippa
visited England, and this trip may have helped to spread his
reputation in that country. By 1569 his *De vanitate* had found

28. For a detailed look at Agrippa's debts to Ficino and Pico, see ibid., pp.
122–25.
29. Quoted in ibid., p. 202.
30. Ibid., p. 202.
31. Agrippa, *Of the Vanitie*, f. 59^{r-v}.
32. *The Life and Art of Albrecht Dürer*, pp. 168–71.

an English translator who attests to Agrippa's magical reputation in his preface: "For it is saide, and his workes testifie
the same, that he exercised the Arte Magicke, and therein
farre excelled all other of his time."[33] John Dee, whose seven-
thousand-volume library was perhaps England's best, owned
two editions of the *De occulta*: the 1533 first edition and the
1550 edition, which had appended a spurious fourth book that
made Agrippa seem a much more radical and goetic magician
than the original three books suggest. Dee was evidently not
only an owner but also a reader of Agrippa's book, since he
cited it on at least one occasion.[34] Among many English literary references to Agrippa[35] is Thomas Nashe's portrayal of
him as a trickster: bringing back Tully for Erasmus to see,
showing the Earl of Surrey his love in a magic glass, and displaying perfect memorization of a two-thousand-book library.[36] The most famous reference to Agrippa occurs, of
course, in Marlowe's picture of the goetic magician:

> 'Tis magic, magic, that hath ravish'd me.
> Then, gentle friends, aid me in this attempt,
> And I, that have with concise syllogisms
> Gravell'd the pastors of the German church,
> And made the flowering pride of Wittenberg
> Swarm to my problems as the infernal spirits
> On sweet Musaeus when he came to hell,
> Will be as cunning as Agrippa was,
> Whose shadows made all Europe honour him.[37]

Agrippa's reputation seems to have been twofold: he was
known as a goetic magician and a learned philosopher. Sidney,
who used Agrippa's *De vanitate* in his *Defense of Poesie*,
seems to regard him as a philosopher and makes no mention
of him as a magician. The duality of Agrippa's reputation appears in Sanford's preface, in which he first remarks how
much Agrippa knew and how wise he was and then goes on
to recount the story of Agrippa's black dog, a demon disguised, which Agrippa on his deathbed accused of having

---

33. *Of the Vanitie*, trans. James Sanford, sig. *iii^v.
34. "Mathematicall Preface," *The Elements of Geometrie of the most auncient Philosopher Euclide of Megara*, trans. Sir Henry Billingsley, sig. Ciiii^r.
35. A. C. Hamilton, "Sidney and Agrippa," pp. 152–53, lists a number of
English literary references to Agrippa.
36. "The Vnfortunate Traveller," *The Works of Thomas Nashe*, ed. Ronald
B. McKerrow, 2:252–55.
37. Christopher Marlowe, *Doctor Faustus*, ed. John D. Jump, 1.1.109–17.

damned him and which then promptly ran and drowned itself
in the river.[38] A similar ambivalence between philosophical
and practicing magician marks many of the magicians who
appeared on the Elizabethan stage.

Thus, while there is little evidence that English writers
were familiar with the magical theories of Ficino and Pico, a
goodly number of them had probably heard of Agrippa. If neoplatonic magic had not already found students in England,
Agrippa's works and the later visit of Giordano Bruno (1548–
1600) may have aroused interest in philosophical magic.

Bruno's visit to England in 1583 seems to have been more
of an event than Agrippa's earlier sojourn. While there, he
published two books, one dedicated to the French ambassador
and the other to Philip Sidney, and participated in a philosophical debate at Oxford, where—one spectator scornfully
noted—he quoted great chunks from Ficino without giving
him any credit.[39] The debate left Bruno contemptuous of the
Oxford "pedants" and apparently did not give the faculty
there a much higher opinion of him. More positive, however,
was his acquaintance with Sidney (who seems involved in one
way or another with several magicians, for he was a friend of
John Dee and a participant in his study circle, the subject of
which was probably neoplatonism).[40] There is no evidence
that Dee and Bruno ever met, but Sidney must have provided
a mutual contact, so that they were at least aware of one another's interests. Though Sidney undoubtedly knew some of
Bruno's works, there is no certainty that he knew much or
anything about his magic, since Bruno's treatises specifically
on magic, De magia and De vinculis in genere, were probably
not composed until after Sidney's death and were not published until the nineteenth century.

Perhaps partly for this reason, Bruno did not have the same
magical reputation as Agrippa, and only in fairly recent scholarship have his magical interests received emphasis. Much of
Bruno's magic derived from Agrippa's De occulta, though he
omitted the angels that Agrippa insisted can be summoned by
theurgic magic. Instead Bruno envisioned an ascending scale
for the magician to mount: "From sense to elements, demons,

38. Of the Vanitie, trans. James Sanford, sig. *iii^v.
39. Yates, Bruno, pp. 208–9.
40. Richard Deacon, John Dee, p. 91. Yates also mentions this study circle
(Bruno, pp. 187–88).

stars, gods, thence to the soul of the world or the spirit of the universe, and from thence to the contemplation of the one simple Optimus Maximus, incorporeal, absolute, sufficient in itself."[41] Since reaching the demons is one of the early steps in the ascent, Bruno seems to believe unabashedly in demonic magic.

How much of Bruno's magical belief was in evidence to his English friends cannot be determined. Some scholars believe that Bruno's English contacts were limited to a small circle and that his works were little known in England until years after his visit.[42] Others seem almost overanxious to find evidence of his influence in literary works of the period. Yates has speculated that the character Berowne in *Love's Labour's Lost* is modeled on Bruno, and A. W. Ward in his 1887 edition of *Friar Bacon and Friar Bungay* suggested that the magical contest in that play may reflect Bruno's Oxford debate.[43] Such conjectures are interesting but speculative. What can be ascertained is that Bruno, an outspoken believer in neoplatonic magic, was present and publishing in England and evidently acquainted with English literary figures. He provides another means by which knowledge of neoplatonic magic may have entered England.

Even more familiar to English writers might have been their countryman John Dee (1527–1608). Philosopher, scientist, book collector, consultant to the royal navy, adviser to Queen Elizabeth, and acquaintance of Philip Sidney, Dee was also a practicing magician and alchemist. In fact, he left written transcriptions of conversations with angelic spirits whom he had summoned with the help of the medium Edward Kelley.

Dee was a neoplatonist,[44] though his theories contained elements from other philosophical schools as well. Certainly his ideas on the intellectual quest for wisdom sound familiar.

> Thus, can the Mathematicall minde, deale Speculatiuely in his own Arte: and by good meanes, Mount aboue the cloudes and sterres; And thirdly, he can, by order, Descend, to frame Naturall thinges to wonderfull vses: and when he list, retire home into his

41. Yates, *Bruno*, pp. 264–65.
42. F. R. Johnson, *Astronomical Thought in Renaissance England: A Study of English Scientific Writings from 1500 to 1645*, p. 168, approvingly cites Oliver Elton, "Giordano Bruno in England," *Modern Studies* (London, 1907), pp. 1–36, on this point.
43. Yates, *Bruno*, pp. 356–57. She refers to Ward's suggestion on p. 210.
44. See Calder, "John Dee Studied as a Neoplatonist."

owne Centre: and there, prepare more Meanes, to Ascend or Descend by: and all, to the glory of God, and our honest delectation in earth.[45]

Dee's library contained works by both Pico and Ficino, and his writings show evidence of their influence, yet his magic most resembles that of Agrippa. Like Agrippa, Dee believed that to practice the highest form of magic, "Thaumaturge or divine magic," one must seek "communion with goode angels by purifyinge of the soul."[46] What is unusual about Dee is his interest in doing what he theorized about. Notice in the excerpt quoted above that there is a descent mentioned as well as an ascent, and all is for our "delectation in earth." Dee evidently intended that the wisdom gathered from the mystical ascent would be put to use in the natural world. Eugene Rice in *The Renaissance Idea of Wisdom* speaks of a debate over two conflicting views of wisdom: *sapientia* or contemplative wisdom and *scientia* or practical, utilitarian wisdom.[47] Dee seems to combine these two views of wisdom in ways the Italian theorists did not. (Ficino is something of an exception, perhaps, for he hoped to use the wisdom he gained from spiritual communications in his medical practice.) Dee's journals and diary[48] indicate that he tried and believed he had succeeded in communicating with the spirits, something other magicians had theorized about but left no record of actually trying. In addition, Dee committed himself and his family to several years in Europe, primarily at the court of Rudolph II, by whom he was hired for the express purpose of producing the philosopher's stone. Though the visit was ultimately a fiasco, Dee's initial commitment to it suggests his confidence in his ability to produce material good from his magical activities.[49]

Until recently, Dee's reputation rested largely on tales of his

45. "Preface to Euclid," sig. Ciii^v.
46. Quoted in Deacon, *John Dee*, p. 41. He gives no source for the Dee quotation.
47. Pp. 73–74.
48. *The Private Diary of Dr. John Dee and the Catalogue of His Library of Manuscripts*, ed. James Orchard Halliwell; Meric Casaubon, *A True and Faithful Relation of What Passed Between Dr. John Dee and Some Spirits*.
49. R. J. W. Evans, *Rudolph II and His World: A Study in Intellectual History, 1576–1612*, presents a fascinating study of Rudolph's court, perhaps the most humanistic and the most interested in the occult to be found in sixteenth-century Europe. For a discussion of Dee and Kelley's visit, see pp. 218–28.

communication with angels, and often the other sides of his
varied career were ignored.[50] He was first suspected of being a
conjuror after he staged Aristophanes's *Peace*, in which an
elaborate mechanical beetle appeared to fly. The stagecraft
was so ingenious that his audience was convinced he had used
magic, and from then on his reputation spread. His relationship with Elizabeth dates from the time she was a princess
and out of favor during her sister Mary's reign. Dee apparently
cast favorable horoscopes for her, predicting that she would
one day rule. However, Dee's prognostications caught up with
him. He was suspected of conspiring with Elizabeth to do
away with the queen by sorcery[51] and formally accused of sorcery against Mary, though acquitted by the Star Chamber in
1555. During Elizabeth's reign, Dee seems to have been called
in for occasional consultations by the queen, and his diary
records visits by her to him at his house at Mortlake. Other
entries in the diary suggest that he was kept busy casting horoscopes, teaching and advising friends, and at various times
performing jobs for the queen or traveling at her request. In
addition, Dee wrote treatises on a number of different subjects,[52] though none specifically on magic. Dee conducted a
number of scientific experiments, invented useful naviga-
tional devices, and was reputed to be an excellent mathematician. He was, all told, one of England's best examples of the
"Renaissance Man" and deserves F. A. Yates's succinct observation that "no more complete mirror of the Elizabethan age
could be found than John Dee."[53] True to Pico's symbol, this
Renaissance man was, in addition to all his other attributes,
a magician.

Yet many of his fellow Englishmen feared Dee as a conjuror,
a spirit-summoner, and this reputation greatly distressed Dee,
partly because it was dangerous to be suspected of conjury in
England at that time, and partly because Dee was apparently
horrified to be suspected of commerce with the devil. Several
of his later writings contain long complaints about the pillage
of his library (which seems to have been a deliberate act of
destruction against the "conjuror" carried out while Dee was

50. The most complete study of Dee to date is Peter J. French, *John Dee:
The World of an Elizabethan Magus*.
51. *The Mirror for Magistrates*, ed. Lily B. Campbell, p. 29.
52. For Dee's own list of his published and unpublished works, see *A Letter, Containing a Most brief Discourse Apologeticall*, sigs. A3ᵛ–B1ᵛ.
53. *Theatre of the World*, p. 8.

abroad) and about the rumors that he was a "Caller of Deuils"
and "Arche Coniurer, of this whole kingdom."[54] Dee wanted
to make the distinction between a philosopher who experi-
mented (which he considered himself to be) and a conjuror
(which he was reputed to be). In the following warning, however, Dee, like many writers on magic, struck a note of condescension toward the vulgar and unlearned who presume to
judge his activities:

> Let all such, therefore, who, in Iudgement and Skill of Philoso-
> phie, are farre inferior to Plinie (who called Moses a magician)
> take good heede, leaste they ourshoote them selues rashly, in
> Iudging of Philosophers straunge Actes, and the Meanes, how they
> are done. But, much more, ought they to beware of forging, deuis-
> ing, and imagining monstrous feates, and wonderfull workes,
> when and where no such were done: no, not any sparke or likeli-
> hode, of such, as they without all shame, do report.[55]

But Dee's protestations had little effect, and as an old man in
1604 he was still petitioning King James to clear his name of
the label of *conjuror*. Despite all Dee's unhappiness with his
image, he is remembered primarily as a magician, thanks in
good part to Casaubon's publication in 1659 of parts of Dee's
journals. His magical paraphernalia—his table, crystal globes,
and the black obsidian mirror cherished by Horace Walpole as
the "Black Stone into which Dr. Dee, used to call his
Spirits"[56]—are housed in the British Museum for all to see,
evidence that Dee was an operator as well as a theorizer about
magic. To his contemporaries he must have been an obvious
example of a magician, perhaps more useful as a model than
Ficino or Pico because he actually practiced what he wrote
about.

Turning theory into practice, however, changed philosophical magic. What had been for Pico a symbol of man's potential, and for Ficino a theory of how to obtain infinite wisdom,
became for Agrippa and Dee an increasingly concrete and
practical way of operating in the world. The uninitiated and
uninformed misperceived this magic and, through rumor,

54. John Dee, *General and Rare Memorials Pertayning to the Perfecte Arte
of Navigation*, sig. △iii[v].
55. Dee, "Mathematicall Preface," sig. Aiii[r].
56. Hugh Tait, "The Devil's Looking-Glass: The Magical Speculum of Dr.
John Dee," pp. 206–7. Tait speaks of the fate of a number of Dee's posses-
sions.

transformed it into cheap tricks. Writing of the medieval church, J. Huizinga commented:

> But was she able to stand against this strong need of giving a concrete form to all the emotions accompanying religious thought? It was an irresistible tendency to reduce the infinite to the finite, to disintegrate all mystery. . . . Even the profound faith in the eucharist expands into childish beliefs—for instance, that one cannot go blind or have a stroke of apoplexy on a day on which one has heard mass. . . . While herself offering so much food to the popular imagination, the Church could not claim to keep that imagination within the limits of a healthy and vigorous piety.[57]

Such making tangible of the intangible Christian mysteries is similar to what happened to spiritual magic as it filtered down to broader public awareness. The vulgarization of spiritual magic merely added to the continuum of varieties of magic from which the writer of Elizabethan and Jacobean England could draw.[58]

What contemporary philosophical magic made available to the dramatist was a climate of interest in the magician. Despite the strictures of the church, the dramatist had the pos-

57. *The Waning of the Middle Ages*, p. 155.
58. At the very end of this continuum, and of very little influence in the literary portrayal of magicians (except in those works, such as *The Alchemist* and *The Wizard*, that debunk magic), is "popular magic," practiced in villages much as medicine was practiced. The village wizard, however, came from a very different tradition than did the philosophic magician and was primarily interested in healing, giving advice, predicting the future, and looking for things lost or stolen. Keith Thomas, *Religion and the Decline of Magic: Studies in Popular Beliefs in Sixteenth and Seventeenth Century England*, p. 228, remarks on the differences: "By this period popular magic and intellectual magic were essentially two different activities, overlapping at certain points, but to a large extent carried on in virtual independence of each other. Most of the magical techniques of the village wizard had been inherited from the Middle Ages, and had direct links with Anglo-Saxon and classical practice. Many can be paralleled in other primitive societies. They were only slightly affected by the Renaissance revival of magical inquiry or by the learned volumes which were its most characteristic product. . . . So although virtuosi and university-based magicians can be shown to have been much influenced by Renaissance speculations on magic, the same is not true of the village wizards." Reginald Scot's *Discoverie of Witchcraft* deals to a large extent with popular magic, which is often distinguished from intellectual magic simply by being termed *witchcraft*. For a detailed and fascinating account of village magic, Thomas's book is invaluable. Though for the purposes of my study popular magic is pretty much dismissed in this footnote, the distinctions between it and intellectual magic were neither simple nor clearly demarcated for the Elizabethans. The practices and beliefs of popular magic served to further confuse the terminology and interpretations of magic available to both dramatists and their audiences in Tudor-Stuart England.

sibility of presenting "white" or "natural" or "spiritual" magic as a positive force. In addition, he could develop the magician as a fully fleshed character: wise, intellectually oriented, using verbal rituals, music, perfumes, and special clothing to accomplish his ends. The magician could be as human as, though a good deal more exotic than, the village shoemaker; that is, he could be treated realistically within the drama.

II.

What contemporary magic could not have provided, however, was much for the magician to *do*. Philosophic magicians did not, after all, perform tricks, heal the sick, or assist those in trouble. They read, they meditated, often they advocated severing all ties to the world around them. Even John Dee's angelic conversations—perhaps the most sensational action reported by a philosophical magician—are hardly the sort of material a dramatist could use for plot.

But there were other traditions of magic, literary ones, to which dramatists could have turned for help in motivating their magicians and involving them in plot action. The most fruitful of these traditions to examine for examples of "literary" magic seems to me to be the medieval narrative romances (their possible link with the drama is clear when we remember that English stage magicians appeared first in dramatic romances, which were often clumsy adaptations of longer narrative romance materials). Filled with magic and with stereotyped, unrealistic characters, romance had no need to correspond closely to the real world. Thus, the medieval romances took a relaxed, unconcerned attitude toward magic. It exists everywhere in the romance world and is good or bad according to the motives of the magician or the effect it has on plot.

The magician as a character in romance is quite different from the character suggested by the writings of the neoplatonic philosophers. The romance magician, who can be either male or female, is usually set apart from the other characters by some physical or spiritual peculiarity: Merlin is unnaturally hairy and has a devil rather than a human for his father; Clinschor (in Wolfram von Eschenbach's *Parzival*) has been castrated; Morgan le Fay (*Gawain and the Green Knight*) and

Cundrie (*Parzival*) are incredibly ugly. Rarely does a magician have a family, close friends, or a lover. Merlin, in his several romances,[59] is something of an exception, but even so—since his relationship with his mother receives little emphasis after he grows up, and his mistress shuts him up forever in a rock— he can hardly be seen as part of a warm familial group. In a genre much interested in reconciliations between long-lost families or lovers, the magician generally remains apart and aloof.

In the narrative romances, magicians generate their own magic; they have no need to employ spirits or to perform elaborate ceremonies. Occasionally a magician—such as Malory's Morgan le Fay, Cundrie in *Parzival*, or the Clerk in Chaucer's "The Franklin's Tale"—is learned or uses books, but such references are always casual. There is none of the association between magic and learning mandatory in theories of philosophic magic. Most magicians seem born to their trade, whether—like Merlin—because of a nonhuman or magical relative, or because of a prediction that they will have magical skill. The romances spend little or no time explaining the motivation for or methods of magic; what is important is the effect the magician has on the plot. On the stage, such undeveloped, unexplained magic occasionally occurs in plays, like *The Birth of Merlin*, that seem directly derived from narrative romance.

Much of the magic in the romances has no particular source. Magical rings, enchanted springs, deadly beds, and magical potions abound, and often the writer makes no effort to explain how they came to be enchanted. Examples of romances containing such magical effects include *Floris and Blancheflour* (with its magic ring and a stream to detect adulterous maidens); Chretien de Troyes's *Yvain* (protective rings and an enchanted spring); *Sir Launfal* (magic purse, horse, and dwarf); and *Sir Tristrem* (magic potion). Whole faerie or magical worlds may exist (as in *Sir Orfeo* and *Sir Launfal*) without

59. The Merlin romances from which my general remarks about Merlin are derived include Henry Lovelich, *Merlin: A Middle-English Metrical Version of a French Romance*, ed. Ernst A. Kock; *Merlin or the Early History of King Arthur: A Prose Romance*, ed. Henry B. Wheatley; *Of Arthour and of Merlin*, ed. O. D. Macrae-Gibson; Geoffrey of Monmouth, *Vita Merlini*, ed. Basil Clarke; and Thomas Malory, *The Works of Sir Thomas Malory*, ed. Eugène Vinaver.

explanation of their origin. No magician need be involved in creating them. But sometimes a specific magician is responsible for providing characters with invulnerable magical props (as Clinschor creates the enchanted bed in *Parzival*). In such cases, however, emphasis is invariably on *what* magic accomplishes rather than *how* it is performed.

The magical equipment associated with romance magicians is varied. Sorceresses seem to favor magic potions, rings, and swords, while male sorcerers often prefer larger projects—enchanted castles, magical beds, or invulnerable battle dress. The variety itself is informative, however, because it suggests there is no required or mandatory equipment for performing magic. The magician is usually self-sufficient and needs little help from spirits or objects to produce his effects.

What magicians in narrative romance do is facilitate plot action and provide spectacular effects. A miraculous transformation is their most usual way of producing results. Merlin, for example, is fond of changing the weather, raising fogs or mists to bewilder the enemy. The Green Knight is a shape changer, changing from the host to the Green Knight with apparent ease. Merlin, too, has vast shape-changing powers. His most famous change, of course, is the transformation of Uther Pendragon into the likeness of the Duke of Tintagel so that Uther may sleep with Tintagel's wife and beget King Arthur. Not all Merlin's shape changes are so utilitarian. He frequently appears to his acquaintances in disguise for no reason other than his apparent joy in bewildering others and in variety. This delight is frequently carried beyond all reasonable bounds, as when, to attract Julius Caesar's attention, he transforms himself into a stag and goes running through the palace of the emperor.[60] Although Merlin is by far the most ubiquitous romance magician, his powers are fairly typical of those possessed by less well known magi.

The production of surprising effects and spectacle, as well as of disguises, has implications that are carried further in dramatic literature. The disguises, of course, are associated with role-playing; in many ways the magician is an actor. Even more, however, he is a director, a presenter of spectacular shows for the discomfort, edification, or entertainment of

60. *Merlin*, ed. Wheatley, p. 423.

spectators. Although these qualities of the magician are only suggested, and never carefully developed, in the romances, they do exhibit the potential available to a writer to portray the magician as director or as creative artist. Merlin and his counterparts "create" illusion; their magic produces temporary changes that affect man's senses but eventually dissolve back to reality. In medieval romance, then, more than in contemporary magic, the Tudor-Stuart dramatist could have found the association between the magician and the artist, the magician and the director of spectacle.

A traditional function of magicians that receives emphasis and development in romance is prophecy. E. K. Chambers has gone so far as to suggest that Geoffrey of Monmouth invented Merlin solely as a mouthpiece for prophecy.[61] Whether or not Chambers is right, romance authors repeatedly fall back on the device of the enigmatic prediction to hold the reader's attention. In the Merlin romances, for example, Merlin is apparently tricked into predicting three different deaths for the same man (who keeps disguising himself as part of an effort to discredit Merlin); all of the death predictions are, of course, fulfilled. Nearly all romance magicians, villains or heroes, have similar prophetic powers, though evil magicians are necessarily blind to their own downfall.

Evil magicians are fairly generously scattered through the medieval romances. Good magicians appear more rarely, and when they do they are usually paired with an evil magician. This scarcity of good magicians apparently results more from problems of plotting and suspense than from any feeling about the impossibility of good magic. A villainous magician provides a worthy opponent to a hero; victory over the magician's special powers enlarges the hero's triumph. Thus, Clinschor's magical traps in *Parzival* make Gawan's adventures exciting as he manages to defeat the evil magic. But the entrance into a romance of a powerful good magician requires some magical competition just to keep the plot alive. In the Merlin romances, Fortager's wise men compete with Merlin for the king's patronage. Once they are defeated, Merlin interests us because he is on the side of the underdog, working against overwhelming odds. After Arthur is crowned king,

61. *Arthur of Britain*, p. 96.

these romances lose much of their interest and become little more than a series of battles, ingeniously led and won by Merlin. Merlin's role throws Arthur into deep shadow; although he is a king, Arthur is apparently incapable of making an intelligent decision without Merlin. Probably Thomas Malory foresaw this difficulty when he constructed his tales, for he shut Merlin up in a rock very early in the narrative. An active Merlin would prevent Arthur's emergence as a hero. And for the short time that Merlin is active, Malory provided him with a rival: Morgan le Fay, constantly plotting against Arthur, gives magical assistance to his enemies.[62] Merlin is finally defeated by the magic of Nyneve, the beautiful woman to whom he has taught his own art. Good magicians threaten to diminish plot interest unless they are provided with worthy challengers, and thus they appear more rarely than villainous magicians, both in the romances and, later, in drama. Like the romancers, dramatists who do create good magicians almost always give them magical competition (as in *Friar Bacon and Friar Bungay*, *John a Kent and John a Cumber*, and *The Tempest*, where Prospero's magic is stronger than that of Sycorax).

Finally, romance magicians are generally amoral. Though they are heroes (and therefore good) or villains (and therefore bad), ordinary moral or religious standards are usually not applied to them. Despite the malice of Clinschor, for example, nothing indicates that he is the agent of any diabolic power. Merlin, though fathered by the devil, is clearly on the side of good. Yet in all versions of his story he does some fairly immoral things. In arranging for the begetting of Arthur, for example, Merlin acts as the manager of an adultery; he frequently serves as a pander in the romances. Malory, as is frequently the case, followed his source and made Merlin seem even less attractive: Merlin orders Arthur to destroy all children born to lords and ladies on May Day in an effort to kill Mordred, Arthur's bastard, who will one day be his murderer. This action is reminiscent, of course, of Herod's slaughter of the innocents, and just as futile—a good reminder that magical counsel is not always infallible.[63] Although Merlin is generally on the right side, moral and religious issues run a poor second to interests of plot.

62. Malory, *Works*, p. 59.
63. Ibid., p. 44.

Missing from romance treatments of the magician is any sense that he has entered into an agreement with the devil in order to obtain his powers.[64] Indeed, the only conjuring in the romances I have read is done not by a magician but by a "good man [who] toke a stole aboute hys neck and a booke, and than he conjoured on that booke. And with that they saw the fyende in an hydeous fygure, that there was no man so hardé-herted in the worlde but he sholde a bene aferde."[65] Here the "good man" merely wants to know if a priestly colleague who has been killed is damned or saved; the devils are being asked to provide information (as are the spirits who are summoned in Chapman's *Bussy D'Ambois*), not to perform any evil acts. Occasional references indicate that authors were well aware of the possible identification of magicians and devils: Malory has a sorceress who, when her temptations fail, disappears, only to be identified as the devil himself.[66] Here and in similar references, however, the tone is casual. The romances are not anxious to explore the moral implications of magic or to characterize it as "white" or "black," natural or demonic.

What is important to notice is the possibility of good—or even merely "neutral"—magic in medieval literature. In this respect romance magic is similar to the magic of the later philosophers: good magic can exist and, indeed, be a desirable attribute. Of course, both traditions also acknowledge the existence and danger of bad magic, but neither sees magic as exclusively bad.

Where the two sorts of magic differ radically, however, is in their emphases. The medieval romances show little or no interest in theories of magic. Instead, they develop the magician for literary use. Competition between magicians, magical prophecy to provide suspense or foreshadowing, humor and practical jokes arising from magical powers, and plot interest heightened by miraculous occurrences were all useful in the romances. Many of these same techniques were also used by dramatists in the portrayal of stage magicians.

64. Pacts with the devil frequently occur, however, in medieval religious literature as well as in fabliaux. For one example, see Walter Map, "Of the Lad Eudo, who was Deceived by the Devil," in *De nugis curialium*, trans. Montague R. James.

65. Malory, *Works*, p. 671.

66. Ibid., pp. 668–70.

III.

The combined influence of these two traditions of magic, the fictive and the philosophical, perhaps first appeared in a nondramatic form, the romance epic. Boiardo, Tasso, Ariosto, and Spenser all included magic and magicians in their epics. Their magicians generally resemble medieval romance magicians: they move the plot; they create and use magical equipment; they frequently compete with one another; they prophesy. But these characters also show certain differences from magicians found in medieval romance.

For example, epic magicians are clearly learned in a way romance magicians are not. All of Spenser's magicians are dependent on books for their magic: Busirane and Merlin work from texts and write "straunge characters" that seem to be some sort of magical hieroglyphics (3.3.14; 3.12.31).[67] Archimago, in his deception of the Red Cross Knight, goes into his study to search his magic books; after his first attempt fails, he "searcht his balefull bookes againe" (1.2.2).

A similar association of magic with books appears in the Italian epics. Ariosto carried his portrait of the bookish magician almost to absurdity when he portrayed Atlantes astride the flying hippogryph, his magic shield on one arm and his open book in the other hand, reading aloud magical incantations. In fact, Bradamant defeats Atlantes partly because the magician has carelessly left his book behind:

That wretched man, the volume by whose aid
He all his battles fought, on earth had laid. (4.25)[68]

This growing reliance on books and stress on learning suggest that philosophic magic was influencing Renaissance writers' conception of the magician.

A second important change is the almost formulaic association of the magician with spirits or demons. The most famous Spenserian lines suggesting this connection are those on Archimago's flies:

67. All references to *The Faerie Queene* in my text are to *The Poetical Works of Edmund Spenser*, ed. J. C. Smith and Ernest de Selincourt, vols. 1 and 2.
68. Ludovico Ariosto, *Orlando Furioso*, trans. William Stewart Rose, ed. Stewart A. Baker and A. Bartlett Giamatti. All subsequent references in my text are to this edition.

> And forth he cald out of deepe darknesse dred
> Legions of Sprights, the which like little flyes
> Fluttering about his euer damned hed,
> A-waite whereto their seruice he applyes. (1.1.38)

But Merlin, too, has legions of "sprights" working underground, and his strange writing serves a purpose: "With . . .
[it] the stubborn feends he to his seruice bound" (3.3.10–14).
These associations are not only Spenser's. At one point in *Orlando Furioso*, Melissa, a magical assistant to the dead but
still vocal Merlin, calls up a parade of demons, but only after
drawing a circle around Bradamant and tying a pentacle to her
head to protect her from the spirits. In *Jerusalem Delivered*,
Tasso tried to distinguish between evil and good magicians in
terms of their demonic associations. The great magical feat in
the poem is Ismen's creation of the enchanted forest, which
he accomplishes by assigning a demon to every tree and bush.
The conjuration scene, described in great detail, produces "legions of devils."[69] To balance this overtly demonic magic,
Tasso portrayed a hermit, a good magician, who practices only
natural magic:

> Nor yet by help of devil or aid from hell
>   I do this uncouth work and wond'rous feat;
> The Lord forbid I use or charm or spell
>   To raise foul Dis from his infernal seat;
> But of all herbs, of every spring and well,
>   The hidden power I know and virtue great,
> And all that kind hath hid from mortal sight,
> And all the stars, their motions and their might. (14.42)

Yet this hermit, conspicuous in his disclaimer of demonic
magic, is the exception. Most epic magicians had passed beyond strictly natural magic and unabashedly employed demons, whether they themselves served God or the devil.

Increased dependence on books and demonic aid is important not only as an indication of the possible influence of philosophical magic on the literary conception of the magician
but also for his development as a character. The need for
books and for assistance from spirits moves the magician
closer to the ordinary man. If—like most romance magicians—he is granted special powers from birth and is thus

---

69. Torquato Tasso, *Jerusalem Delivered*, trans. Edward Fairfax, 13.11. All
subsequent references in my text are to this edition.

able to work magic with no help, then he is a creature set
apart from the rest of mankind. But if his magical ability
comes from study and if his magical acts are actually performed by spirits, then the magician can be human.

Peopled as it is by stereotypes and allegorical characters, the
romance epic is hardly the place for realistic character development. But the beginnings of a more human magician can
be seen in a character like Spenser's Archimago. Far from infallible, Archimago constantly reveals human weaknesses,
despite his considerable magical ability. Having created the
false Una, for example, "The maker selfe [Archimago] for all
his wondrous witt, / Was nigh beguiled with so goodly sight"
(1.1.45). Archimago is no more able to detect deceptive appearances than the good characters and is fooled by Bragga-
dochio's fine armor into choosing him as a worthy foe to Gu-
yon and Red Cross Knight. Archimago is sensually tempted
and easily fooled because, like all of Spenser's heroes (with
the exception of Arthur), he is subject to human failings. Far
from being the devil personified, Archimago is a man, as dedicated to evil as Gloriana's knights are to good, but as prone
as they to fall short of his goal. Similar fallibility coupled with
magical ability is seen repeatedly in stage magicians; indeed,
it becomes part of a stock formula for both good and evil magicians.

Another element of this stock formula that found early development in the romance epic is the portrait of the magician
as artist, as creator and director of spectacle, pageant, and
masque. Commenting on Archimago, Donald Cheney remarked, "Spenser directs his emphasis in particular toward
the suggestion of a demonic figure of the artist. He is repeatedly the victim of his own art."[70]

Magicians specialize, as do artists, in the creation of illusion, and it is not surprising that the one becomes a symbol
for the other. Though the Italian epics also have creative magicians, the best example of the magician as artist is Spenser's
Busirane. Creator of the enigmatic Mask of Cupid and apparently chief curator of his house filled with lovely works of art,
Busirane exercises a power that resides not in his "vile" self
but in his artistic creations. Despite his frequent identification with Lust, Busirane has not built another Bower of Bliss

70. *Spenser's Image of Nature: Wild Man and Shepherd in "The Faerie
Queene,"* p. 46.

that tempts by direct physical sensuality. Rather his house is a temptation through carefully selected art, a temptation to believe the didactic message that tapestry, statuary, and masque all convey: Love is cruel and painful as well as erotic. But Spenser, supremely aware of the dangers of illusion, foils Busirane with a heroine who pushes beyond the art to its source: "Bold Britomart . . . / Neither of idle shewes, nor of false charmes aghast," pushes through to the plain third room, not meant to be seen, from which the magician operates.

Busirane is, in many ways, typical of the Renaissance magician as he will develop onstage. The magical creation of pageant and masque will recur repeatedly (Prospero's wedding masque and Faustus's necromantic pageants are simply the two most obvious examples). As a creator, the magician can be compared to other creators, and new realms of possible significance attach to him. From a religious perspective, for example, creation is an imitation of God, and to create sensual lures is to rival God and to work against his purposes. So in the *Faerie Queene* all the "bad" magical figures (Archimago, Busirane, Acrasia, and the witch) create illusions or false duplicates of real characters. But Merlin, the good magical figure, creates a mirror that reveals truth and a shield before which everything false or illusory crumbles.

From another perspective, the creator is also the artist, and Busirane is very much the dramatic artist, directing all from behind the scenes. The pageant he creates is described in clearly dramatic terms:

[Ease appears] as on the ready flore
Of some Theatre, a graue personage,
That in his hand a branch of laurell bore,
With comely haueour and count'nance sage,
Yclad in costly garments, fit for tragicke Stage. (3.12.3)

In Spenser's moral framework, such dramatic illusion can only be negative. But in other contexts, the metaphor of magician as artist can be (and is) exploited more positively. Busirane's connection with masque is only an early example of the magician as artist. The tradition of associating masque and magician, and the verisimilitude of stage illusion to magical illusion, strengthens as the drama develops.

The changes in the portrayal of the magician in the romance epics open up a series of new and complex possibilities for the magician as a character. How will he use his abilities? At what price comes his power over spirits? How do his contacts with the world of spirits change his life on earth? Will human weakness limit his magical power? The conflicts with which it is now possible for the writer to endow the magician pave the way for his development as an interesting stage character. While in some plays he remains a set piece, a conventional, undeveloped figure, in others he is a complex, often morally perplexed man.

Robert Fludd, *Utriusque cosmi*, 1619 (courtesy Cornell University Library).

2

The Magician in Minor Tudor and Stuart Drama

The Development of Stereotypes

The relatively late development of secular drama in England made it possible for playwrights to draw not only from literary sources but also from philosophical theory and from contemporary life in creating the stage magician.[1] Though he was a minor character in the early dramatic romances, the magician was both durable and versatile. For the fifty years from 1570 to 1620 at least two dozen plays involving magicians, conjurors, and enchanters are extant; the plays include comedies, tragedies, and romances, and the magicians' parts range from walk-ons to starring roles.[2]

The common critical premise that mars studies of magical drama is that the magician was automatically viewed as evil by an Elizabethan audience. One exponent of this view, Kurt Tetzeli von Rosador, argues, for example, that the magician is

1. Robert West, *The Invisible World: A Study of Pneumatology in Elizabethan Drama*, argues that the stage magician is drawn solely from real-life models: "The 'practicing magician' was the magician of contemporary actuality as distinguished from the legendary Merlin, a wholly literary figure" (p. 57).

2. The most complete survey of the use of magic in the drama of the period is Robert R. Reed, Jr., *The Occult on the Tudor and Stuart Stage*. Reed explains much of what happens onstage as a reflection of contemporary society; the supernatural elements in the plays "were as realistic and mundane to [Elizabethan playgoers] as was London Bridge or the apprentice riots on Fleet Street" (p. 18).

a special development of the Vice, sharing with him the automatic moral condemnation of the audience, though, like the Vice, the magician may be the most active and entertaining character in the play. Since the magician is morally suspect from his first moment onstage, Tetzeli continues, a playwright who wishes a positive magician must in some way neutralize his character's pejorative connotations:

> Will der Dramatiker aber die allgemeine Anrüchigkeit und moralische Problematik der Magie neuen Zwecken dienstbar machen, will er diese Problematik entgegen der Publikumserwartung umdeuten oder gar aufheben, so muss er sich bestimmter Mittel und Techniken bedienen, um den Magier von seinem teuflischen Ursprung zu lösen und umzuwerten.[3]

> If the dramatist wants to make the general disreputableness and moral problem of magic subservient to new ends, if in opposition to public expectation, he wishes to explain or neutralize entirely this problem, then he must make use of definite means and techniques to loosen the magician from his demonic origins and revalue him.

Such assumptions about magicians burden them with a sobriety and a moral significance at odds with the tone and pace of many of the plays in which they appear. Moreover, as has been seen, good magicians and benevolent magic existed in literature, and important thinkers wrote philosophical defenses of theurgistic magic. While the magician may duplicate the functions and features of the Vice in some plays, his origins are outside the morality tradition, and he does not carry the moral weight of the Vice.

To view the magician as a development of the Vice seriously distorts two of the major roles he plays in the drama. Frequently, he functions as a symbol of the artist, creating shows and taking responsibility for otherwise unexplained but entertaining spectacle. In many dramas this produces little more than diversion and entertainment, but in plays such as *The Tempest* the magician-as-artist motif is fully developed. To burden such a character as Prospero with negative connotations would destroy much of the play's effect and make any serious examination of the role of the artist impossible.[4]

3. *Magie im Elizabethanischen Drama*, p. 27.
4. In fact, a number of critics do view Prospero and his magic very negatively: Clifford Leech, in *Shakespeare's Tragedies and Other Studies in Sev-*

Some of the most complex treatments of the stage magician present him as a man both admirable and flawed. His considerable magical powers are qualified and frequently destroyed by human weakness. In the plays that carefully develop this theme, the magician becomes a symbol of man's ambiguous place in the universe: a creature supremely talented but doomed to fail. To see the magician as evil from the beginning destroys the ambiguity on which this characterization depends.

I.

To understand the complexities of characters like Faustus and Prospero, however, we will do well to look first at their less fully developed forebears, the earliest English dramatic magicians.

The first stage magicians apparently appeared in popular romantic drama of the 1570s and 1580s. Only three representatives of early dramatic romance are extant: *Clyomon and Clamydes*, *Common Conditions*, and *The Rare Triumphs of Love and Fortune*.[5] Of these, two have active magicians, though the villain of *Clyomon and Clamydes*, Brian Sans Foy, is very different from the kindly Bomelio of *The Rare Triumphs*. Both plays are hybrids, romances interwoven with strong elements of the morality tradition.

In *Clyomon and Clamydes*, the morality influence is evident in the inclusion of the Vice, Subtill Shift, though the plot deals with the adventures and love affairs of knights. The play contains several villainous characters, but the most prominent is the enchanter, Brian Sans Foy. The Vice and the enchanter have similar functions in the play; in fact, some of

enteenth Century Drama, pp. 142–58, is one of the earliest to systematically criticize Prospero and his "puritanical" behavior; D'Orsay W. Pearson, "The _Tempest_ in Perspective," mounts the most complete attack against the play's magic, calling Prospero "a type of potentially damned sorcerer"; most recently, Anthony Harris, _Night's Black Agents: Witchcraft and Magic in Seventeenth-Century English Drama_, argues that Prospero's magic is evil and must be renounced (pp. 129–48).

5. To speculate on the nature of lost plays such as Skelton's _The Necromancer_ is futile, but awareness that such plays may have had a significant effect on the dramatic portrayal of the magician reminds us that assumptions about the development of the figure are tentative at best. For a discussion of romance as a dramatic genre, see Betty J. Littleton's edition of _Clyomon and Clamydes_, pp. 53–54, 195–98. All references to _Clyomon and Clamydes_ are to this edition.

the Vice's traditional role is duplicated or absorbed by Brian; Shift himself remarks several times on their "consanguini-tie." Both characters are cowards, for example; both disguise their true identities—Brian goes to court as Clamydes, and Subtill Shift uses the alias *Knowledge*—and both exist primarily to complicate the plot with their evil mischief. But though Brian is eventually unmasked and sentenced to languish in prison until he dies, Subtill Shift completely escapes the traditional unmasking and judgment that normally befall the disguised Vice. His true name is never revealed to the other characters, and he receives no punishment. The enchanter has evidently absorbed the ending usually given the Vice. What this peculiar duplication of roles suggests is that, as romance and morality merged, the Vice and the romance villain (here the wicked magician) filled similar roles. Brian seems not so much an outgrowth or development of the Vice as an alternative to him.

This suggestion is supported by the vaunt characteristic of both the magician and the Vice, a feature Tetzeli cited as partial proof of their common source.[6] Shift's numerous short vaunts serve the purpose of introducing the Vice and his knavery:

> For I promise you, I entend not very long to be his
> man;
> Although under the tytle of Knowledge my name I do faine,
> *Subtill Shift* I am called, that is most plaine.
> And as it is my name, so it is my nature also,
> To play the shifting knave wheresoever I go. (Lines 210–14)

Shift's speech exhibits a joy in hypocrisy absent from Brian's introductory vaunt, which sounds more like a discussion of his weaknesses than a boast of his abilities, despite the vaunt formula of the opening line:

> Of *Brian Sance foi* who hath not heard? not for his
> valiant acts,
> But well I know throughout the world, doth ring his
> cowardly facts.
> ....
> ... I in *Venus* yoke,
> Am forst for want of valiancie, my freedome to provoke:
> Bearing the name and port of knight, enchantments for

6. *Magie im Elizabethanischen Drama*, pp. 65–71.

to use,
Wherewith full many a worthy wight, most cowardly I
 abuse. (Lines 549–62)

Brian's magical ability is his compensation for lack of courage,
for human weakness. Far from proud, Brian is one of the most
shamefaced villains ever to walk onstage. In Brian's mind
magic is apparently but a poor substitute for courage. Though
he manages to put Clamydes to sleep by enchantment, Brian
is outwitted by Shift, is so terrified that he travels by night
when no one can see him, and finally is frightened into con-
fessing his deception. Though he shares certain qualities with
the Vice, Brian is far weaker and more vulnerable.

Throughout the play, Shift is more a commentator on the
plot than an integral part of it. He emphasizes the fictional,
formulaic quality of the play, distancing both himself and the
audience from involvement in it.

What is all things finished, and every man eased?
Is the pageant packed up, and all parties pleased?
Hath each Lord his Lady, and each Lady her love? (Lines
 2130–32)

Brian, more involved in the play's action, never achieves such
distance: unlike Shift, who apparently loves mischief for its
own sake, Brian has a motive for villainy, his lust for Juliana.
He is unable to dissociate himself from his cowardice and desire and to survey the other characters objectively as Shift
does. Magic for Brian (as for a number of other dramatic magicians) is an attempt to compensate for a particular personal
weakness. In contrast to the pride and aplomb of the Vice,[7] a
frequent characteristic of the magician is his recognition of
his human weakness, whether such recognition is present
from the start as with Brian or is painfully learned by a character like Friar Bacon.

Magic is also a crutch for Bomelio in *The Rare Triumphs of
Love and Fortune*, a means of partial retaliation for his unjust
banishment. But magic has had little effect on Bomelio's unhappy life; his magical abilities are not even revealed until far
into the play. Though able to strike Armenio dumb, Bomelio
apparently has very limited power, for he has lived as a mis-

7. See Patricia Russell's discussion of the role of the Vice in romances,
"Romantic Narrative Plays: 1570–1590," in *Elizabethan Theatre*, ed. John
Russell Brown and Bernard Harris, pp. 118–21.

erable exile for a number of years without remedying his situation. Though he says he can ensure through his magic that the love of his son and Fidelia will be secure, his vulnerability is clear when he becomes totally helpless at the loss of his magic books. Imposing further limitations on Bomelio's pathetically weak magical powers is the contest for mastery between Venus and Fortune that frames and controls the action taking place on earth, for what little Bomelio does manage to accomplish through magic is really a manipulation by one of the goddesses involved in the heavenly power struggle. When Bomelio strikes Armenio dumb, it is a minor victory for Venus, just as the destruction of the magic books is a victory for Fortune. Even more than in *Clyomon and Clamydes*, the limitations put upon magic in this play make it almost a bad joke, an apparent power that is ironically ineffective.

Like a number of other elements in *The Rare Triumphs*, magic is treated both chaotically and inconclusively. But the magician does have features that are interesting in so early a play. For example, the moral connotations attached to Bomelio's magic are extremely ambiguous. Bomelio is a positive character because of his unjust suffering and his basic kindliness. As a benevolent figure, abetting true lovers, he is a crude ancestor of such later love-assisting magicians as John a Kent, Peter Fabell, and Prospero. But, despite the general positiveness of his portrait, fear of Bomelio's magic and an interpretation of it as evil creep into the play with his son's reaction to his father's magic books:

> And therfore I perceiue he strangely vseth it,
> Inchaunting and transfourming that his fancy did not fit.
> As I may see by these his vile blasphemous Bookes,
> My soule abhorres as often as mine eye vpon them lookes.
> What gaine can counteruaile the danger that they bring,
> For man to sell his soule to sinne, ist not a greevous thing?
> To captiuate his minde and all the giftes therin,
> to that which is of others all the most vngratious sinne. (Lines
>   1354–61)[8]

Bomelio's son burns his father's books, an act that drives the old man mad. His madness is characterized by a terrible fear of the devil:

8. *The Rare Triumphs of Love and Fortune.* All references to the play are to the edition cited in the bibliography.

What canst thou tel me, tel me of a turd, what and a come I con-
iure thee foule spirit down to hell, ho ho ho the deuil, the deuil, a
coms, a coms, a coms vpon me and I lack my books. help, help,
help, lend me a Swoord, a swoord, oh I am gone. (Lines 1506–9)

Such mad talk implies that Bomelio's magic had operated
through his control of the devil, a control that, without his
books, he can no longer exert. But this is the only evidence
the play offers of diabolic magic. The devil does not appear
despite Bomelio's ravings, and the significance of this speech
is perhaps qualified by its madness. Later, after Bomelio has
been returned to sanity by the intervention of Venus and Fortune, no mention is made of his magic. He does not recant or
apologize for magic, nor is he punished further. Whether his
son was right or wrong to destroy the books is not clear.
Though the son's words echo one contemporary view of
magic—"of others all the most ungratious sinne"—his act
produces his father's madness. The bonfire may be a good
thing, for though it brings temporary madness, Bomelio is
eventually freed from involvement with magic. The son's
speech and Bomelio's mad rant give support to such a reading.
On the other hand, the fire may be simply another complication imposed by Fortune to prevent the happy love conclusion that Bomelio's magic is promoting. This alternative
reading is supported by the positive tone of Bomelio's
characterization and by the praiseworthy goals of his magic.
The play itself forces neither view.

In neither of these romances is magic treated comprehen-
sively or consistently. Though in many ways Bomelio and
Brian seem to have stepped straight from narrative romance,
their magic is actually diminished when it reaches the stage,
in part because of the necessary compression of voluminous
romance materials into a performance of a few hours. Littleton remarked on the reduction of certain characters' importance when transposed from their romance source into *Clyomon and Clamydes* and spoke specifically of what happened
to the magician in the transition:

The arch-enemy of all the knights of the Franc Palais, a powerful
enchanter who is the only descendant of the enchanter Darnant,
becomes the cowardly, "ignomius" Brian Sans Foy, whose enchantments make up for his "want of valiancie." In fact, the marvellous that pervades *Perceforest*—enchantments, prophetic

dreams, marvellous beasts and the like—is reduced in the play to
one enchantment.[9]

Just as the smallness of acting troupes had an effect on the
plotting and scene sequences of the sprawling romances,[10] so
did limitations in staging techniques apparently reduce the
spectacular effects of magic. In these two plays magic is responsible for one sleep-enchantment and one case of dumb-
ness, neither requiring any particular stage effects. The plays
are not devoid of special stage techniques—both call for heavenly descents, for example—but techniques designed to produce magical effects were perhaps still rudimentary, or perhaps ways to make magic visible onstage had simply not yet
occurred to authors who were adapting romance narratives to
the stage. In any case, in these two plays the magic was not
visually impressive. Of course, this early limitation on stage
magic, perhaps produced by lack of technical skill, was overcome in later drama where sophisticated stage techniques
often made magic visually spectacular. But the theme of the
limitations on magic remained even in later dramas in which,
like Bomelio and Brian, magicians almost always come to realize the limitations their humanity imposes upon their magical powers.

II.

The rapid advance in sophistication of magic onstage is evident in Peele's *Old Wives Tale*, staged about 1590. It is one
of a spate of magical plays of that particular period: *Friar Bacon and Friar Bungay*, *John a Kent and John a Cumber*, *Dr.
Faustus*, and *John of Bordeaux* were probably all written between 1588 and 1592.

Unlike the magicians just examined, Peele's Sacrapant is no
minor character. By kidnapping two women, he provides motivation for the *Tale's* two plot strands, and it is his defeat that
resolves the various plot complications. More interesting than
his central role, however, are the numerous magical effects he
creates. He strikes one character blind and another deaf—as

9. *Clyomon and Clamydes*, ed. Littleton, pp. 39–40.
10. David M. Bevington, *From "Mankind" to Marlowe: Growth of Structure in the Popular Drama of Tudor England*, discusses the suppression of
characters in the transplanted romances and notes the limitations this need
for suppression placed on the native sprawl of the romance form (pp. 193–98).

Bomelio made one dumb—with visible and audible side effects that Bomelio did not produce: "A voice and flame of fire" (line 555, s.d.), "thunder and lightning" (line 415, s.d.), and "two furies" who appear to carry out a number of tasks for the magician.[11] In addition, he provides the best wine in France and the best meat in England at Delya's request and nourishes his precious lamp of life, which insures the survival of his magic. While none of these effects, except the fire and lightning, calls for particularly impressive stage techniques, the role of magic and the abilities of the magician have broadened considerably from Brian and Bomelio's feeble and largely undramatic magic. Peele's use of props, the incantation Sacrapant intones for the bread and wine, the provision of a Friar and the two furies as assistants to Sacrapant—all are dramatically effective. No longer do magical effects occur at a mere word from the magician; now there are books, lights, thunder, and spirit assistants, all emphasizing by their presence the power and importance of magic.

But though Sacrapant's powers are well advanced over those of his predecessors, his general state of mind is no more cheerful. That his powers have not made him happy is apparent from his first lines:

Each thing rejoyseth underneath the Skie,
But onely I whom heaven hath in hate:
Wretched and miserable Sacrapant. (Lines 337–39)

Going on to tell of his birth and his abduction of Delya, "the Mistress of my heart," he points to her as she enters: "She . . . from whence my sorrows grow." Frank Hook found Sacrapant's sorrow puzzling:

At l. 353 Sacrapant says that Delya is a source of sorrow for him; he does not explain why, but we gather that his love for her is unrequited (a situation that must rather undermine our respect for his powers of enchantment). . . . The relationship between these two is a fairly murky business. Peele faced a problem: Sacrapant's power could not be made too strong, because Delya must be kept pure for her rescuer. Even so, one can raise questions about the presentation: Does she love him or not? Just how enchanted is she? When does she get the potion?[12]

11. *The Old Wives Tale*, ed. Frank S. Hook, in *The Life and Works of George Peele*, ed. Charles Tyler Prouty, 3:299–443. All references to the play are to this edition.
12. *The Old Wives Tale*, ed. Hook, pp. 349–50.

The relationship is certainly less ambiguous than Hook suggests. Delya is thoroughly enchanted, for she never shows any reservations toward her handsome captor (as do Amoret and, later, the Lady in *Comus* when faced by similar situations). In fact, Delya comments at one point: "heavens! how am I beholding to this faire yong man" (line 584). Until her brothers arrive, Sacrapant has no need to make Delya forget her name and relatives, but with their appearance he finds a potion of forgetfulness necessary.

Sacrapant apparently has no problem enchanting Delya, but he does face limitations with regard to himself. His opening speech suggests why he regards Delya as the source of his sorrows. He recounts how he

> . . . stole away the Daughter to the King,
> Fair Delya, the Mistres of my heart:
> And brought hir hither to revive the man [Sacrapant himself]
> That seemeth yong and pleasant to behold
> And yet is aged, crooked, weake and numbe.
> Thus by inchaunting spells I doo deceive,
> Those that behold and looke upon my face;
> But well may I bid youthfull yeares adue. (Lines 345–52)

Surely his is a case of a willing mind but a weak body, and Delya has been less able to "revive" that weak body than Sacrapant had hoped. Able to enchant others and to change his exterior appearance, Sacrapant lacks power over his own physical incapacities. Like Tithonus, who was immortal but capable of infinite aging, Sacrapant thinks he cannot die, thanks to his magical light, but he can grow old, and he has. Delya has occasioned lustful desires that he is incapable of satisfying. His human weakness qualifies his magical power, and thus Sacrapant, too, is an unhappy magician. Even his light, which Sacrapant thought safe because of the magical charm protecting it, is extinguished. With the light disappears the magic that seems to promise Sacrapant so much but delivers so little.[13]

But *The Old Wives Tale* is not so serious, of course, as my discussion may make it sound. Lest the audience become too involved in the tale, the interruptions of Frolic and Fantastic

13. For an informative discussion of Sacrapant's relation to the appearance/reality theme in the play, see Werner Habicht, *Studien zur Dramenform vor Shakespeare: Moralität, Interlude, romaneskes Drama*, pp. 229–32.

constantly remind us of our distance from it. Again and again they tell us that this is but an old wives' tale. The relative importance of the magician is reduced by Madge's tendency to forget about him:

> Oh Lord I quite forgot, there was a Conjuror, and this Conjuror could doo anything, and hee turned himselfe into a great Dragon, and carried the Kinges Daughter away in his mouth. . . . O I forget: she (he I would say) turned a proper yong man to a Beare in the night . . . and made his Lady run mad. (Lines 119–28)

Like the distancing Vice and the debates that frame the two earlier romances, the frame of Peele's play constantly emphasizes that all is fictional within. Sacrapant's dominant ancestor comes from literary romance and not from real life. The play's magic is to be enjoyed and to be amazed at but produces no horror or terror and very little moral message.

Deliberate distancing is a trademark of romance. It is not so readily found in genres where realism has some importance. In romantic comedy, the emphasis is usually on the real world—somewhat idealized—rather than on faraway lands and exotic lovers. The differences between romance and romantic comedy are perceptible when we compare *The Rare Triumphs* and *The Old Wives Tale* with a group of magical plays that have romance affinities but are clearly comedies: all share a strong romantic interest, a magician who furthers the love story, some emphasis on local history or nationalism, and a general lightness of tone.

Since all these plays deal with magicians who, unlike Bomelio, are clearly identified from the beginning and whose primary plot function is to exercise their magical abilities, they present the same problem in plotting that Merlin presented in the narrative romances. Given a good magician with extraordinary powers, what opposition can be created for him that is not too easily toppled? The most usual solution is suggested by the very title of the "wretched *John a Kent and John a Cumber* of the ballad-maker Anthony Munday."[14] A rival "not-so-good" magician provides plot conflict. And in *John a Kent* the two sides line up very symmetrically: the brides and their true lovers are on one side assisted by John a Kent and his half-boy/half-spirit, Shrimp; on the other are the un-

14. Muriel C. Bradbrook, *The Growth and Structure of Elizabethan Comedy*, p. 80.

wanted lovers and the girls' parents, aided by John a Cumber
and his hired bevy of clowns. The plot is a series of magical
contests between the magicians, with the winner taking the
girls as wives for his set of lovers. What makes the play less
than good (though perhaps not so "wretched" as Muriel Bradbrook suggests) is that its entire movement is left to the magicians; compared to them, the other characters are manne-
quins.[15] Once, although John a Kent has actually won the
ladies and united them with their true loves, he gives them
up again to the opposition so that he may have another contest.[16] His sense of responsibility for plot complication is revealed early in the play when he first brings the lovers together:

> but must these ioyes so quickly be concluded?
> Must the first Scene make absolute a play?
> no crosse? no chaunge? what? no varietie?
> One brunt is past, alas, whats that in looue? (Lines 529–32)

The play demonstrates the difficulty of tying the magical contest and the love plot too closely together. The lovers are
likely to lose all character, as they do here, and become mere
pawns in the magicians' games.

This problem is avoided in the double-plotted *Friar Bacon*,
in which the primary magical contest is a matter of national
glory and has nothing to do with the love plot. Friar Bacon
participates, of course, in both plot lines, but his dual involvement prevents him from dominating the lovers in the way that
Munday's magicians do. Similarly, in *John of Bordeaux*, the
competition between Bacon and Vandermast initially has
nothing to do with the cruel plot to separate husband and
wife, though eventually that, too, becomes part of the struggle
for mastery between the two magicians.

Another feature of *John a Kent* common to a number of
magical plays is a sense, never clearly focused, of regionalism,
of local pride and loyalty. John a Kent is Welsh, as is one of

15. I. A. Shapiro, "Shakespeare and Munday," feels differently about the
play's quality: *John a Kent* "has an extremely ingenious plot, full of surprises
and turns which are always plausible, provided we accept the Elizabethans'
belief in natural magic. . . . It is true that the interest is chiefly in plot and
situation, but the characters are not mere puppets, and the two male lovers
are nicely distinguished" (p. 28).

16. Anthony Munday, *John a Kent and John a Cumber*, lines 1467–91. All
references to the play are to the edition cited in the bibliography.

the lovers he assists, while Cumber and one of the rejected lovers are Scottish. Though the play contains the potential for a struggle for regional honor, the idea never really comes to the fore in the play's development. A good deal of talk about things Welsh occurs in the play (the two brides are also Welsh), but Kent's victory comes more as a personal triumph than as a victory for Wales. (The tradition of Welsh magicians is strong, recalling, of course, Owen Glendower, mentioned in *John a Kent* and one of the few magicians whom Shakespeare puts onstage.) The emphasis on place in such plays makes it clear that magicians can represent or champion particular regions and be looked on as heroes rather than as unsavory characters. So in a moment of crisis, Moorton shows his faith in his local magician:

> Ile post to Scotland for braue Iohn a Cumber,
> the only man renownde for magick skill.
> Oft haue I heard, he once beguylde the deuill,
> And in his Arte could neuer finde his matche. (Lines 694–97)

Magicians as national champions also appear in the two Friar Bacon plays, where Bacon acts as England's champion against Vandermast, the German magician.

Munday's play also contains the strange creature called Shrimp, Kent's spirit-assistant. Shrimp belongs to the same family as Puck and Ariel, though he is far less attractive and poetic than they (as his name suggests). Munday is very careful, however, in his presentation of the magicians. He never permits John a Kent to claim power over spirits, though the clowns testify that he is popularly believed to command devils (lines 1038–77). Griffin asks him about such powers:

> Canst thou my freend, from foorth the vaultes beneathe,
> call vp the ghostes of those long since deceast?
> Or from the vpper region of the ayre:
> fetche swift wingde spirites to effect thy will? (Lines 108–11)

But Kent evades the question with rhetorical questions of his own:

> Can you my Lord, and you, and you, and you,
> goe to the venson, for your suppers drest:
> and afterward goe lay ye downe to rest? (Lines 112–14)

Though such a response is a tacit positive answer, Kent never clearly says he has power to summon spirits, and we never

witness any hint of necromancy on his part, though Shrimp
is obviously more than mortal in his abilities to become invisible and to produce misleading music from thin air. Cumber, on the other hand, derives much of his fame from having
"ourreachte the deuill by his skill," but he is the worse of the
two magicians, and perhaps Munday means to make this clear
by suggesting that Cumber's magic has necromantic roots.

Munday does attempt to distinguish between the two magicians' magic. John a Kent, for example, claims to deal with
reality and scorns Cumber's use of "shaddowes" for his tricks:

> I know not what this play of his will prooue,
> But his intent to deale with shaddowes only,
> I meane to alter, weele haue the substaunces. (Lines 1089–91)

Throughout, Cumber's magic rests on visual tricks. Its weakness is underscored by Moorton's comment, as he views the
real characters whom he mistakenly assumes are Cumber's
spirits: "And trust me I was not a little moou'de, / Prince Grif-
fins shape so led her by the hand: / but that I credit arte more
then mine eye" (lines 1337–39). Greater reliance on art than
nature, than visible reality, is always dangerous in literature of
the period. And Moorton's comments suggest that he, and all
of Cumber's adherents, are thoroughly confused as to the
proper hierarchies. Art may beautify nature but never entirely
supersede it, as Spenser makes clear in the Bower of Bliss. In
the play's final contest, Kent again distinguishes between
shadow and substance, refusing to let his lovers don disguises
to get by the watching Cumber and into the marriage chapel:

> Tu[sh] weele no shapes, nor none of these disguysings,
> they [h t]ofore seru'de bothe his turne and myne,
> As no[ ] ye are, so shall ye passe the gate. (Lines 1558–60)

But, despite verbal attempts to make Kent the magician of
reality and Cumber that of appearances, the plot itself con-
fuses the issue.[17] Kent does disguise himself and deceive the
sight; and, though the lovers do not wear disguises in the final
attempt to win their brides, Kent creates a "sillie dazeling

17. Habicht, *Studien zur Dramenform*, pp. 220–23, also comments on the
appearance/reality conflict in the play. He believes that it is carefully worked
out by Munday and that it has serious moral implications for the play's interpretation (John a Kent is explicitly benevolent; John a Cumber is explicitly
evil).

mist" that blinds Cumber into allowing them to pass. Kent sees nothing wrong in deceiving the vision of the other magician, though he will not allow his lovers to go to their weddings, into God's presence, in disguise.

Munday's play demonstrates his awareness of the issue of appearance and reality (shadows and substance) as it can be related to magic, a theme that is emphasized in several other magical plays by the presence of the magician's magic glass. (Cumber has one here, but it is mentioned only once in passing.) A magic glass may either focus or distort reality—and these two possibilities offer potential for dramatization of the real versus the apparent. The crudity of Munday's attempt to incorporate the theme of appearance versus reality in his play is undeniable, but that he makes the effort at all indicates that magic has the potential not merely to entertain or startle on the stage but also to carry some of the important thematic business of the play.

Though *John of Bordeaux* is clearly a sequel to the popular *Friar Bacon and Friar Bungay*, it deals with quite different themes and speaks in a more somber tone than the earlier comedy.[18] The play, available to modern editors only in a mutilated manuscript copy probably written by an uneducated scribe from dictation,[19] has no extant ending, though its plot conclusions are pretty clear. Even with an ending, it would not rank high on anybody's list of favorite Elizabethan plays, but its lack of artistic polish enables us to see how its anonymous author (possibly Greene himself)[20] attempted to use magic in his play.

In his second stage appearance, Friar Bacon repeats the scholarliness of his approach to magic, which was suggested, more lightly, in *Friar Bacon and Friar Bungay*. Upon his arrival in Germany, Bacon makes clear that his visit is no pleasure jaunt.

18. Though *Friar Bacon and Friar Bungay* comes chronologically before *John of Bordeaux*, I postpone detailed discussion of the play until the next chapter, where the complexity of its treatment of magic can be fully discussed.

19. *John of Bordeaux or the Second Part of Friar Bacon*, pp. xii–xiii. All references to the play are to the edition cited in the bibliography.

20. Waldo F. McNeir, "Robert Greene and *John of Bordeaux*," presents a strong, though by no means conclusive, argument for Greene's authorship of the play.

... Bakon left not his Inglish skolls to gayne<
a broud wealth or promotion desier of deper skill mad me<
cost vnto the Iermayne clime. (Lines 41–43)

Throughout the play Bacon remains essentially serious,
though he occasionally resorts to a silly demonstration of his
magical abilities. His association of magic and philosophy, as
well as his continual search for wisdom, is reminiscent of the
magical theories of the neoplatonists. Indeed, *John of Bordeaux* is the only play discussed thus far where their influence is clear. Bacon's advice to the scholar, somewhat garbled
though it is, suggests the philosophical base upon which he
rests his magic:

> Bacon: her in I like thy mynd and humble bent for who so wanders
> in phelosophe must read and thinck and thincking read agayne
> for more the soyll is tild the better frute and more a man doth
> studdie more his skill [here me my son the] entraunce in to art
> as oft the stragerit with cunning showes is like the ayer vnto
> the [subtill] Carlies eie whos subtill essence flotes and flies
> away but when the eie trannsfers vnto the hart the straung Idea
> of so rare a being then gines the mynd to work of thing*es* devine
> it tremling work*es* vpon the movers myght who seinge nature
> perfeted by art the bonus Ienivs myghtie in his pouer let*es* lose
> the Raynes of reason to conseve thing*es* past belefe here of con-
> iecturd is that poeat*es* wrighte Sapience dominabeter astri[e]s
> Scoller: my mynd is heved beyonnd the commane reatch and now
> in shadose I be hould no more but se in substaunce what trew
> wisdom is
> Bacon: how far thow art young man from Iudgement yet or sight
> of thing*es* acording as the ought Ill lerne the straight. (Lines
> 731–46)

Though Bacon refers to Aristotle and not Plato here, he rec-
ommends a progression from the eye, the sight of the visible
object, to the idea in the mind, which accords with the gradual progression in wisdom and understanding that Plato and
the neoplatonists describe. And Bacon's advice to study, with
the assurance that wisdom rules the stars, echoes in very general and simple terms what many neoplatonists had said. Of
course, such ideas are so general as to require little familiarity
on the author's part with particular philosophers. But such
weighty words in Bacon's mouth are far removed from the
usual trivia of the romance magician. Contemporary neoplatonic philosophy, which associated wisdom with magical
powers and saw the initiate attaining wisdom, understanding,

and magical ability only by degrees, surely had some influence on this speech. Bacon's scholar is a beginner, not an initiate, and though he believes Bacon's words make him understand more clearly (they are hardly a model of clarity to us), he is assured by the magician that he is still far from the true "sight of thing*es*."

Though this passage suggests interesting possibilities about the author's conception of the magician and his function, it remains, within the texture of *John of Bordeaux*, an undigested lump of rhetoric. There is no need or any excuse for such a passage, given the themes and plot of the play. Perhaps the author wished to contrast the "low" tricks of Bacon's clown assistant and the magic of wicked Vandermast with Bacon's own "superior" magic. If so, he did not succeed, for some of Bacon's magical effects are silly and pointless. Though the philosophical view of the magician is interesting here, it merely contributes to the general unevenness and inconsistency that mark the play. In no way do the high sentiments Bacon expresses fit the triviality of his onstage magic (as is also the case in *Doctor Faustus*).

Accompanying its insistence on the philosophical base of Bacon's powers is the play's equal insistence on his Christianity. *John of Bordeaux* combines two plot lines: the magical contests and the story of a war hero wrongly disgraced in a war against the heathens. The latter plot line is much in the background, but it does serve to emphasize the theological commitments of the various characters. Bacon feels himself supported by God, for he consoles Bordeaux's poverty-stricken and beleaguered wife, assuring her that God will soon relieve her. Since Bacon himself is the means of her final restoration to her position and her husband, he is apparently the promised instrument of "riteous god [who] will never fayle the Iust" (line 993). Even more persuasive of Bacon's Christianity is his confrontation with Astrow, one of his spirits, who suddenly refuses obedience to Bacon because "the hellish sperrit*es* ar no mor at thy commaund / thy tyme prefickst thy pour hath a nend / and thow art ours both bodie and soull" (lines 1141–43). As happens in *Faustus*, the time allowed in the magician's pact with the devil is over, and Bacon should, according to all expectations, be dragged to hell. Instead, he calmly responds: "Away presuming speright away thow hast no / pouer over a Cristian fayth" (lines 1114–45). And he is apparently right, for Astrow is soon busily carrying out his commands once again. The point seems to be that magic rightly applied in the search for wisdom and in the service of a just God has no limits. Within the play, Bacon is omnipotent; since there is no end, we cannot be sure that Bacon does not again renounce magic as he did in *Friar Bacon and Friar Bungay*, but it seems extremely unlikely given his consistent triumphs. He is one of the few stage magicians who displays no sense of limitation, except for the bounds imposed by a Christian faith, bounds that apparently were lenient enough in this case to permit a pact with devilish spirits.

The German magician Vandermast, on the other hand, fits all requirements for a "bad" magician. Employed by the King's son to procure the sexual services of Bordeaux's wife, Vandermast uses his magic for a series of immoral and deceptive purposes. He knows, however, the limits to which evil magic can be employed:

> ha ferdenand the mynd is such a thinge as is beyonnd
>   the reach
> of ani art she that is chast cannot be won with charmes (Lines
>   310–11)

Like Sacrapant, John a Cumber, and Brian Sans Foy, Vandermast is restricted; he has neither the magical power nor the moral strength of "Inglish Bacon." Though *John of Bordeaux* begins as a continuation of the nationalistic magical contest between England and Germany, it quickly broadens into an exemplum on the differences between good and evil magic. England's magician, of course, remains the moral and magical victor.

A major part of the magician's role in the two comedies just discussed has been his job as stage manager, purveyor of sensory delights—visual, auditory, and even gustatory. John a Kent provides alluring music and arranges a scenario that bewilders and enrages his rival. Cumber himself has previously staged a little musical play of "Antiques" that enables the fathers and wrong lovers to capture the castle and the girls. The range of "shows" is even greater in *John of Bordeaux*. Numerous spirits are called onstage by both Bacon and Vandermast; some appear in their own shapes, others impersonate real characters. In addition, Bacon calls up a banquet, served by nymphs, to feed the starving hero. Later, to demonstrate to the King his son's lust, Bacon brings on a dumb show of the rape of Lucrece. In addition to shows clearly described, the manuscript (probably a prompter's text) contains suggestions of scenes not described: at line 446, for example, the stage direction reads, "Exent Bacon to bring in the showes as you knowe." Thus, despite a growing involvement with plot and theme in certain plays, magicians continued to function on-stage (as in Spenser's epic) as masters of ceremonies, bringing on set-piece entertainments for the other characters and the audience.

One of the few magicians who does not create such shows is Peter Fabell, better known as the Merry Devil of Edmonton. Fabell does, however, share other characteristics with his contemporaries in romantic comedy. The play in which he is tit-ular hero is notable mostly for its lightness of tone, its swiftly moving plot, and its unique induction. Like the other come-dies, it stresses locality; Fabell is clearly placed in the pro-logue as a native of Edmonton, though he evidently spent much time at Cambridge. History here is only local, however; no king or prince frolics, only small-time landowners and clownish deer poachers. Fabell's magic is unusually subdued for such a late play (1602). It consists of disguisings, a bit of foreknowledge, and a pair of roadhouse signs that get switched long enough to confuse the lovers' parents and allow the wedding to be performed. Fabell, when the moment comes at the play's end for him to explain his role, makes it clear that he has not transgressed into black magic:

> I vsde some pretty sleights; but I protest
> Such as but sate vpon the skirts of Art;
> No coniurations, nor such weighty spells
> As tie the soule to their performancy. (5.2.140–43)[21]

The usual magical contest is avoided, for, as Fabell describes the situation, a different sort of contest is underway:

> Let vs alone, to bussell for the set;
> For age and craft with wit and Art haue met. (1.3.135–36)

The old, crafty parents will battle the young, witty lovers and their friend Fabell, and the nature of the struggle suggests why the magic is so subdued—too many spectacular effects by Fa-

---

21. *The Merry Devill of Edmonton*, in *The Shakespeare Apocrypha*, ed. C. F. Tucker Brooke, pp. 265–84. All references to the play are to this edition.

bell would make it no contest at all. Yet there is no doubt that
Fabell, like Bacon, derives his powers from study and from
"the liberall Arts, / The Metaphysickes, Magicke, and those
parts / Of the most secret deepe philosophy" (1.3.14–16). No
more than this is said of Fabell's power, and the play concen-
trates far more on the lovers and the clowns who poach deer
than on magic.

The aspect of *The Merry Devil of Edmonton* worth a second
glance here is its induction. In it the most severe charge that
could be brought against a magician, a pact with the devil, is
affirmed onstage and then, in effect, brushed off. The prologue
prepares the audience for the fiend's arrival to claim Fabell's
soul and by its language suggests the paradoxical nature of
what is about to happen.

> Sit with a pleased eye, vntill you know
> The Commicke end of our sad Tragique show. (Prol., 40–41)

Coreb, a demon, wakens Fabell and informs him that his hour
has come. Faustus-like, Fabell attempts to stall, moaning elo-
quently about his situation and summarizing beautifully the
spiritual condition of the overreacher who pridefully wishes
to know too much:

> The infinity of Arts is like a sea,
> Into which, when man will take in hand to saile
> Further then reason, which should be his pilot,
> Hath skill to guide him, losing once his compasse,
> He falleth to such deepe and dangerous whirlepooles,
> As he doth lose the very sight of heauen:
> The more he striues to come to quiet harbor,
> The further still he finds himselfe from land.
> Man, striuing still to finde the depth of euill,
> Seeking to be a God, becomes a Deuill. (Prol., 50–58)

Nowhere in Elizabethan drama is there a clearer summary of
the paradoxical position of the philosophical magician. Seeking to know more than is granted to man, but limited by his
very humanity, trying to become like God he falls into evil.
Yet at the same instant these solemn words are uttered, Fabell
is somehow trapping Coreb in the necromantic chair. He
beats the devil at his own game and exacts from him another
seven years of life. With as much confidence as Bacon assuring
Astrow that demons have no power over Christian faith, Fabell tricks Coreb and then goes off to make merry with his

friends. The theological view that the magician who made a pact was damned was evidently not always applicable onstage. Potential tragedy is turned to comedy here; man has beaten the devil, at least temporarily, and all rejoice.[22]

What this induction suggests—and the suggestion is reinforced by the similar scene between Bacon and Astrow—is that an Elizabethan audience could tolerate pacts and black magic without immediately condemning the character who engaged in them. Perhaps it was the ends of magic, not its means, that largely determined audience response. Magicians who used black magic for purely selfish purposes, to satisfy lust, to gain money or position, or to harm others, were condemned. But magicians who were supportive of the community or nation, who used their magic to restore order, to right wrongs, or to assist true love, were supported and seen as "good" no matter what the details of the magic they practiced. These plays seem to disprove the claim that all magicians carried negative connotations with them onto the stage. In *The Merry Devil*, the playwright insists on immediately presenting Fabell in the most compromising spiritual situation possible and then goes on to reverse and minimize that situation, allowing the magician to frolic through the play and emerge victorious with no shadows to mar his complete triumph. This play's popularity suggests that the Elizabethan audience approved and applauded Peter Fabell, "devil" though he might be.[23]

Aside from Friar Bacon and Friar Bungay, there are few other magicians in Tudor-Stuart romantic comedy. Two unusual magicians, slightly different from those already considered, deserve comment, however. One is a magician/tutor like Fa-

22. Tetzeli (*Magie im Elizabethanischen Drama*, p. 110) views Fabell in a more serious way: "Dennoch fühlt sich auch hier der Autor verpflichtet, seinem Magier, obgleich dieser für die Liebeshandlung keine magischen Funktionen ausübt, eine Apologie in den Mund zu legen—allzu festgelegt sind Publikumserwartung und orthodoxer Rigorismus, allzu problematisch und verwerflich ist magische Betätigung." (Nevertheless the author feels obliged here to put in the mouth of his magician an apology, although this one practices no magic function for the love plot—so fixed are public expectations and orthodox rules, so problematical and doubtful is magical activity).

23. Ben Jonson mentions the play's popularity in the prologue of *The Devil is an Asse*, in *Ben Jonson*, ed. C. H. Herford and Percy and Evelyn Simpson, 6:163: "If you'll come / To see new Playes, pray you affoord vs roome, / And shew this, but the same face you haue done / Your deare delight, the *Diuell of Edmunton*." W. W. Greg lists four editions of the play before 1630 (*A Bibliography of the English Printed Drama to the Restoration*, vol. 1, no. 264).

bell who appears in a late play called *The Two Merry Milk-maids* (1619). This play is notable only for its obvious attempt to capitalize on all the formulas that had produced successful plays in the past. This is apparent from its prologue:

> We hope, for your owne good, you in the Yard
> Will lend your Eares, attentiuely to heare
> Things that shall flow so smoothly to your eare;
> That you returning home, t'your Friends shall say,
> How ere you vnderstand 't, 'Tis a fine Play:
> For we haue in't a Coniurer, a Deuill,
> And a Clowne too; but I feare the euill,
> In which perhaps vnwisely we may faile,
> Of wanting Squibs and Crackers at their taile. (Prol., 10–18)[24]

Clearly, by 1619 the conjuror was established as a stock character.

The play's plot is extremely complex, and in it magic has only a secondary role. The opening scene is the one where magic figures most prominently. There Bernard, pupil of the magician-scholar Landoffe, reads from his teacher's magic books in a vain effort to conjure a spirit who will help him in his love affair. Landoffe overhears and resolves to disguise himself as a spirit and help Bernard:

> Ile follow him, attending still vpon him,
> As if I were the Spirit he guesses me:
> And if there shall be cause, Ile play my part
> So well, that men shall prayse the Magick Art. (B3ʳ)

The chief act of magic in the play is the procurement of an everfresh garland by a spirit, an incident borrowed, like almost everything else in the play, from Chaucer's "Franklin's Tale," in which a magician performs an impossible love task and all the principals outdo themselves in courtesy, each refusing to take advantage of the other. In *The Merry Milkmaids*, the compromised lady's husband, led on by a suspicious courtier, is not as understanding as Chaucer's husband, and much plot complication results from his jealousy.

Despite the enormous complexity of the play's action, the plot is all played out by the end of the fourth act, and the fifth act, anticlimactically, consists simply of entertainments—a

24. *The Two Merry Milkmaids*. All references are to the edition cited in the bibliography.

masque and a sonnet-writing contest—devised by the magician for the court's pleasure. Already presented as a scholar-magician, Landoffe is given a second, common role as a masque-deviser. A few lines of dialogue smooth the transition: a courtier asks, "Is not the Poet amongst them [the revellers]?" and the reply comes:

> Yes, and which is a miracle a Masquer,
> The learned Landoff who more although he be
> A professed Acamedian,
> Has laid aside his grauer waightier studdies,
> To exercise his skill not yet forgotten,
> Being brought vp a Page at Court, and practis'd
> Much in that quallity. (N4^v)

The consistency of thematic development and even the conception of character itself have been sacrificed to a series of formulaic stereotypes that do not even fit together. This example suggests that the magician's role on the public stage was, by this time, almost played out, though he continued to appear in masques, where stereotypes and ritual magic still served a function.

The second unusual play, *The Birth of Merlin*, is peculiar because it is simply a dramatization of a medieval prose romance. Though the play was probably staged about 1608, and thus came between the two most human and humanistic stage magicians—Faustus and Prospero—Merlin is much like a magician from narrative romance. He is a freak, the offspring of a devil and Joan Goe-too't; he talks as soon as he is born and is given great powers from birth. Though the name and character of his mother and the presence of her clown brother show the playwright's conscious updating of the romance to provide the almost mandatory stage clowns, the anonymous author does little to change the conception of Merlin himself. There are traditional plot elements (magical contests and masquelike visual shows of Merlin's abilities), but there is no weakness or humanity in Merlin. He has no doubts and needs no scholarship or additional wisdom. At one point he is caught reading a book by his mother; when asked why he reads, Merlin replies: "To sound the depths / Of Arts, of Learning, Wisdom, Knowledge" (3.4.24–25).[25] But this is the

---

25. *The Birth of Merlin*, in *The Shakespeare Apocrypha*, pp. 351–82. All references are to this edition.

play's only line about the scholarly life, and Merlin is obviously born knowing more than can ever be found in books. He is completely self-sufficient, able to defeat even his father. The play works almost entirely in terms of plot complication and verbal wit; the reader is not at all interested in its characters.

Though most playwrights had abandoned medieval romance as a source by 1608, *The Birth of Merlin* recalls for us how similar the original stage magicians were to magicians in the romances. And the play suggests, by its very oddness in its time, how far most playwrights had moved from stock romance material in their use of magic.

III.

The magician who walks onstage in tragedy and didactic drama[26] is very different from the jovial, love-assisting character so often found in romantic comedy. In fact, magicians in didactic drama are not, by and large, important characters. Aside from Faustus and Pope Alexander in *The Devil's Charter*, no magician has a major role in these plays. Most are minor accessories to more important characters, useful to accentuate the evil of those with whom they conspire.

Such is the case in *The Wars of Cyrus* (1588), which portrays the good ruler and contrasts virtue with vice to demonstrate virtue's superiority. Araspas, one of Cyrus's lieutenants, is put in charge of a beautiful female prisoner of war and immediately falls in love with her. Cyrus himself refuses even to look at her:

> Nothing can more dishonour warriours
> Then to be conquered with a woman's looke. (1.3.340–41)[27]

Not only conquered by her look but also determined to conquer her physically, Araspas engages a magician to prepare a magic charm so that the woman will love him. The magician accepts the job confidently:

26. With the term *didactic drama* I refer to those plays—like *The Wars of Cyrus* and *A Looking Glass for London and England*—that are serious and didactic in tone (and thus not comedy or romance) and yet that are not proper tragedies or histories. It is difficult to find a generic name for such plays.

27. *The Wars of Cyrus*, ed. James Paul Brawner. All references to the play are to this edition.

Doubt not the operation of this charme,
For I haue tride it on *Dianas* nymph
And made her wanton and lasciuious.
If *Panthea* be a Goddesse, she must yeeld. (3.2.766–69)

Panthea does not yield but repulses Araspas once more. When
the disappointed lover returns to complain of the charm's failure, the magician gives him an answer that seems to belie his
earlier assurances:

Araspas: Must Magicke yeeld to vertue? Wherefore then
          Didst thou assure me she should be in loue?
          ....
Magician: Reason, my Lord, was the predominant;
          Her intellectuall part striued against loue,
          And Magicke cannot commaund the soule. (3.2.860–
          67)

Araspas finds out what most magicians know—magic has
limits. The playwright's point is primarily didactic: Panthea's
virtue and self-control are so great that they can withstand
even the power of magic. As Vandermast made clear in *John
of Bordeaux*, magic cannot force one to love against one's will.
Magic is used in *The Wars of Cyrus* only in this one short
scene. The play extols the good ruler and the virtuous
woman; one resists the temptations of feminine charm, the
other clings, like the lady in Milton's *Comus*, to a chastity so
strong that even magic is powerless against it.

Limitations of a different sort are experienced by the magicians who play a minor role in Greene's *A Looking Glass for
London and England*. Concerned primarily with retelling the
biblical story of the fall of Nineveh (London, of course, is to
see itself in the mirror of corrupt Nineveh and reform), the
play presents a ruler, Rasni, who practices almost every vice
known to man. He is proud, lustful, gluttonous, cruel, and
incestuous. To complete the picture of his evil, he employs a
corps of magicians to carry out some of his more extravagant
schemes. Here, too, the purpose is didactic, for the plot is a
series of magical contests between Rasni and his magicians
and God and his prophet, Jonah. Rasni commands his magicians to create an arbor for his sister/fiancée: "The Magi with
their rods beate the ground, and from under the same riseth a
braue Arbour" (line 495, s.d.).[28] But the magicians' spectacle

28. Robert Greene and Thomas Lodge, *A Looking Glasse for London and*

is no sooner completed and the incestuous sister installed in the arbor than God sends a wind that knocks it down and kills Rasni's sister. At another point in the play, God creates a spectacle of his own by sending a hand from a cloud to warn the king of his sins. But the magicians, called upon to interpret this phenomenon, miss its point entirely. They explain it away with garbled astronomical terms: "These are but clammy exhalations, / Or retrograde coniunctions of the starres" (lines 1560–61). After numerous warnings from God and Jonah, Rasni and his court repent, and even the magicians are brought to acknowledge the superior power of God. Thus, magic is employed both to intensify the audience's awareness of the evil of those who use or commission it and to demonstrate, by its inevitable defeat, the superior power of virtue and, in this play, of God himself. Such evil magic is often employed to accentuate the power of God and virtue and is, of necessity, limited in its power and effectiveness.

A much more extensive use of magic in a didactic drama occurs in Barnabe Barnes's anti-Catholic play, *The Devil's Charter*. The play begins spectacularly with a dumb show in which the soon-to-be Pope Alexander VI bribes cardinals and then makes a pact with the devil in exchange for the triple crown of the papacy. Many of the details—including repeated attempts by the conjured spirit to find a shape pleasing to Alexander (a cleric's shape is finally chosen) and the letting of Alexander's blood—resemble the much longer pact scene in *Doctor Faustus*. But once this opening show is over, magic is used primarily for spectacle and not to any real thematic purpose.

The central point of *The Devil's Charter* is that Alexander and his family are totally corrupt. The play is Senecan in its delight in poisonings and general slaughter. Though Alexander has magical powers (or, more exactly, the powers of a witch), he employs a series of poisoners to dispose of his gallery of victims rather than using his magic. The Pope is fond of claiming that his ambitious climb to power has been for the good of his children: "All my misty machinations / And Counsels held with black *Tartarian* fiends / Were for the glorious sunne-shine of my sonnes" (lines 339–42).[29] But he

England, in *The Plays and Poems of Robert Greene*, ed. J. Churton Collins, 1:137–214. All references to the play are to this edition.
29. Barnebe Barnes, *The Devil's Charter: A Tragedie Containing the Life*

quickly becomes reconciled to the fact that one son has killed the other and later even arranges the poisoning of his daughter Lucrezia, with whom both he and his oldest son have had incestuous relations. In fact, Alexander—like Rasni—is involved in almost every gruesome crime and sin imaginable. He not only commits incest and then has his daughter murdered, he also has homosexual relations with a young, unwilling nobleman and then murders him with asps to gain his estates. He poisons countless political and religious leaders. In such a man, magic is only one more evil to swell his catalog of crimes, and in Barnes's play it is only one more spectacle to divert an audience from the play's many shortcomings.

The play's most spectacular scene is also perhaps the most elaborate conjuration in Jacobean drama. (Conjurations appear only in plays about evil magicians; evidently the actual rite performed onstage was considered damning and thus was to be avoided when presenting sympathetic magicians. Faustus is something of an exception here, as I suggest in Chapter 4). Having seen in his magical glass that his youngest son has been murdered, Alexander summons spirits to show him the murderer. His equipment is complex—robes, a bell, a rod, a book, coals in an earthen vessel, and perfumes. His ceremony is clearly astrological, for he calls on the spirits of the month and the hour and prepares a special fumigation of "red sandall" to attract a particular set of spirits. Robert West has shown that the scene follows in many of its details the *Heptameron* of Peter of Abano, a detailed handbook on magic. But West concludes:

> The dominant impression from the play's conjuration is of that utter nonsense which orthodox authorities so scornfully insisted magicians relied on. . . . It may be thought, then, either that Alexander's conscious practice was rather more diabolical than the actual rituals of the time required, or that the scene in the play is addressed to the audience as a stripping of magic to its insensate fundamentals.[30]

Ironically, the result of his elaborate and much protracted ceremony is the revelation to Alexander of what the audience already knows—the son has been killed by his older brother, and their sister Lucrezia has murdered her husband. This in-

and Death of Pope Alexander the Sixt, ed. R. B. McKerrow. All references to the play are to this edition.
30. *The Invisible World,* p. 128.

formation, its impact lessened by the audience's prior knowledge, is all that magic accomplishes in the play. Here as elsewhere, magic is revealed as a deceptive power, spectacular and promising much, but in practice weak and empty.

In the last spectacle of the play, the devil intervenes in one of Alexander's elaborate poisoning attempts. By switching cups, the devil poisons Alexander and his son instead of their intended victims. Though this scene may have been simply another spectacle for Barnes, it is a surprisingly good way to end a play that has not had a single strong and good character. If the evil Alexander is to be punished, then the devil himself had better do it. None of the human characters is strong or intelligent enough to defeat Alexander. All the dogmatism and horrors of *The Devil's Charter* are summarized by the groveling Pope's final didactic speech:

> Learne miserable wretched mortall men,
> By this example of a sinfull soule,
> What are the fruites of pride and Auarice,
> Of cruell Empire and impietie,
> Of prophanation and Apostacie,
> Of brutish lust, falsehood, and perfidie,
> Of deep dissembling and hypocrisie,
> Learne wicked worldlings, learne, learne, learne by me
> To save your soules, though I condemned be. (Lines 3239–47)

It is merciful that the black magician functioning as a play's chief character has so few representatives on the English stage. A spectacular example of evil, he is a static character, incapable of change or growth. Plays in which he appears usually have a distinctly religious flavor and are often anti-Catholic. In such plays, magic is only one of a gallery of evil practices to be reformed or defeated by representatives of good and morality.

The evil magicians mentioned so far have been used by playwrights primarily for didactic or plot purposes. But often the magician's role is so minor that even his plot function is lost, and he becomes purely a purveyor of spectacle. With regard to such spectacles, Louis Wright remarked:

> Certainly the conjuror was a favorite performer with the populace; he took rank with the clown and devil; the uncritical crowd cared little about the dramatic requirements of the play; they wanted to see the conjuror's spectacles, extraneous or otherwise. . . . Players and playwrights [sometimes] simply inserted extraneous exhibi-

tions of jugglery and conjury in order to satisfy the popular craving
for sensational shows.[31]

Though Wright perhaps overstated a bit the extraneous nature
of most of the magicians, there certainly are plays in which
magicians appear solely in "cameo" roles. A prime example
of such a play is the anonymous comedy *The Wisdom of Doctor Dodypoll* (1599).

Among the varied and tangled love plots in *Dodypoll* is an
episode in which a once-loved but now rejected maiden, Lucilia, pursues her former lover into the woods, much as the
scorned Helena pursues Demetrius in *A Midsummer Night's
Dream*. In the wood is an Enchanter out hunting for his fairy
servants. They have stolen away his jeweled cup and are using
it to provide a banquet for an amazed peasant who has happened by and suddenly finds food and drink before him. Practical, he seizes the cup and leaves with it, scorning to stop
even for the food that remains. Just as the Enchanter arrives
on the scene so do Lucilia and her Lassingbergh, and the Enchanter overhears Lassingbergh's rejection of his former love.
Much attracted by Lucilia, the Enchanter puts both her and
Lassingbergh under a spell, moves them to a green bank, has
a banquet brought in, and tries to convince Lucilia, now
awake but suffering from amnesia, that she and he are really
husband and wife. When she doubts, he begins to describe
their courtship in terms similar to Volpone's temptation of
Celia or Comus's attempted seduction of the Lady:

> Why loue, doubt you that?
> Twas I that lead you through the painted meades,
> Where the light Fairies daunst vpon the flowers,
> Hanging on euery leafe an orient pearle,
> Which strooke together with the silken winde,
> Of their loose mantels made a siluer chime.
> Twas I that winding my shrill bugle horne,
> Made a guilt pallace breake out of the hill,
> Filled suddenly with troopes of knights and dames,
> Who daunst and reueld whilste we sweetly slept,
> Vpon a bed of Roses wrapt all in goulde,
> Doost thou not know me yet? (Lines 1087–98)[32]

31. "Juggling Tricks and Conjury on the Stage before 1642," pp. 278, 284.
32. *The Wisdom of Doctor Dodypoll*. All references to the play are to the
edition cited in the bibliography. Edgar Wind, *Pagan Mysteries in the Renaissance*, pp. 59, 70, discusses the incorporation of a modified epicureanism by

Interrupting this seduction come the peasant and a number of the main characters, drawn on by the cup the peasant has shown them and by his story of how he came by it. Lucilia's father, a jeweler, is among them, and he has with him a ring that dissolves enchantments. Immediately the Enchanter, his spirits, and all traces of the banquet are borne away, and we hear no more of the episode. Only the cup remains in the play. There is no reason for the scene; it changes nothing, helps no character grow, and even the cup is of no importance to the plot. The Enchanter is simply stage diversion, providing a break in an admittedly overextended plot, allowing for two banquets, the sight of fairy attendants, a song and music, and a seduction scene. Although the Enchanter clearly intended Lucilia no good, he has no didactic weight, for he is not really a character but only a prop, a diverting piece of stage machinery that disappears once it has served its purpose. Such magical scenes function almost as unlabeled masques within their plays. Like masques, they usually have one-dimensional, stereotyped characters, set speeches, visual spectacle, music, supernatural elements, and the magician himself, who is responsible for providing all the effects.

Doctor Dodypoll's Enchanter, as a magician who has no connection with the rest of his play, is certainly an extreme example of such a character. But the magicians who appear in such plays as Shakespeare's *Henry VI* (1591), Chapman's *The Gentleman Usher* (1602), Dekker's *The Whore of Babylon* (1606), and Webster's *The White Devil* (1612) have very little more connection with the central issues of their dramas. Such examples only reemphasize the familiar stereotype of the stage magician.

Perhaps the best way to summarize the stereotyped features of both good *and* evil magicians is to look at one final play, *Two Noble Ladies and the Converted Conjuror* (1622?). This play is similar to its near contemporary *The Two Merry Milkmaids* in its compositeness, the anonymity of its author, its use of a completely formulaic magician, and its overall wretchedness. The play concerns two love affairs that are vastly complicated by a Christian-pagan war. When Antioch

---

neoplatonists. The emphasis on the sensory aspects of magical ceremonies discussed above reinforces this point. Thus, the association between neoplatonic magic and epicureanism may be partially responsible for the epicurean sensuality with which many dramatists endow their magicians.

is sacked by the Turks, Cyprian, a scholar and magician, is brought to the Souldan's court by the greatest Turkish warrior, Lysander. In front of Lysander, Cyprian, and his whole court, the Souldan announces his intention of marrying his own daughter. Horrified, she flees the court leaving Lysander, her lover, to mourn her absence. Cyprian becomes a mentor to Lysander and tries to comfort him. He diverts Lysander with a masque that reveals Lysander's previously unknown parentage.

As soon as the masque ends, however, an angelic spirit appears:

Cyprian: whence comes this sound? this heau'enly harmonie?
          what apparition's this rais'd without mee?
Angell: Thou by whose skill anothersfate was showne
          shalt finde thy selfe ignorant of thine owne.
          Read here, and learn thyne owne catastrophe.
Cyprian reads.
          Cyprian borne at Antioch, bred in arts
          of deep caldean learning, by whose skill
          Wonders are wrought, since in him vertuous parts
          are found, it is the gracious heauens will,
          that now ere long, this learned heathen man
          shall renounce Magicke, and turne Christian.
          ....
Angell: I come not by the call of magicke spells;
          but by that pow'r that in yond pallace dwells
          am sent to tell these news. (Lines 1101–19)[33]

Until this point in the play, Cyprian has been the perfect "good" magician, humane, considerate of Lysander, willing to further true love. So far Cyprian has done nothing for which he has any reason to repent.

But with the introduction of the contest—Cyprian's show for Lysander is bettered by God's show for Cyprian—Cyprian must be blackened so that he can convert convincingly. The playwright provides a series of plot twists that turn Cyprian into a typically "evil" magician. He rescues Justina, a Christian lady in distress, falls madly in love with her, and resolves to use a love charm on her. He makes an epicurean temptation speech (lines 1583–99), but it does no good. Cyprian's most sensuous temptations do not succeed with the chaste Chris-

33. *The Two Noble Ladies and the Converted Conjuror.* All references to the play are to the edition cited in the bibliography.

tian, and he resorts to more powerful aids by calling up devils
to make her yield: "hell shall force her / to offer vp that Iewell
of delight" (lines 1637–38). But Justina remains firm, and,
moved by her faith, Cyprian is finally convinced that Christianity is stronger than magic. Cyprian throws away his
charmed rod and his magic books and renounces his magic.

> . . . O how haue I mispent my tyme
> That in my studdys could not finde this faith!
> I did beleeue that Arte could teach the vse
> and rule of all the world. Was not this ffaith?
> I did beleeue that Arte could reach to hell
> and thence fetch secrets vp surpassing arte.
> Was not this ffaith / I did beleeue that hell
> could all desires accomplish: But I finde
> Beleefe is but deluded in this kinde. (Lines 1803–11)

So Cyprian becomes the "converted Conjuror" and returns to
good following the renunciation of his magic. Most of the
traits of the good and the evil magician are combined in Cyprian. First a tutor, a love-assister, a benevolent, nonreligious
magus, he suddenly turns would-be rapist, aligned with hell
and devils, ready to use his magic to satisfy his personal desires. The combination of these two seemingly mutually ex-
clusive stereotypes suggests not only how bad the play itself
is, but also how barren of originality and life stage magic had
become by the 1620s.

The title page of the second edition of *Friar Bacon and Friar Bungay*, 1630 (courtesy University of Pennsylvania, Van Pelt Library).

3

Friar Bacon

The Educable Magician

Though every Tudor-Stuart dramatic magician was to some extent composed of the stereotyped traits examined in the previous chapter, not all of them were wooden or ridiculous. In a few instances, magic—far from merely amusing or terrifying the audience or distracting it from the play's central concerns—contributed importantly to the play's development. The period faced several unresolved questions about magic: whether it was good or evil, demonic or daemonic, effective or mere charlatanism. The complex responses that such questions provoked provided material that could be used in literary treatments of magic, and certain playwrights took full advantage of this potential material. The plays discussed in this and the following chapters are cases in point: *Friar Bacon and Friar Bungay*, *Doctor Faustus*, *Bussy D'Ambois*, and *The Tempest* all include magicians whose practice of magic is in some way essential to a full understanding of the play. Each playwright saw magic from a slightly different perspective, but all raised the questions of how much achievement, power, or knowledge is permitted to man, and what are his possibilities and his human limitations.

I.

Much of the critical attention paid to Robert Greene's *Friar Bacon and Friar Bungay* concerns the character of its leading magician, Friar Bacon. A poor Oxford scholar, working night and day on a wall to protect England, willing to help almost anyone from a prince to homesick schoolboys, and entertaining visiting royalty with harmless magic tricks, Friar Bacon seems a prototypical good magician. Frequent descriptions of him by other characters as the "jolly" and "frolic" friar add to the general amiability of his portrait. Yet his use of necromancy, his apparent willingness to further Edward's lust for Margaret, and his self-proclaimed responsibility for the deaths of the young scholars seem more appropriate to a black magician. Indeed, some recent scholars regard the frolic friar as a dangerous and overproud man who escapes damnation only by his timely and heartfelt repentance. One critic has suggested that his magic "leads Bacon to reflect in himself or foster in others each of the traditional Seven Deadly Sins,"[1] while an editor of the play has called it a tragicomedy in which the happiness of the lovers is seriously "threatened by sorcery."[2] Such readings of Greene's play suggest something quite different from the festive romantic comedy most earlier critics assumed it to be.[3]

Bacon's character, with its blend of evil and benevolent traits, encourages debate over the genre and didactic purpose of the play. Greene manages to hold Bacon's good and evil traits in a precarious balance, unlike the less successful author of *The Two Noble Ladies and the Converted Conjuror*, where Cyprian was first everything good, then everything evil, and then miraculously good again.[4] Indeed, Bacon is not the only character in the play who shows an apparently intentional two-sidedness. Disguises, character transformations, and much ambiguous descriptive imagery suggest that simple moral evaluation of characters in Greene's play is impossible.

1. Albert Wertheim, "The Presentation of Sin in 'Friar Bacon and Friar Bungay,'" p. 275.
2. Daniel Seltzer, introduction to Robert Greene, *Friar Bacon and Friar Bungay*, p. xvi.
3. Among the critics who read the play as festive and Friar Bacon as benevolent are Waldo F. McNeir, "Traditional Elements in the Character of Greene's Friar Bacon"; Muriel C. Bradbrook, *The Growth and Structure of Elizabethen Comedy*, pp. 80–81; and Peter Mortensen, "*Friar Bacon and Friar Bungay*: Festive Comedy and 'Three-Form'd Luna,'" p. 200.
4. Wertheim, "The Presentation of Sin," argues that Bacon's magic becomes increasingly evil as the play progresses, but this reading gives trouble in several scenes, most notably when Bacon wins his patriotic victory over Vandermast.

Friar Bacon and Friar Bungay explores conflicting tendencies in man: love and lust, social concern and selfishness, humility and pride. Though good finally triumphs, and reason, friendship, love, and good intentions are affirmed, the triumph comes only after the play has laid bare some of the less attractive attributes of man and after four characters have been killed. *Friar Bacon* goes beyond the simple celebratory frolic it seems at first glance to be.

The disguisings and role reversals so evident in the play provide an introduction to the uncertainty and ambiguity that underlie its surface. In the first scene, Prince Edward talks of his recent disguise as a "frolic courtier," a disguise adopted in order to hunt unrecognized—both deer and women. The Prince, frolicking incognito with his companions or lustfully attempting to buy a country girl's favors, is quite different from the noble young man who later meets and weds the Spanish Princess Eleanor. Like Shakespeare's Prince Hal, and like Bacon himself, Ned has two sides to his character. He remains interesting and important in the play only as long as there is uncertainty about which of the two personalities will dominate. The King's fool, Rafe, disguises himself for a period as Prince Edward, and Lacy disguises himself as a farmer in order to woo Margaret for Edward. Such disguises are one indication of tensions within the world of play.

Indicative of more seriously troublesome ambiguities and uncertainties than the disguises reflect are the transformations or role reversals that take place during the play. Lacy woos Margaret for Edward, acting in fact as a pander for his master's lust, hoping to buy Margaret for the Prince. But after meeting and falling in love with her himself, Lacy is transformed from a pander to a lover. He casts off both his role as pander and his disguise as a farmer early in the play when he stands in the church ready to marry Margaret. Yet his original willingness to deceive Margaret qualifies his character. He is not the easy foil to Edward—loving suitor versus the lustful seducer—that he is sometimes assumed to be.[5] Later in the play, his scheme to test Margaret's love suggests that he is subject to suspicion and doubt about the woman he claims to love. Like Prince Edward, Lacy is not an idealized but rather a slightly flawed character.

5. For two examples of this point of view, see note 9 below.

Margaret's character also has its inconsistencies.[6] Delight-
fully straightforward and frank in her admission of love for
Lacy, she is less frank about admitting this love when con-
fronted by the proposals of the two landowners. She could
easily have told them that she loved someone else; yet she
stalls and asks for time to choose. Margaret is often given
credit for having the power, through her beauty, to transform
Lacy from willing go-between to equally willing suitor. But if
she is to be credited with this beneficial transformation, she
must also bear the responsibility for transforming the two
squires, by the same beauty, from best friends to dueling enemies. Just as Margaret, though she is only a deerkeeper's
daughter, is elevated by her frequent comparison to classical
beauties such as Daphne, Semele, and Helen, so the landowners, changed by their love for her, assume the role of chivalric
champions battling for the love of a maiden. Margaret's delay-
ing tactics give the two men false hope and make her as responsible for their deaths as Bacon is responsible for the
deaths of their sons.

Like Lacy and Ned, Margaret also undergoes a transformation of sorts, though hers is temporary. Having learned that
Lacy will marry someone else, Margaret enters holy orders
and becomes a nun. She forswears all the vanities of this
world, including love:

> Now, farewell, world, the engine of all woe;
> Farewell to friends and father; welcome, Christ.
> Adieu to dainty robes; this base attire
> Better befits an humble mind to God
> Than all the show of rich abiliments.
> Love, oh love, and with fond love, farewell. (14.29–34)[7]

Such a withdrawal no more reflects Margaret's true nature
than the role of farmer fits Lacy, the role of simple courtier
describes Prince Edward, or the role of Prince can be convincingly played by Rafe. Lacy has only to ask, "Whence, Peggy,

6. Calling Margaret "an uneasy compromise between two conventions,"
Kenneth Muir also pointed out the inconsistencies in her character and found
her ambiguities a flaw, thereby dissenting from the host of critics who praise
her. See "Robert Greene as Dramatist," in *Essays on Shakespeare and Elizabethan Drama in Honor of Hardin Craig*, ed. Richard Hosley, p. 50.

7. *Friar Bacon and Friar Bungay*, ed. J. A. Lavin. All further references to
the play are to this edition.

comes this metamorphosis? / What, shorn a nun?" (14.65–66), and she is stopped short, her transformation reversed: "Off goes the habit of a maiden's heart" (14.89). Her vows forgotten, Margaret reassumes her rightful role as virtuous and constant loved one.

All the major characters have similar moments of change and vacillation. The play's only tragic moments, the deaths of the Lamberts and Serlsbys, occur when characters take their adopted roles too seriously. The fathers' assumption of chivalric roles and their duel for Margaret result in death for both of them and, indirectly, for their sons. Most other transformations and disguises are reversed or disappear by the play's end, but the landowners carry their role-playing too far, into death.

Despite the presence of a good deal of magic in the play, magic is responsible for none of these transformations or disguises. Though known for its metamorphic power, magic here reveals disguise rather than assists it (like Merlin's magic in *The Faerie Queene*). In fact, magic's chief purpose in the play is to reveal truth, though often the revelation is untimely. Thus, Bacon reveals the "truth" of Burden's scholarly endeavors of the night before by bringing in the Henley hostess who is his mistress, and he strips Prince Edward and Rafe of their assumed identities:

> Edward, King Henry's son and Prince of Wales,
> Thy fool disguised cannot conceal thyself.
> I know both Ermsby and the Sussex earl,
> Else Friar Bacon had but little skill. (5.67–70)

In addition, he reveals to Edward exactly what his supposed agent, Lacy, is doing with Margaret. In a similar way, Bungay is able to tell Margaret the true identities of the disguised courtiers, Edward and Lacy. Nowhere in the play is the magic of Bacon or of Bungay deceptive. It is occasionally petty (as in the scene with the hostess), and it may have monetary motives (Edward promises Bacon money if he will stop Lacy and Margaret's wedding). But it is never specifically evil or deceitful. Even the deaths for which Bacon has received so much blame, and for which he blames himself, occur through what seems to be innocent magic. The prospective glass shows only what is actually happening. What kills is literally truth, not

magic. Similarly, there is nothing obviously wrong with Bacon's most ambitious magical feat, the creation of the brazen
head. Bacon's intentions are patriotic:

> And I will strengthen England by my skill,
> That if ten Caesars lived and reigned in Rome,
> With all the legions Europe doth contain,
> They should not touch a grass of English ground,
> The work that Ninus reared at Babylon,
> The brazen walls framed by Semiramis,
> Carved out like to the portal of the sun,
> Shall not be such as rings the English strond
> From Dover to the market place of Rye. (2.57–65)

But something goes wrong despite Bacon's good intentions.
Magic power has its possible dangers as well as its possible
good effects, just as Margaret's beauty, usually positive in the
play, indirectly produces the deaths of her two country suitors.
Empson surely struck to the heart of the play when he wrote,
"The process [of the double-plotting of *Friar Bacon*] is simply
that of dramatising a literary metaphor—'the power of beauty
is like the power of magic'; both are individualist, dangerous,
and outside the social order."[8]

Greene indicates the parallelism of Bacon and Margaret in
a number of ways. Most obviously, both share responsibility
for the deaths in the play, and both undergo a religious withdrawal of sorts. Margaret takes the vows of a nun and bids
farewell to the world, repentant for her worldly vanity. Bacon,
in the scene that directly precedes Margaret's vows, also repents:

> Bungay, I'll spend the remnant of my life
> in pure devotion, praying to my God
> That he would save what Bacon vainly lost. (13.106–8)

Later, both retract their vows, at least partially. Margaret rejoins the world as Lacy's wife, and Bacon returns, in a limited
way, to his magical skills with the prophecy that ends the play.
Though Margaret's and Bacon's powers have been shown to be
dangerous and easily misused, neither beauty nor magic is
essentially evil. Despite their potential danger, both magic

---

8. William Empson, *Some Versions of Pastoral*, p. 31.

and beauty have a place in a proper order, as Margaret's and Bacon's final positions in the play suggest.[9]

That this is the point of much of the play is suggested by two prophetic image patterns. With regard to Margaret and her beauty, the image that recurs is that of Helen, most beautiful and dangerous of women. Margaret herself introduces the allusion when she compares Lacy, first, to Paris disguised as a shepherd courting the nymph Oenone (2.64–65) and, later, to the Paris who tempted Helen:

> His personage, like the pride of vaunting Troy,
> Might well avouch to shadow Helen's scape. (6.31–32)

In scene 10, Lambert calls Margaret "Suffolk's fair Helen"; indeed, she will be as fatal to him as Helen was to Troy. Margaret also, in that same scene, realizes the dangers of her beauty:

> Shall I be Helen in my froward fates,
> As I am Helen in my matchless hue,
> And set rich Suffolk with my face afire? (10.93–95)

Margaret's beauty produces ambivalent results and is carefully qualified by the imagery Greene chooses to describe her.

In much the same way, Bacon's nationalistic fervor is qualified. Though he serves well as England's magical champion

9. In an article that also argues that Greene carefully structured his play by means of parallel scenes and characters, Werner Senn ("Robert Greene's Handling of Source Material in *Friar Bacon and Friar Bungay*") calls Margaret a very minor character and sees the parallels between her and Bacon as "misleading; Margaret is kept in total ignorance of her suitors' fate and never feels any guilt on that score. The obvious parallels between the renunciation scenes of Bacon and Margaret further enhance the confusion of response. Margaret is never blamed, not even implicitly, for the deaths of Lambert and Serlsby, nor is it her reason for renouncing the vanity of a worldly life" (p. 553). Senn argues instead that the important parallel is between the situations of Edward and Bacon: "Both . . . are seen indulging in presumptuous projects, one, to debauch a girl, the other, to erect a brass wall around England. . . . To questions concerning their ambitions both answer with a curt, hostile 'what of this?'" (p. 551). For another statement of the parallels between Edward and Bacon, see Mortenson, "Festive Comedy," p. 200. Greene may well parallel Edward and Bacon, but to see such a parallel as the play's focus, as Senn does, forces him to conclude that only the first half of Greene's play is successful and that the playwright loses control of his structure in the second half, where Edward hardly appears. The Bacon-Margaret parallels— whether or not Margaret is conscious of her guilt, a guilt the Helen imagery surely suggests—are both those most obvious to an audience and those that hold the two plots in balance until Margaret and Bacon appear onstage together in the play's final, ritually ordered scene.

against the German magician, Vandermast, Bacon's attempt
to wall all England is carefully undercut by the imagery of the
play. As King Henry welcomes his foreign guests, his speech
is studded with images of walls:[10]

> Great men of Europe, monarchs of the west,
> Ringed with the walls of old Oceanus,
> Whose lofty surge is like the battlements
> That compassed high-built Babel in with towers,
> Welcome, my lords, welcome, brave western kings,
> To England's shore, whose promontory cleeves
> Shows Albion is another little world. (4.1–7)

The King of Castile replies in terms of other walls:

> England's rich monarch, brave Plantagenet,
> The Pyren Mounts swelling above the clouds,
> That ward the wealthy Castile in with walls,
> Could not detain the beauteous Eleanor. (4.13–16)

England is already walled with the ocean, and the trip from
Spain to England has been a difficult surmounting of a series
of walls for the visitors. England's glory can best be served not
by shutting her off from the rest of the world with Bacon's
wall but rather by allowing her communication and inter-
change with other countries. England can hold her own with
the best of Europe (as Bacon shows in the contest with Vandermast); there is no need for, but rather danger in, England's
withdrawal behind brass walls. The openness and richness of
the country are suggested by Henry's last speech in which he
portrays his kingdom as a kind of Eden, graced by the rulers
of other nations:

> But, glorious commanders of Europa's love,
> That makes fair England like that wealthy isle
> Circled with Gihon and swift Euphrates
> In royalizing Henry's Albion
> With presence of your princely mightiness;
> Let's march. (16.64–69)

In such a context, Bacon's ambitious desire to ring all England
with his wall seems as mistaken and misguided as his willingness to let the scholars have free access to his glass.

10. Mortenson, "Festive Comedy," p. 205, also notices the imagery concerning walls, remarking that nature has already done for England what Bacon proposes to do by unnatural means.

The qualifications these image patterns suggest about the powers of Margaret and Bacon disappear only in the final scene. There, Margaret rejoins the world, firmly within the social order as Lacy's wife and no longer a beautiful temptation.[11] In much the same way, Bacon uses his magic in the last scene for a proper purpose. His prophecy, supportive of the king and his successors, affirms the political order. This has been a chief responsibility of good English magicians since Geoffrey of Monmouth first created Merlin. Within the world of Greene's play, both beauty and magic have found their places in an ordered and convivial society.

II.

As we have seen, *Friar Bacon and Friar Bungay* is a play dealing, in part, with the proper place of magic within a stable social order. But acknowledgment of that place presupposes recognition and acceptance of the limits of magic's legitimate sphere of action. Because magic, like nearly everything and everyone else in the play, is ambiguous, its treatment is important as a clue to Greene's thematic intentions in the play as a whole.

Just as striking as the similarities among various characters is that among the various magic scenes in the play. Apart from the final prophecy, there are three kinds of scenes involving magic in *Friar Bacon*: transportation scenes, in which a person is carried on- or offstage by devils; prospective-glass scenes; and scenes that test magicians' skill (the contest scene and the later scene with the brazen head). Apparently unconcerned about repetition of effects, Greene created four transportation scenes, two scenes using the glass, and two magical contests. The repertoire of stage effects available to Greene could have furnished him with many more various and spectacular tricks than those he put onstage. But deliberate repetition with variation allowed Green to qualify and

11. Wertheim, "The Presentation of Sin," claims: "Counterpoised to the basically destructive magic of Bacon is the richly affirmative romantic magic of Margaret and Lacy." But if their love is so consistently affirmative, why does Lacy test Margaret and why does Margaret make her temporary renunciation of love? Surely, the final scene, with what Wertheim describes as "the traditional hymeneal festivities, here embellished with a magnificent prognostication of England's future prosperity" (p. 286), makes us realize that *both* Margaret and Bacon return to their proper roles in the larger society.

shade his presentation of magic just as he shaded his characters.

The contest scenes provide the most complete view of the magic in which the play is interested. In the public contest, all three magicians appear, and each is given an opportunity to speak and to perform feats of magic. What is striking is how similar the three men are. All are academics, learned, involved with philosophical magic. They differ only in their opinions as to which branch of astrological magic is most efficacious and in the degree of their learning and hence of their power.

In making his magicians so similar, Greene differed markedly from his source, *The Famous Historie of Fryer Bacon*. There, as both Lavin and Seltzer have pointed out,[12] Bacon's magic is whitewashed. Strong emphasis is placed on his piety, and he is given no connection with necromancy, whereas both Bungay and Vandermast are reported to have given the devil three drops of blood in exchange for their powers.[13] In addition, it is Bungay, not Bacon, who in the source is on the side of the lustful courtier and in opposition to the true lovers. Greene might thus have used available traditional material to portray Bacon as a relatively innocent, good magician opposed to the diabolical Bungay and Vandermast. But Greene did not adopt this ready-made pattern for his magician. Instead he deliberately introduced ambiguous elements into the characterization of Bacon and minimized the differences between him and his magical rivals.

The power of Greene's three magicians arises from their knowledge of how to command and bind spirits rather than from demonic pacts, such as Faustus made. The academic basis of their magic is demonstrated by the debate between Vandermast and Bungay about whether pyromancy or geomancy is the strongest form of magic. Vandermast claims to have carried on similar disputes and contests with scholars from all over Europe (as indeed some of the wandering philosophers of the time, such as Giordano Bruno and Henry Cornelius Agrippa, probably had, though their disputes were not necessarily about magic):

12. Seltzer, "Introduction," *Friar Bacon*, pp. xiii–xiv; J. A. Lavin, Introduction to Robert Greene, *Friar Bacon and Friar Bungay*, p. xv.

13. *The Famous Historie of Fryer Bacon*, in *Early English Prose Romances*, ed. William J. Thoms, 1:243.

I have given nonplus to the Paduans,
To them of Sien, Florence, and Bologna,
Rheims, Louvain, and fair Rotterdam,
Frankfort, Utrecht, and Orleans;
And now must Henry, if he do me right,
Crown me with laurel, as they all have done. (9.110–15)

Such a contest clearly involved national honor and was a test of rival nations' scholarship and learning as well as, in this literary example, their magicians. Bacon's victory in the contest is important, for he upholds England's honor. Just as she has a prince attractive enough to draw Eleanor over the seas, so too England has a scholar able to put foreigners to shame, worth coming to England to see and hear.

But the victory does not come in verbal debate (Bacon does not debate at all, for he scorns to dispute unless his opponent "were more learned than Vandermast" [9.129]). Before Bacon enters, Bungay and Vandermast have switched from debate to a contest of magical tricks. When Bacon does appear, he wins by performing the most impressive trick, by turning Vandermast's own magic against him. More stage time is devoted to visual spectacle than to scholarly debate. Although such spectacles were clearly not an aspect of the real-life debates and contests mentioned above, the overt magical demonstration is very much a part of literary magical tradition from Merlin to Munday's John a Kent and John a Cumber. Such visual spectacles were far more common onstage than the scholarly debate.[14]

In this contest scene, Greene provides a perfect example of the combination of the two traditions of magic we have been examining: the debate (often with nationalistic overtones) had a pattern found in his own time and country; the contest of magical spectacles had literary roots. A number of the traditional characteristics of the magician used by Greene in this play are found also in literary romance, as Waldo F. McNeir has pointed out.[15] But other elements of the magician's portrayal come not so much from literary as from contemporary sixteenth-century historical models. The references to cabal-

14. I know of no other Elizabethan or Jacobean play with a verbal debate about technical aspects of magic, though a number emphasize scholarship as an attribute of their magicians. The magical contest, on the other hand, is portrayed in several contemporary plays.
15. "Traditional Elements," pp. 174–75.

istic and hermetic magic, the university connections and philosophical bent of the magicians, and the debate itself (which may have been suggested by Bruno's debates with Oxford scholars during his 1583 visit to England)[16] are all related to the magic being practiced or discussed by learned men throughout Europe in the fifteenth and sixteenth centuries.

The explanation for this particular combination of verbal contest and magical competition may have to do with the playwright's attempt to make philosophical magic dramatically appealing. The real-life verbal debate may have brought interested scholars to Oxford to witness the play of contesting wits, but such a debate is hardly appropriate for lengthy development onstage. Even Greene's version of the debate is a bit too complex for a largely untrained audience to follow easily. Greene may have begun with the debate to set a high tone for the occasion and then developed the actual magical contest to help sustain audience attention. Such a double magical presentation—intellectual, largely theoretical magic with no spectacular effect, combined with sensational magical tricks—was fairly common on the Elizabethan stage (particularly in *Doctor Faustus*, where it was handled far less smoothly than by Greene in *Friar Bacon*). Greene used the double tradition to his advantage, for magic's two sides provide one more example of the doubleness that is a hallmark of the play.

In the contest before the kings of England and Spain, Bacon's magic is praiseworthy; it demonstrates learning and supports both King Henry and England's national honor. Had Bacon confined his magical endeavors to such demonstrations, he would have had little need to repent. But though he appears omnipotent in the scene with Vandermast, Bacon is human. He has good intentions but sometimes makes mistakes, is jovial and triumphant one moment and in despair the next. If the magical contest reveals Bacon at the peak of his magical powers, praised by both kings and fellow magicians, the scene with Miles and the brazen head shows him in a very different light.

16. J. D. McCallum, in "Greene's *Friar Bacon and Friar Bungay*," argues that Vandermast is a satirical portrait of Bruno and that the debate in *Friar Bacon* is modeled upon Bruno's Oxford debates, which were attended by the visiting Polish Prince Alasco. According to Frances A. Yates, *Giordano Bruno and the Hermetic Tradition*, p. 21, n. 2, this suggestion was made even earlier by A. W. Ward in his 1887 edition of Greene's play.

When Friar Bacon returns to the stage after the contest with Vandermast, his situation is very different from what it had been when he displayed his magic before the kings. Bacon's contest here is with the supernatural head he has created, not with rival magicians. The three-way contest was public and took place in daylight; here the whole scene takes place at night within the confines of Bacon's cell with only Miles as witness. Earlier Bacon was in complete control, confident and self-reliant. Here he is tired, forced to depend on his undependable servant:

> Bungay and I have watched these threescore days,
> And now our vital spirits crave some rest.
> If Argus lived, and had his hundred eyes,
> They could not overwatch Phobetor's night.
> Now, Miles, in thee rests Friar Bacon's weal. (11.21–25)

Bacon's human limitations are apparent. Wertheim interprets Bacon's inability to stay awake as an example of sloth.[17] But Miles's impartial testimony—"So. I thought you would talk yourself asleep anon; and 'tis no marvel, for Bungay on the days and he on the nights have watched just these ten-and-fifty days" (11.39–41)—suggests that no blame be attached to Bacon's inability to stay awake; he has simply reached his human limits. It is appropriate that these limitations should appear in this scene, for Bacon is overreaching. His attempt at personal glory, his secret endeavors to animate the brazen head, are not as praiseworthy as his public work for the glory of his country and ruler. Bacon proudly articulates for the audience his overreaching even as he tries to explain the experiment's failure:

> But proud Astmeroth, ruler of the north,
> And Demogorgon, master of the fates,
> Grudge that a mortal man should work so much.
> Hell trembled at my deep commanding spells;
> Fiends frowned to see a man their overmatch.
> Bacon might boast more than a man might boast. (9.104–9)

That Bacon's attempts to do more than any man are foiled by his human weariness and reliance on a dull-witted servant demonstrates how vulnerable his power is.

The messages that the head speaks—"Time is. . . . Time

17. "The Presentation of Sin," 282–83.

was. . . . Time is past"—are also important for understanding Bacon's limitations. They remind Bacon and the audience that men are subject to time, are mortal. The head is a memento mori, as Miles's flippant comment reminds us: "I thought, Goodman Head, I would call you out of your memento" (11.49). When Bacon hears from Miles the words the head has uttered, he suddenly realizes the effect of time on himself and his fame: "Ah, villain, time is past; / My life, my fame, my glory, all are past" (11.92–93). Shocked by the failure of his beloved project, Bacon does not yet see that he is primarily responsible for his own defeat. At this point in the play, he still regards the debacle of the brazen-head experiment as Miles's fault totally. Only a later scene, and a more serious accident, suffice to bring Bacon to awareness and acceptance of his own fallibility.

Despite the relative seriousness of the contest scenes, Greene did not neglect magic's potential for comedy. The transportations are all comic. For each, Bacon summons a devil or spirit to carry one or another character on- or offstage. Though he repeated the trick four times, Greene altered its mechanics each time in order to retain some variety. In the first such scene, Bacon actually conjures onstage, and a devil appears, bringing the Henley hostess and her shoulder of mutton to show in the flesh the "book" that one of the learned academics had been pondering the night before. The scene ostensibly demonstrates Bacon's power to the Oxford dons, but the trick's sexual implications only make the scholars look foolish. The scene is strictly comic and adds little except lightness of tone to the play.

The second transportation is part of the larger scene with the prospective glass in which Bacon interrupts the wedding of Margaret and Lacy. Part of the effect of the transportation depends on the split stage, with Lacy, Margaret, and Bungay performing an unconscious play-within-a-play for an audience of Bacon and Edward. Though Margaret is really frightened when a devil enters to carry Bungay away, the audience knows that the friar is only going to Oxford for dinner, and the scene remains comic. The transportation of Bungay and the laugh with which Edward responds to it suggest early in the play, I think, that Edward is not as angry as he pretends to be and that his intentions toward the lovers are not particularly malicious.

Spiriting Bungay away to Oxford for dinner lightens what has been a fairly serious scene; in like manner Vandermast's transportation back to Germany at the end of the magical contest and debate assures the audience that *frolic* is still the play's key word.[18] Despite serious moments in nearly every scene, the dominant and constantly resurfacing tone of *Friar Bacon* is comic. The comedy in Vandermast's transportation lies primarily in the ironic circumstance of his forced departure at the hands of a spirit whom, only a few moments before, he had himself commanded. But this demonstration of Vandermast's ephemeral power offers a comic foretaste of the defeats that Bacon will later suffer in his turn.

Greene's final variation on this kind of scene is perhaps his most outrageous flouting of traditional stage business and tone and carries the possibilities of transportation by devils to their extreme. A devil, initially annoyed by Bacon's order to seek out Miles, is, in effect, taken over by that intrepid clown. Miles *wants* to go to hell, hoping for a job as tapster there. Provided the devil gives him transportation, he will go voluntarily, and, when the devil offers his back, Miles straps on his spurs to ensure that he will have control over the gait of his unusual steed. The scene reverses both in tone and in circumstance the conventionally edifying but horrible spectacle of the condemned soul being dragged screaming off the stage.[19] Miles willingly anticipates the trip to hell where he will finally get a job appropriate to his talents. This final and most unusual transportation assures the audience that nothing can for long overcome the comic tone of the play. Prepared earlier by a series of comic transportations, the viewer laughs quite as readily at this one, for Miles clearly has no fear about his destination or his reception. Thus the "magical" feat of transportation, used by Greene as his most common visual demonstration of Bacon's power, reveals the comic aspects of an art that in other scenes is treated seriously.

The final kind of magical scene in Greene's play reveals other facets of the play's magic. The prospective-glass scenes with the divided stage are really plays-within-the-play. In making Bacon the creator of such "shows" (as he calls them

18. For a very different view of Greene's tone at this point, see Wertheim, "The Presentation of Sin," p. 280.

19. See *Friar Bacon*, ed. Lavin, p. 91, n. 62, for comment on the extraordinary nature of Miles's departure.

when repenting), Greene followed the tradition of the magician as master of ceremonies or stage manager. But Bacon creates for the audience something quite different from what he and Edward experience. For the two in Oxford, the glass is only a visual aid; they see but do not hear what happens in the church at Fressingfield—Lacy's wooing of Margaret for himself instead of the Prince, and their about-to-be-performed marriage—while the audience both sees and hears. Bacon and Edward actually witness a dumb show, an effect common to magical spectacles within plays (*The White Devil* and *Bussy D'Ambois* provide other examples). The tradition of the magically produced dumb show demonstrates quite graphically the limits of magic. Its creative powers, though often great, are not able fully to re-create reality. In Greene's play, magic produces sights but not sounds. Edward's inability to hear the lovers may partially explain the extreme response of the Prince, for a dumb show is always much more schematic, much less delicately shaded, than actions accompanied by dialogue. Edward only sees that Lacy kisses and is about to marry Margaret; he does not hear Lacy debate his love and his loyalty, nor does he hear the conversation between the lovers.

Even the prospective glass may have carried, for an Elizabethan audience, a double set of connotations that would have made ambiguous the moral implications of its use.[20] John Dee's "Mathematicall Preface" to Henry Billingsley's English Euclid mentions two kinds of glasses. Of the deceptive (and perhaps magical) glass, Dee wrote:

> Thynges, farre of, to seeme nere: and nere, to seme farre of. Small thinges, to seme great: and great, to seme small. One man, to seme an Army. Or a man to be curstly affrayed of his owne shadow. Yea, so much, to feare, that, if you, being (alone) nere a certaine glasse, and proffer, with dagger or sword, to foyne at the glass you shall suddenly be moued to giue backe (in maner) by reason of an Image, appearing in the ayre, betwene you & the glasse, with like hand, sword or dagger & with like quicknes, foyning at your very eye, likewise as you do at the Glasse.[21]

20. According to the *OED*, a prospective glass was "a magic glass or crystal in which it was supposed that distant or future events could be seen." Alternatively (and this is clearly only a secondary meaning for Greene's play), "prospective glass" could be used interchangeably with the earlier "perspective glass" to mean "spy-glass or telescope," a scientific instrument.

21. "Mathematicall Preface" to *The Elements of Geometrie of the most auncient Philosopher Evclide of Megara*, trans. Sir Henry Billingsley, sig. bl[v].

This description of a deceptive glass helps explain Edward's response to Bacon's glass. He lunges at it with his sword. Completely deceived by it, he believes that he can actually strike Lacy.

But the other kind of reference to perspective in Dee's "Preface" assumes that the assistance given by perspective and optical glasses to scientific observation is basic to the mathematical science that Dee is discussing:

> I speake nothing of *Naturall Philosophie*, which, without *Perspectiue*, can not be fully vnderstanded, nor perfectly atteined vnto. Nor, of *Astronomie*: which, without *Perspectiue*, can not well be grounded: Nor *Astrologie*, naturally Verified, and auouched. That part hereof, which dealeth with Glasses (which name, Glasse, is a generall name, in this Arte, for any thing, from which, a Beam reboundeth) is called *Catoptrike* and hath so many vses both merueilous, and proffitable. (Sig. bl^v)

Thus, according to the usage of the period, though Bacon's glass was primarily a magical device, a potentially deceptive object, it might also have carried connotations of the scientific tool that served to bring into view events far away without distorting or marring the image. Bacon's glass is both deceptive and accurate, of course, for it fools Prince Edward and, at the same time, truly shows what is happening at Fressingfield.[22]

Though the first prospective-glass scene is often regarded as evidence of Bacon's corruption—he is willing to serve Edward's lust in return for the promise of money—it can be read more positively. The play contains no other evidence of Bacon's greed. In fact, much is made of the modesty of his scholar's life, and he himself says nothing about money when Edward offers it. Perhaps Bacon helps Edward because he feels that seeing at a distance is, in this case, the best thing. After all, it is the glass, not Lacy, that absorbs Edward's initial sword-thrust. Bacon clearly feels in this scene that he is in

---

Lily B. Campbell, *Scenes and Machines on the English Stage during the Renaissance*, remarks on the tremendous interest shown by the public in mirrors and perspective glasses—"every means of distorting reality and deceiving the sight" (p. 149). Ernest B. Gilman, *The Curious Perspective: Literary and Pictorial Wit in the Seventeenth Century*, examines the Renaissance fascination with lenses and other devices for creating perspective (pp. 30–66).

22. This deliberately ambiguous aspect of Bacon's magic occasioned the debate between Frank Towne and Robert H. West over its nature: see Towne, "White Magic in *Friar Bacon and Friar Bungay*?," and West, "White Magic in *Friar Bacon*."

control, that he can handle Edward. Indeed, he rather cava-
lierly refers to the spectacle in the glass as a "comedy," calling
attention to the play-within-the-play, but also suggesting that
he knows or can bring about a happy ending. In any case, the
general tone of the prospective-glass scene is one of calm control on Bacon's part. Perspective pictures, as Ernest B. Gilman
has described them, play with a viewer's perceptions in a way
curiously apposite to the way Greene plays with his audience's perception of Bacon and his magic, and indeed of the
entire play:

> [The viewer] finds that he is no longer able to see the world un-
> equivocally—with the eye of cool reason—from a secure point of
> view. Instead he confronts an enigma that demands to be figured
> out, and his own relationship with the work becomes problemat-
> ical as it engages him in a process of puzzlement and revelation.[23]

Though the prospective glass is conventional magical equipment, its inclusion so prominently in *Friar Bacon* serves to
alert the audience to issues of perspective and its attendant
ambiguities.

The second prospective-glass scene is very different from
the first, both in tone and in outcome. It opens with Bacon
melancholy, worried about the loss of his fame and glory. He
knows that something bad will befall him but is not sure
what. This emphasis on his own difficulties, his self-concern,
somehow blurs the arrival of the two scholars to use his glass.
Almost indifferently he allows the young men access to the
glass, though he apparently does not know, as he did in the
case of Edward, what the glass will show. Once the glass focuses on the combat, Bacon does not interfere but advises his
visitors to "Sit still . . . and see the event" (13.63). Only when
both fathers and both sons are dead does Bacon speak again;
he has evidently been too helpless, too self-involved, or too
indifferent to interfere. Unlike the earlier scene, in which he
had perfect control, here he is unsure and preoccupied; somehow the deaths occur, and he does not prevent them. Once
the event is over, Bacon takes full blame and destroys his
glass:

> Bacon, thy magic doth effect this massacre.
> This glass prospective worketh many woes;
> . . . .

23. Gilman, *The Curious Perspective*, p. 66.

The poniard that did end the fatal lives
Shall break the cause efficiat of their woes.
So fade the glass, and end with it the shows
That nigromancy did infuse the crystal with. (13.75–76, 80–83)

But perhaps Bacon's abrupt turnabout is as excessive as
Margaret's decision to enter the convent. Both turn to God
out of disappointment; both have failed to get what they
wanted. Bacon's glass and his magic have not been evil,
though Bacon should have been more discriminating about
the purposes for which his magic was used. When he mourns
the loss of the Head not for what *England* has lost but for the
harm to his *own* reputation, Bacon shows himself too proud,
too self-interested, to continue unchecked. The practice of
magic for self-aggrandizement, for personal fame and glory, is
wrong; but magic for the good of others and of the country
should not be renounced. This is why the prophecy at the end,
announcing Bacon's return to patriotic magic, is important.
Bacon has learned, like Margaret, to curb and control his
power in the service of proper goals.

Like many other scenes in this carefully structured play, the
two prospective-glass episodes work as foils to each other,
showing the positive and negative aspects of magic, much as
the contest and the brazen-head scenes contrast public, patriotic magic with less commendable secret magic practiced for
selfish motives. Neither Bacon's glass nor his magic is bad—
he is as impulsive as Edward when he breaks the glass. Their
apparent flaws are rather Bacon's own, for he has failed to control carefully the conditions of their use. Bacon is powerful,
but he is also human and prone to human mistakes. This is
what he comes to admit within the play. After two serious
setbacks—the failure with the Head and the deaths of the
Lamberts and Serlsbys—a much humbler and more subdued
Bacon describes himself, at the beginning of his final prophecy, as:

Repentant for the follies of my youth,
That magic's secret mysteries misled,
And joyful that this royal marriage
Portends such bliss unto this matchless realm. (16.36–39)

Though Bacon officially renounces magic, he prophesies
the happy future of the realm, a traditional function of literary

magicians, and it is difficult to take his renunciation as total and irrevocable.[24] Bacon perhaps purges his magic of some of its elements, but, more important, as the final prophecy suggests, he learns to use it wisely and for proper purposes.

III.

The deaths of the Lamberts and Serlsbys qualify to some degree the frolicsome tone of the play, even though they are deemphasized (the men are onstage only a few moments, certainly not long enough to win much sympathy from an audience, and they are not noble characters). But if the ambiguities of character and of the play's magic have not provided adequate evidence of a serious foundation under the play's mirth, the deaths surely do. Even in a world of sport and frolic, death is not far away. Magic and love have no power to ward off the results of human folly or the passage of time. The qualifications of both love and magic that the play effects provide a balance in tone and theme. Like *Love's Labour's Lost*, *Friar Bacon* suffers no serious diminishment of joy and celebration, but both plays, by briefly introducing death into their worlds, acknowledge a darker, more complex side to life than their surfaces would seem to suggest.

Greene took advantage of the ambiguities associated with magic and turned them to his own ends, using the doubleness of magic and magician to underline the basic themes of his play. None of the major characters in the play is entirely consistent; each is in some way qualified so as to escape, at least for part of the play, an audience's wholehearted approval. Bacon, of course, is the play's best example. By a series of checks and balances, Greene produced a sophisticated and ambiguous portrait of a magician who is powerful and well inten-

24. Seltzer also stresses the alteration in Bacon's magic rather than its abandonment: "When [Bacon] repents, the art which had taught him prophetic powers becomes implicitly virtuous, for his learning–now similar to Prospero's—has become an ordered control of nature born of Christian contemplation" (p. xx). (I see little evidence that Bacon's new magic or art is specifically Christian in nature.) The continuator of the Bacon story, whether Greene or someone else, also did not take seriously Bacon's abandonment of magic. For though the Friar has no glass in *John of Bordeaux* (it has been shattered—a deliberate reference to *Friar Bacon*), his magical abilities are intact, and he uses them in the service of God and the good, in a way far more overtly Christian than anything in the earlier play.

tioned but also proud and fallible.[25] Endowed with extraordinary powers, able to do "more than a man might boast," Bacon also is brought to realize his human limitations and to accept his proper place in the society of which he is a part.

25. Lavin sees the ambiguity of Bacon's portrait not as a strength but as an "inconsistency" and an "incomplete artistic integration" (*Friar Bacon*, p. xxix).

Rembrandt, sometimes labeled *The Inspired Scholar*, or *Faust*, circa 1652 (courtesy New York Public Library, Prints Division).

4

Doctor Faustus

Master of Self-delusion

The ambiguities with which Greene hedged *Friar Bacon* were surely deliberate. When we turn to Marlowe's *Faustus*, ambiguity is again everywhere, but here it seems less purposeful, more accidental. Indeed, the play presents almost insoluble problems: its date of composition is in doubt, and it exists in two very different texts, neither of which modern scholars think to be wholly Marlowe's.[1] These extant texts, confused and mutilated as they are, have understandably been susceptible to a multitude of critical interpretations. Yet the very fascination that *Faustus* holds for critics suggests something of the power that the play retains, even in its imperfection.

Ambiguity and irony—key words in almost every discussion of *Faustus*—are frequently used to explain the play's various dichotomies. For underlying almost all explication of *Faustus* is a sense that the play's words and actions do not match: Faustus's rhetoric and his deeds are incommensurate, and the play's beginning and end frame a number of prosaic

1. Most critical opinions accept, as I do, W. W. Greg's argument for a 1592 date for *Doctor Faustus* (*Marlowe's "Doctor Faustus" 1604–1616: Parallel Texts*, ed. W. W. Greg, pp. 1–12). However, for a cogent argument supporting an earlier date, see Curt A. Zimansky, "Marlowe's *Faustus*: The Date Again." Greg's discussion of the texts (pp. 15–139) is generally accepted as the best explanation of the state of the 1604 and 1616 editions yet given. His arguments for preferring the 1616 text are generally followed by John D. Jump in his edition of *Doctor Faustus*, cited throughout my discussion.

and dull scenes in which Faustus seems totally unlike the
scholar of the play's opening.[2]

Among the reams of *Faustus* criticism are some treatments
of Marlowe's use of magic. But most of this work has sought
sources for the magical techniques and terminology Marlowe
uses and possible models for Faustus himself.[3] Very little has
been said about the importance of magic to the play's theme
and structure,[4] though the ambiguity and uncertainty commonly associated with magic make it a particularly appropriate concern for this much-debated play.

In a thorough review of Faustus's magic, Paul Kocher
termed it witchcraft and asserted, "Marlowe's play maintains
a thoroughly orthodox basis in theology, ethics, and astronomy; it makes no departure from consistency in its witchcraft
theory."[5] Kocher is correct, in the main, for as soon as Faustus
signs the pact with Mephistophilis he crosses the border that
separates magician from witch.[6] From this point on, Faustus
does not control but is controlled, as Mephistophilis demonstrates repeatedly.

But Faustus himself does not subscribe to the orthodox
theory that Kocher found predominant in Marlowe's play. In
the first scenes, he obviously has no intention of becoming a
witch or of subjecting himself to any power—godly or de-

2. Two critical camps have formed with regard to this problem. Some assume a split between the poetic scenes and those of farcical prose and call
this split a weakness in the play; see, for example, F. P. Wilson, *Marlowe and
the Early Shakespeare*, p. 74; J. B. Steane, *Marlowe: A Critical Study*, pp.
122–24; and *Doctor Faustus*, ed. Jump, pp. lix–lx. Others find the discontin-
uity functional within the argument of the play; see G. K. Hunter, "Five-Act
Structure in *Doctor Faustus*"; Muriel C. Bradbrook, "Marlowe's *Doctor Faustus* and the Eldritch Tradition," in *Essays on Shakespeare and Elizabethan
Drama in Honor of Hardin Craig*, ed. Richard Hosley, pp. 83–90; and Robert
Ornstein, "The Comic Synthesis in Doctor Faustus," in *Marlowe's "Doctor
Faustus": A Casebook*, ed. John D. Jump, pp. 165–72.

3. Most notable among the source-hunters are Paul H. Kocher, *Christopher
Marlowe: A Study of His Thought, Learning and Character*, pp. 150–73;
Bradbrook, "Marlowe's *Doctor Faustus*," pp. 83–90; and Beatrice Daw Brown,
"Marlowe, Faustus, and Simon Magus."

4. Two important exceptions to this generalization are Robert H. West,
"The Impatient Magic of *Doctor Faustus*," and William Blackburn, "'Heavenly Words': Marlowe's Faustus as a Renaissance Magician."

5. *Christopher Marlowe*, p. 170.

6. The simplest distinction between a magician and a witch is that a magician coerces, attracts, or controls spirits but is never in their control, while
a witch completely abandons himself to damned spirits, usually by some sort
of pact or blood bond. See Robert H. West, *The Invisible World: A Study of
Pneumatology in Elizabethan Drama*, p. 3.

monic—beyond his own. In his expansive imagination, Faustus sees himself controlling spirits:

> Shall I make spirits fetch me what I please,
> Resolve me of all ambiguities,
> Perform what desperate enterprise I will? (1.78–80)

Apparently speaking for Faustus and Cornelius as well, Valdes offers an apt metaphor for the relationship that they expect to prevail between themselves and the spirits:

> As Indian Moors obey their Spanish lords,
> So shall the spirits of every element
> Be always serviceable to us three. (1.120–22)

Though Faustus may intend to practice magic of dubious moral value, he envisions a straightforward situation in which he will compel spirits to do his will. He intends to be a magician "as cunning as Agrippa was" (1.116). Agrippa rejected magic that subjected man to the devil but accepted magic by which man could compel the devil to do his will. At this point in the play, Faustus—filled with dreams of personal power— would surely make a similar distinction about his intentions with regard to magic.

The path Faustus is attempting to walk is very narrow. Pico's famous *Oration* makes clear what is at stake:

> Magic has two forms: one consists entirely in the operations and powers of demons . . . which appears to me to be a distorted and monstrous business; and the other . . . is nothing other than the highest realization of natural philosophy. . . . The disciple of the first tries to conceal his practices because they are shameful and unholy; while cultivation of the second has always been the source of highest glory and renown in the arena of knowledge. No philosopher of merit, eager in the study of the beneficial arts, ever devoted himself to the first. . . . For just as that first form of magic makes man a slave and a pawn of evil powers, so the second form makes him their ruler and lord. That first form cannot lay claim to being either an art or a science; while the second, filled as it is with mysteries, comprehends the most profound contemplation of the deepest secrets of things and, ultimately, the knowledge of the whole of nature.[7]

Obviously, Faustus desires the power and knowledge made possible by Pico's second kind of magic; command of such

7. Pico della Mirandola, *Oration on the Dignity of Man*, in *Renaissance Philosophy I: The Italian Philosophers*, ed. and trans. Arturo B. Fallico and Herman Shapiro, pp. 164–66.

magic would be an appropriate next step from the accomplishments he has already to his credit. Though somewhat self-
centered, Faustus's aims for his magic are basically good:

> I'll have them read me strange philosophy
> And tell the secrets of all foreign kings;
> I'll have them wall all Germany with brass
> And make swift Rhine circle fair Wittenberg;
> I'll have them fill the public schools with silk
> Wherewith the students shall be bravely clad. (1.85–90)

He plans to be a benevolent magician who, like Agrippa, or
Greene's Friar Bacon, will command spirits for good, or at
least harmless, purposes. His rationale for turning to magic
suggests that he expects full control of the spirits with whom
he will deal.[8]

Faustus already has a number of the qualifications necessary to practice theurgic magic. He relies on his "wit" to
make him an effective magician, after a few lessons in ele-
mentary magic techniques from Valdes and Cornelius. Magic
is to be the crown of his intellectual achievements, the dis-
cipline that will be the real test of his abilities. The two student magicians clearly believe that Faustus will have powers
greater than theirs due to his greater intellect: "Faustus, these
books, *thy wit*, and our experience / Shall make all nations to
canonize us" (1.118–19, my italics). Cornelius lists requirements for the skilled magician: "He that is grounded in astrology, / Enrich'd with tongues, well seen in minerals, / Hath
all the principles magic doth require" (1.137–39). This list is
comparable to, though not as extensive as, Giambattista della
Porta's requirements for a magician: he must be a philosopher, a physician, an herbalist, know metals and distillation,
understand mathematics, especially astrology, and be skillful
in optics. "These are the Sciences," Porta concludes, "which
Magick takes to her self for servants and helpers; and he that
knows not these, is unworthy to be named a Magician."[9]

8. James Robinson Howe discusses at length Marlowe's familiarity with
neoplatonic and hermetic magical theories in *Marlowe, Tamburlaine and
Magic*, pp. 15–85. Robert H. West denies, however, that Faustus even thinks
of philosophic magic: "I have to believe that critics are ignoring the text to
think that Faustus began his magical enterprise in a spirit of high challenge,
much less that with the failure of coercive magic his ready consent to unre-
served demonolatry was a continuation of some creditable humanism" ("The
Impatient Magic of *Doctor Faustus*," p 232).

9. *Natural Magick in XX Bookes*, p. 3.

Faustus, with his considerable knowledge, is clearly the sort of person Porta describes.

As sources for Cornelius's enumerated requirements for magic, Kocher suggested a number of contemporary treatises on magic and witchcraft, but he deliberately refused to distinguish between what is necessary for a magician and what for a witch.[10] By failing to distinguish, Kocher lost one of the crucial ironies of the magic scenes. For none of Faustus's reliance on intellectual achievement, proper qualifications, or elaborate incantation is necessary for contact with demons if Faustus merely wishes to make a demonic pact, to become a witch. The concerns he expresses suggest that he is preparing to command spirits, as Agrippa asserted man might do.

But Faustus's preparations are careless and inadequate;[11] he constantly violates the rules set forth by the very treatises Kocher suggested were Marlowe's sources. In his haste to become immediately powerful—a haste characteristic of Faustus, who far too briefly considers and rejects his accomplishments in all major branches of learning—he neglects an important rule of magic, black or white. He resolves to conjure at once, and thus effectively makes impossible the purification, the ritual preparations, recommended by magical handbooks. (Such haste is not present in Marlowe's source, for in *The Damnable Life* Faustus has practiced magic for a long time before he calls up Mephistophilis to be his servant.)[12]

Kocher briefly summarized the handbooks' recommended magical procedures and drew conclusions about their omission from Faustus's preparations:

> The magician cleanses himself by fasting and prayer to God for nine days before the act of magic. When the time for conjuration arrives, he consecrates the circle and all his instruments. If he prays, it is to God, and he never salutes the fiends but wields

10. *Christopher Marlowe*, p. 138, n. 1. Reginald Scot complained about a similar lack of discrimination in sixteenth-century England. Scot himself distinguished between the two terms and noted, in another section of his book, that witches and conjurors are treated very differently by society, even for the same offense (*The Discoverie of Witchcraft*, pp. 245, 44).

11. In much of this discussion I am in agreement with William Blackburn, "'Heavenly Words,'" but he argues that Faustus "knows nothing about magic" and attributes his failure in magic to his basic ignorance (p. 5).

12. *The Historie of the Damnable Life, and Deserved Death of Doctor John Faustus*, in *The Sources of the Faust Tradition from Simon Magus to Lessing*, ed. Philip Mason Palmer and Robert Pattison More, p. 136.

against them the adverse power of holy names. Theoretically, the wizard is still on the side of the angels. Marlowe casts aside this pretense and makes the ceremony a dedication to Satan from the beginning. He is thus falling in with the classical tradition and with the orthodox Renaissance theological doctrine that any kind of conjuring is a worship of the Devil. No attempt is made to show Faustus as engaged in justifiable operations of white magic.[13]

But is it Marlowe or Faustus who casts aside the ordinary procedures? Faustus's haste guarantees that his conjurations will be futile. There is little hope that he will raise spirits to do his will; his methods suggest that he will fail even before Mephistophilis arrives onstage. Intoxicated by his own rhetoric and his desire for power, Faustus clearly destroys any possibility that his magic will actually work. (Lucifer, of course, is onstage from the beginning of the conjuration scene—he enters at 3.1—watching silently. He has obviously come because he wishes to witness the entrapment of Faustus, and his presence onstage makes it clear that hell and not Faustus is in control and that Faustus's conjuration is unlikely to work as he expects.)

Nothing in the play suggests that Faustus would have succeeded had he been more careful. The play rules out theurgic magic as a possibility for Faustus, although it does not make clear whether such magic is impossible because of Faustus's carelessness or because theurgic magic never succeeds. Had Marlowe intended a direct attack on the possibility of theurgic magic, however, he would more effectively have had Faustus follow all its rules and then fail. As it stands, the play chronicles Faustus's failure, not necessarily the failure of theurgy.

Faustus is blithely oblivious to his mistakes. He conjures; Mephistophilis obediently appears; and, filled with self-congratulation, Faustus asserts his power over the spirit.

Fau.   I charge thee wait upon me whilst I live,
           To do whatever Faustus shall command.
           ....
Meph.   I am a servant to great Lucifer
           And may not follow thee without his leave;
           No more than he commands must we perform.
Fau.   Did not he charge thee to appear to me?
Meph.   No, I came hither of mine own accord.
Fau.   Did not my conjuring speeches raise thee? Speak.

13. *Christopher Marlowe*, p. 156.

Meph.   That was the cause, but yet *per accidens*:
        For when we hear one rack the name of God,
        Abjure the scriptures and his saviour Christ,
        We fly, in hope to get his glorious soul;
        Nor will we come unless he use such means
        Whereby he is in danger to be damn'd. (3.38–53).

At this moment, the basis of magic on which the play has apparently been built shifts.[14] Mephistophilis has come voluntarily, not because Faustus compelled him. This is a change from *The Damnable Life*, in which Mephistophilis comes very reluctantly and only after Faustus's repeated commands.[15] Unlike the Faustus of the source, Marlowe's character cannot command spirits by his magic; he is merely a sinner who, by blaspheming against God, attracts the attention of the devil.

Under the circumstances, Faustus sees no hope of obtaining power except by entering into a witch's pact with the devil, and this he immediately proposes to do. He is either so excited by the actual presence of Mephistophilis or so careless about the way he achieves power that he does not mind—or does not notice—that his original assumptions about his control of spirits are being drastically altered. Like his earlier haste to conjure, Faustus's quick offer of a pact is Marlowe's idea; in *The Damnable Life*, Faustus hesitates for some time, trying to find other alternatives to signing away his soul.[16] But Marlowe's Faustus, desperately anxious for the power described by Pico, goes beyond even Agrippa's bounds and subjects himself to the devil. He becomes, although he probably does not realize it, what Pico described as "a slave and pawn of evil powers."

An Elizabethan audience, familiar with witchcraft lore, is likely to have been aware of the radical change in Faustus's position. He is not a magician who, like Friar Bacon, misuses his magical powers but rather a man who has no magical power—much as he desires it—beyond the scraps that the devil permits him in order to mollify him. At the play's open-

14. West, "The Impatient Magic of *Doctor Faustus*," finds no shift here, for he excludes theurgic, humanistic magic completely: "The higher occult philosophy that for a moment of history held the imagination of humanists goes unnoticed in Marlowe's play. What fits that play is the destructive view that orthodoxy took of all spirit magic: it was all one or another stage of devil worship. *This Faustus understood from the beginning*" (p. 229; my italics).

15. *The Damnable Life*, p. 138.

16. Ibid., pp. 139–41.

ing, Faustus could convince us of his potential to achieve much, whether good or evil, through magic and the power of his intellect. But by the end of scene 3, he has been transformed into a man who so covets power that he is willing to give away his soul for its appearance. Ironically, of course, Faustus not only fails to receive true magic power but also relinquishes the power he already had to govern his own life on earth. He gives himself up almost totally to the guidance of Mephistophilis. The only indication that Faustus realizes the enormity of what he has done comes in a slight shift in his rhetoric. Before meeting Mephistophilis, Faustus continually bragged about his future accomplishments by reiterating "I will." Now he includes Mephistophilis as a necessary part of whatever he may accomplish:

> Had I as many souls as there be stars,
> I'd give them all for Mephistophilis.
> By him I'll be great emperor of the world. (3.104–6, my italics)

The subsequent encounters between Faustus and Mephistophilis form a pattern. Faustus imagines or wishes for something: magical control of spirits, a wife, knowledge of the universe, a sight-seeing tour of Rome. Mephistophilis replies that what Faustus wants is forbidden or impossible and offers lesser alternatives: a pact with the devil, any paramour Faustus desires, a pageant, practical jokes on the Pope. Faustus accepts the alternatives, usually without argument. The relationship resembles that between a seasoned horse trader and an arrogant but naive novice. Faustus, cheated every time, hardly knows he loses anything, so great is his self-confidence. Only late in the play does Faustus gradually become aware of the importance of what he has given away.

The sense of loss that fills the play comes not so much from Faustus's own realization of loss as from a general failure of action to live up to words and promises. Faustus's aspirations soar above what he is able to accomplish, and Mephistophilis's promises far outstrip what he delivers. Having promised Faustus anything he wants, Mephistophilis cannot bring him a wife, cannot speak of heaven, cannot really do much to enlarge Faustus's knowledge. This sense of failure and limitation, which permeates the final four-fifths of the play, also accompanies, to a degree, the depiction of magical power in other plays. Bacon, Sacrapant, and the Friar in *Bussy D'Am-*

bois all find magic limited, operable only within certain restraints. In Faustus, however, these restraints are greater, both because Faustus imagines and dreams so grandly and because he is given so little personal power. Through much of the play, in fact, it is not Faustus but Mephistophilis who most resembles the stereotype of the stage magician.

Some deliberate reversals in magical roles early in the play seem to underscore Faustus's essential powerlessness. Functions traditionally the magician's are given in Marlowe's play to Mephistophilis, not to Faustus. Rather than performing in these magical roles, Faustus becomes merely the audience to Mephistophilis's accomplishments.

For example, Mephistophilis assumes the role of promoter of love affairs, as do the magicians in *The Wars of Cyrus* and *John of Bordeaux*. Though finding a sexual companion for Faustus is only a minor job in Mephistophilis's busy schedule, his promises sound very much like those of the magicians:

> I'll cull thee out the fairest courtesans
> And bring them every morning to thy bed;
> She whom thine eye shall like, thy heart shall have.
> Were she as chaste as was Penelope,
> As wise as Saba, or as beautiful
> As was bright Lucifer before his fall. (5.153–58)

No results of this promise ever materialize, though Mephistophilis does, near the play's end, procure the shade of Helen for Faustus's enjoyment. Despite Helen's beauty, her presence in lieu of a live woman can be seen as another of Mephistophilis's deceptions. Faustus gets the shadow and not the substance, though, by the end of the play, the shadow is his own request.

More visually striking and more significant than magical pimping is Mephistophilis's function as spectacle deviser and presenter. Twice, when Faustus falters and seems in danger of repenting, Mephistophilis produces a show "to delight thy mind / And let thee see what magic can perform" (5.84–85). The first show, designed to divert Faustus from the *"homo fuge"* that appears on his arm, is a dance of devils who present Faustus with "crowns and rich apparel." Faustus is mere audience to this scene, which Mephistophilis creates and directs. Almost all of the magicians previously discussed have created spectacle, just as Mephistophilis does here. None has had shows created for him, however, unless God's spectacles designed to bring magicians to repentance in *A Looking Glass for London and England* and *The Two Merry Milkmaids* can be counted as magical shows. The second pageant, the parade of the Seven Deadly Sins, enters in scene 6 to distract Faustus from Mephistophilis's refusal to tell him who created the world. This pageant is far more elaborate than the dance of devils and reminds us (though it fails to remind Faustus) that all the demonic world can offer is immersion in pleasurable sin. (One of the most interesting verbal details in *Faustus* is the shift in emphasis from power to pleasure as the ostensible object of Faustus's quest. Knowledge and power are continually alluded to in the early scenes; pleasure dominates the middle and especially the final scenes of the play.) Faustus is all that Mephistophilis might ask for in the way of enthusiastic audience for his shows, but he is far from behaving like a magician.

Only after the pleasures of witnessing such spectacles have dulled, after Faustus has seen the firmament, earth, and hell, does he attempt to assume the magician's traditional role as controller of spectacle and magical effects. Having been dissuaded by Mephistophilis from sight-seeing, Faustus finally asks that he be allowed some part in the next spectacle:

> Then in this show let me an actor be,
> That this proud Pope may Faustus' cunning see. (8.75–76)

Mild, polite requests have replaced the commands that Faustus once addressed to Mephistophilis. The spirit permits Faustus to participate—"any villainy thou canst devise, / . . . I'll perform it" (8.87–88)—and from this point on Faustus apparently plans much of the magical action. But the scope of such magic is much reduced. There are no more pageants of allegorical figures or reported trips through the firmament. Rather the magic continually narrows, from shape-changing, stealing the Pope's dinner, and calling historical heroes from the dead, to horning a skeptic and providing grapes for a pregnant duchess. At last, the primary locus of the magic becomes Faustus's own body, as his false head and false leg provide clownish humor.[17]

---

17. Such false additions to his body implicate Faustus in the world of multiplicity and disintegration that Leonard Barkan associated with corporeal illusions in *Nature's Work of Art: The Human Body as Image of the World*.

There is something terrifying in these middle scenes, despite their crude humor. Faustus's magic (or what he *calls* "his" magic) literally tears apart his soul. For the sake of magical jokes his body is pulled apart by clowns, as it will later be torn in pieces by fiends. Once Faustus begins to direct the magic, it deteriorates. His once-glorious imagination is reduced to recalling clichéd magical tricks.[18]

Of the change in Faustus, A. Bartlett Giamatti has remarked: "What Faustus does with his power totally undercuts what we heard Faustus claim for his power. . . . Over the play, the magician metamorphoses himself to a court jester, a fool."[19] Perfectly true, except that Faustus is not a magician. He had hoped to be one, dreaming of himself in a far different role than that of witch. But his magical powers are from the start illusory, though he deludes himself about their nature to the end of his life.

Despite his weaknesses, his errors, and his illusions of grandeur and of magical power, Faustus is worthy of interest and respect as a character. Though he fails to become the demigod he aspires to be, his mistakes are symptomatic of his humanity. Faustus's concern is with temporal, worldly matters rather than with eternity. Accordingly, he responds to sensual experiences rather than to disembodied abstractions: "For the skeptical person the senses are the beginning and the end of human knowledge. Faustus, proceeding in the sceptical manner, doubts the existence of things he cannot directly perceive."[20] That this is Faustus's method of cognition is demonstrated by his opening soliloquy, in which he measures his knowledge of logic by his victories in debate, his medical knowledge by his cures, and so on. Only the tangible interests Faustus.

This being the case, Marlowe weighted the dice in favor of hell's appeal over heaven's. Critics often remark on the balance of characters representing heaven and hell, good and evil: Good Angel and Bad Angel, good scholars and wicked scholars, Mephistophilis and the Old Man. But this balance is not as perfect as it first seems. The only "heavenly" character to

18. For my remarks on the nature of comic business in Faustus, I am indebted to Leo Kirschbaum's discussion in his edition of Marlowe's plays ("Comedy in Doctor Faustus," in *The Plays of Christopher Marlowe*, pp. 114–22).

19. "Marlowe: The Arts of Illusion," p. 542.

20. Clifford Davidson, "Doctor Faustus of Wittenberg," p. 518.

appear onstage is the Good Angel; and not only is he balanced
by the Bad Angel, but also Faustus shows no sign that he actually sees either of them. They may be merely external man-
ifestations of his own internal conflict. Hell, on the other
hand, has a number of very visible representatives: Mephistophilis, Lucifer, Beelzebub, and many unidentified devils and
spirits. Their presence is a constant appeal to the senses;
heaven provides almost none (quite rightly, of course, since
heaven's business is the spiritual rather than the sensual).

Evil in the play is palpable and flashy. It intrudes into Faustus's temporal world: the devils put on shows for Faustus, parade riches before him, permit him to raise the dead—the tangible proof he had earlier desired of great medical power. All
this appeals both to Faustus and to his audience. We understand how Faustus chose allegiance to Lucifer and why; we
might have chosen the same way. In contrast to hell, which is
constantly defined, described, and even visited by Faustus and
Mephistophilis, heaven remains silent and unknown. Mephistophilis will not speak of it; it cannot be visited. Heaven
becomes a forbidden, undefined term in the play. Though the
deadly sins are revealed and transformed into a comic show
that amuses Faustus, the virtues never appear. There is no
psychomachia. In the didactic plays discussed earlier—plays
such as *A Looking Glass for London and England* and *The
Two Merry Milkmaids*—God's power is pitted against that of
wicked magic, and heaven displays greater power than evil
does. God and Jonah easily outstrip Rasni's magicians, and
Justina's resolute chastity foils Cyprian's evil charms. But in
Doctor Faustus God does not compete.[21] Even Faustus's punishment is not presented as the active revenge of heaven but
rather as hell claiming its own in the face of Faustus's spiritual inertia.

By some few effects, heaven does signal its presence: Faustus's blood congeals; the inscription *homo fuge* appears on his
arm; and, in the last moments of the play, an empty throne
descends from heaven. In each case, the warning is momen-
tary; the blood soons runs freely again, the inscription disappears, and the throne is simply an emblem of what Faustus

21. On this point Robert West ("The Impatient Magic of *Doctor Faustus*")
has remarked: "God is a force never much exerted in a contest where even
his inaction is overpowering. Yet though doctrine seems to give the game to
God before it begins, dramatic action almost leaves him out of it" (p. 219).

has lost. Even as the throne appears in the air, in fact, hell is "discovered," and it probably emits flame and smoke,[22] while heaven's emblem remains inert and empty. These few signs, two of which are so small as to be visible only to Faustus and not to the audience, hardly balance the many visual wonders provided by the devils.

Faustus's repeated preference for what can be seen, and thus for hell's representatives, is evidenced not only by the ease with which he is distracted by Mephistophilis's shows but also by his response to Lucifer's entrance onstage at a moment when Faustus is apparently ready to turn back to God: "O, what art thou that look'st so terribly?" (6.89). The sight of Lucifer erases all thoughts of God. Against the appearance onstage of the demons, heaven remains an abstraction, an unknown whose joys are promised only in some vague eternity in which Faustus never quite believes.[23]

How this worldly and temporally concerned scholar makes and continues in his fatal choice is understandable, though it is clearly mistaken. David Bevington has written, "Paradox is present in *Faustus*, in its moving tragedy of noble character and its explicit denunciation of moral failure, in its hero's sympathetic aspiration and deplorable degeneracy."[24] Marlowe makes clear that Faustus was wrong, that faith and repentance would have been far better than despair and allegiance to the devil. But the careful onstage presentation of heaven and hell makes sympathetic nonetheless Faustus's terrible mistake.

The highly dramatic and eloquent encounters between Faustus and his demonic visitors usually overshadow the scenes of magical adventure that separate Faustus's pact from his death. The most generally accepted explanation of these scenes is that they show the gradual disintegration of Faustus's mind and body as he comes more and more under the domination of Lucifer and Mephistophilis. The different style

22. Jump suggests such effects in his note on the staging of the scene (*Doctor Faustus*, p. 99 [19.115–115.1, n.]).

23. Heaven's remoteness is emphasized much more strongly than I suggest here in a provocative article by Max Bluestone, "*Libido Speculandi*: Doctrine and Dramaturgy in Contemporary Interpretations of Marlowe's *Doctor Faustus*," in *Reinterpretations of Elizabethan Drama: Selected Papers from the English Institute*, ed. Norman Rabkin, pp. 33–88.

24. From "*Mankind*" to Marlowe: Growth of Structure in the Popular Drama of Tudor England, p. 262.

and tone of the scenes have led many critics to believe they were written in large part by someone other than Marlowe, someone with less talent.[25]

Certainly the magic that appears in these scenes is different from what Faustus envisioned earlier in the play. Though the character of Faustus has been said to portray the contemporary Renaissance magician, unencumbered by traditional literary formulas for magicians,[26] the magic of the central scenes is much like that found in the narrative romances. Faustus's tricks might as well have been performed by Merlin in the course of one of his endless sagas. To fill a large portion of his play, Marlowe chose conventional magic, the sure audience-pleasers, provided by the English Faustbook. This magic distances us from Faustus and sometimes dehumanizes him—as when he is beheaded and delegged—as the romance magicians were often dehumanized. Yet this conventional material has been ordered and shaped to a purpose; the central scenes, awkward though they sometimes are, do more for the play than just represent the passing of twenty-four years.

Faustus had announced his original magical aspirations— to circle Germany with a wall, to stop rivers, to raise tempests, to change the political shape of Europe—when he believed he would be in control, compelling spirits to do his will. None of his ideas was specifically evil or harmful, and several were actually benevolent. This sort of magic, however, the devil is likely to forbid. Just as he can neither describe heaven nor allow Faustus to engage in the sacrament of marriage, Mephistophilis clearly will not permit him any significant magic, nor can he conceivably allow Faustus to perform benevolent magic. To set the Vatican in an uproar, to promote dissension by rescuing the second Pope, to feed the gluttonous desires of a pregnant woman, to raise warlike pagan heroes—these sorts of actions are perfectly all right. But Lucifer will not allow Faustus anything very important or very good. Since Faustus himself is unlikely to wish to do anything particularly evil, what remains is trivial magic that neither seriously helps nor harms anyone.

25. For the most vehement statement of this point of view, see Wilson, *Marlowe and the Early Shakespeare*, pp. 69–74.
26. Kurt Tetzeli von Rosador, *Magie im Elizabethanischen Drama*, p. 97, and West, *The Invisible World*, pp. 58–59.

The process of narrowing the scope of Faustus's desires is gradual. Immediately after the pact is signed, he bombards Mephistophilis with questions about the firmament, philosophy, and the natural world. But, after receiving either no answers or very simplistic ones, Faustus learns to take the easier way, to immerse himself in sensory pleasure, to broach no complicated issues. Mephistophilis is willing to allow Faustus to appear as an ordinary (perhaps even an extraordinary) conjuror who performs standard magical tricks very well, but he allows him no more than this.

Tension arises intermittently in the middle scenes between what Faustus is and what he is believed to be by those around him. Almost all who meet Faustus assume that he is a powerful magician—the Emperor addresses him as "Wonder of men, renown'd magician, / Thrice-learned Faustus" (12.1–2), and Martino calls him "the wonder of the world for magic art" (11.11). In public Faustus puts on an excellent show:

> The doctor stands prepar'd by power of art
> To cast his magic charms, that shall pierce through
> The ebon gates of ever-burning hell
> And hale the stubborn furies from their caves. (12.19–22)

But in a moment of solitude, Faustus reminds himself of his real position: "What art thou, Faustus, but a man condemn'd to die?" (15.21). An audience that has listened to Faustus's early aspirations can hardly watch him strutting and posturing with his petty tricks without feeling a deep sense of irony. Faustus displays a brave front to the world—even his friends, the scholars, learn only at the last moment the source of Faustus's power—and there are moments when he clearly enjoys the tricks he performs. But underlying all these scenes is his growing fear and despair. The confidence of the outer man, the powerful magician, and the indecisiveness of the inner man, the constrained witch, contrast throughout the latter scenes of the play.

If the cheap magic of the central scenes in some ways trivializes Faustus, he is not the only victim. His audiences—popes, Emperor, Duke—deserve the trivial magic he performs and apparently lack the wit to ask for anything more elevated. The Pope is concerned only for the removal of his rival and for the delicacies that furnish his dinner table. The Pope's silliness is best expressed by the words of the curse he orders:

> *Cursed be he that stole his Holiness' meat from the table.*
>   *Maledicat Dominus!*
> *Cursed be he that struck his Holiness a blow on the face.*
>   (9.101–3)

Similarly, the Emperor's most pressing desire is to see the mole on the neck of Alexander's paramour; having seen it he rejoices, "In this sight thou better pleasest me / Than if I gain'd another monarchy" (12.67–68). All Faustus's clients and victims are frivolous and ridiculous, popes and hostelers equally. Faustus is the *least* trivial person in the play (except perhaps for the Old Man), for he intermittently displays concern for important issues and for human achievement.

The magic of the clowns is, of course, a parody of Faustus's magic and clearly points out its inconsequence. By using Faustus's books and attracting devils onto the stage, Robin, Wagner, and Dick show us again that Faustus's own feat was worth nothing; anyone might have called Mephistophilis. The actual magic of the play, as D. J. Palmer has pointed out, is all on a par—and all worthless:

> Faustus soon discovers the limits of the magical powers offered to him by the devil; they do not extend beyond the natural order. . . . Despite its subject matter, then, the world of *Doctor Faustus* consistently excludes the miraculous.[27]

What is important, however, is the relative worth of the characters who attempt magic, as measured by the attention the devils pay to their summoner once they do arrive. Mephistophilis, who would do anything to get Faustus's "glorious" soul (3.51; 5.73), shrugs off the clowns impatiently. Faustus is important enough to be worth a great deal of time and energy; Robin and Dick are not. Mephistophilis's appearance at the summons of Robin has been used to support arguments for a second author on the basis of a textual contradiction:[28] Mephistophilis specifically tells Faustus that he is not compelled to come by a conjuration; yet he arrives, grumbling, at the call of the clowns (10). But Mephistophilis responds to the clowns' blasphemy as he did to Faustus's. When he discovers whom he has come such a distance to tempt, however, he is dis-

27. "Marlowe's Naturalism," in *Christopher Marlowe*, ed. Brian Morris, pp. 171–72.
28. See *Doctor Faustus*, ed. Jump, p. 64 (10.32–34, n.), for one example of such an assumption.

gusted and threatens to turn the clowns into apes and dogs.
Robin and Dick have no power over the spirit; he is quite free
to revile and punish them. The clowns thus serve as foil to
Faustus in two ways: they demonstrate how worthless his
magic is by duplicating it, and they suggest how important he
is as a human being by the very different response they elicit
from the devil. Only Faustus is worthy of serious attention.

One final issue that these central scenes illuminate both
practically and thematically is the difficulty of dramatizing
magic. Nicholas Brooke has been one of Marlowe's most sympathetic apologists in this regard:

> It is impossible to show Faustus acquiring complete knowledge of
> the universe, for the obvious reason that Marlowe didn't possess
> it himself; so he simply states that Faustus did achieve it in two
> fine choruses and leaves the action to what can be shown, the
> power of human interference. The result is such a complete lack
> of balance, that the subject matter of the choruses is often forgot-
> ten, and Faustus accused of mere triviality in those scenes.[29]

To this line of argument, Greg objected, "Much more might
have been done to show the wonder and uphold the dignity of
the quest, and so satisfy the natural expectation of the audience."[30] But the impossibility of staging certain scenes obviously limited Marlowe's creative potential. Much is pre-
vented by the physical limitations of the theater, and much is
impossible because of Faustus's desire to know more than any
man. But simple dramatic considerations of what would play
to an Elizabethan audience must have been responsible for
some of Marlowe's decisions about what sort of magic to show
onstage. To portray a truly philosophical magician whose only
desire is knowledge is not possible; it is far more dramatically
effective to watch Faustus's original desire for knowledge and
power thwarted and perverted into a desire for pleasure and
into cheap juggler's tricks.

For a drama that concerns man's struggle and failure to rise
above the limits imposed by his humanity, Marlowe chose his
scenes wisely. The poetry, the dreams, and the reported
achievements all assure us of Faustus's original vision and
allow us to understand why he does not denounce Mephistophilis as a fraud. But the cheap onstage magic forces us to
see Faustus's limitations despite the magnificence of his vi-

29. "The Moral Tragedy of Doctor Faustus," in Jump, *Casebook*, p. 125.
30. "The Damnation of Faustus," in Jump, *Casebook*, p. 76.

sion. Words alone are insufficient to carry man beyond his station, but words are the only power Faustus possesses.

The power of words, of course, is one of man's greatest assets. Giamatti has suggested the basic analogy between man and the figure of the magician: "Because all men are users of the magic power, language, because all men are performers with words and transformers through words, the Renaissance could figure all men under the single image of the *magus*, the magician."[31] Unfortunately, Faustus's magical powers remain almost wholly rhetorical.[32] He makes his initial impression through magnificent aspirations that impress us for a while. But when the disparity between those words and what Faustus accomplishes is clear, the hollowness of both the magic and the rhetoric is apparent. A major mistake is Faustus's attempt to command spirits solely by words and signs, in contrast to the recommendations of many handbooks on magic that urge, in addition to the ritual preparations, special clothes for the magus, selected perfumes, music, and various pieces of magical equipment as helpful to proper conjurations. But only the language of magic interests Faustus:

> These metaphysics of magicians
> And necromantic books are heavenly;
> Lines, circles, letters, and characters:
> Ay, these are those that Faustus most desires. (1.48–50)

When Mephistophilis first appears, Faustus gloats, "I see there's virtue in my heavenly words" (3.29). This association of magic primarily with language persists throughout the play; even the clowns attempt magic by garbling words from one of Faustus's books. Dependence on words alone, however, does not work for Faustus; instead of the power he envisioned, his ritual words bring him only devilish temptation and a witch's pact.

Doctor Faustus is sometimes read as a humanist play, a great statement of man's ambition and faith in his human potential. But the play presents a very pessimistic view of man's possibilities. Faustus tries to reach beyond himself and fails miserably. Reluctant to give up his dream, he deludes himself

31. "Marlowe: The Arts of Illusion," p. 533.
32. Blackburn, "'Heavenly Words,'" places particularly strong emphasis on Faustus's concern with words: "Faustus's errors and eventual perdition are made possible through his failure to understand the proper use of language" (p. 8).

into thinking that the witch's pact will give him the same power he sought as a philosophic magician. Instead of magic that is to grant him endless power and control over spirits, however, he gets enslavement and terror through his contract with the devil plus the crumbs of power with which Mephistophilis pacifies him. But none of the play's other characters has enough wit to achieve anything significant either. Marlowe's play trivializes rather than elevates mankind. Humanistic magic, which appears in the play only as a dream of Faustus, never becomes more than a dream. The demonic enslavement that replaces it in Faustus's mind and soul proves empty and ultimately degrading. The man who desired to become a magician becomes instead a witch and a slave. Magic indeed "ravished" the scholar of Wittenberg.

From the title page of John Dee, *Letter Containing a Most Brief Discourse Apologeticall*, 1599 (courtesy the Folger Shakespeare Library).

5

Bussy D'Ambois

The Inconsequence of Magic

The magic in both *Friar Bacon* and *Doctor Faustus* is an obvious and important plot factor, not to be overlooked in any reading of the plays. Chapman's *Bussy D'Ambois*, however, contains magic that has no plot value and appears late, in only two scenes in the play. Nevertheless, this magic contributes importantly to the play's meaning by influencing an audience's final assessment of the play's much-discussed hero. The spirits provide Bussy with information offering him a possible means of escape from the trap his enemies have prepared for him. But Bussy chooses to ignore the avenue of escape they provide. His free choice, almost at the last moment of the play, emphasizes the importance of the human will and makes Bussy the master of his own fate. Bussy's choice between the advice provided by the spirits he has summoned, on the one hand, and the appeal of Tamyra's letter, on the other, demonstrates that, unlike other of Chapman's tragic heroes, he is not caught in a deterministic universe.[1] The spirits' willingness to appear before Bussy and the accuracy of their advice give Bussy an alternative other than response to Tamyra's summons. His choice of the human appeal over the advice of the spirits partially explains the heroic aura that surrounds him,

1. Richard H. Perkinson takes an opposite viewpoint: "Chapman elucidates the natural endowments of his super-man, declares that he is foreordained to fall by chance, and blames the almost vicious carelessness of the Nature who has been so generous to him" ("Nature and the Tragic Hero in Chapman's Bussy Plays," p. 269).

despite his fallibility. Even before he sees the disguised Montsurry and exclaims that Behemoth is a "lying spirit," Bussy
has determined that he will obey Tamyra whatever the cost
to himself: "though I die, / My death consenting with his
augury: / Should not my powers obey when she commands, /
My motion must be rebel to my will" (5.3.70–73).[2] Bussy is
not herded to his death but consciously chooses to depend on
his human strength and to ignore his spirit contacts.

To argue that the spirits offer Bussy a possible escape is necessarily to read them not as devilish snares to pull Bussy from
the path of virtue[3] but as a neutral force within the world of
the play. Unlike some of the plays already discussed, in which
a character's involvement with magic merely swells the catalog of his crimes (as in *The Devil's Charter* and *A Looking
Glass for London and England*), *Bussy D'Ambois* contains
magic that is not clearly evil. Indeed, uncertainty about its
nature echoes the central uncertainties of the play. Does
Bussy fall from virtue in his relationship with Tamyra and his
fourth-act promise to use policy, or does he remain heroic, the
man of *virtu*, to the end? Is Tamyra herself a conniving seduc-
tress, or is she a woman swept by passion to violate her strong
moral code? Is the Friar a typical satire of a Roman Catholic
clergyman, corrupt despite his holy words, or is Comolet a
well-meaning and sympathetic friar who (reminiscent in certain respects of Friar Bacon and of Friar Lawrence) assists true
lovers? And is magic wrought by means of demonic spirits
necessarily evil, or is it related to the more positive spiritual
magic discussed by the neoplatonists and their followers?

2. *The Plays and Poems of George Chapman: The Tragedies*, ed. Thomas
Marc Parrott, gives the 1641 text of the play; I quote from his edition. More
recently, Robert J. Lordi (*Bussy D'Ambois*, Regents Renaissance Drama Series
[Lincoln: University of Nebraska, 1964]) also followed the 1641 edition.
Nicholas Brooke in his edition of *Bussy D'Ambois* followed the 1607 version,
though he admitted that some of the revisions in the 1641 text are Chapman's own. The treatment of magic is somewhat more detailed in the 1641
text than in the earlier version: whoever revised these scenes apparently
understood magical theory and terminology. Chapman's knowledge of magic
(see n. 4, below) suggests to me that it is his own hand in the revised text.
Albert H. Tricomi, "The Problem of Authorship in the Revised *Bussy D'Ambois*," argues that Chapman is responsible for the 1641 revisions. For discussion of the play's textual problems, see Brooke's introduction, pp. lx–lxxiv.

3. For such an interpretation of the spirits, see Roy Battenhouse, "Chapman and the Nature of Man," in *Elizabethan Drama: Modern Essays in Criticism*, ed. Ralph J. Kaufmann, p. 142; and Peter Bement, *George Chapman:
Action and Contemplation in His Tragedies*, pp. 122–23.

To take the last first: Chapman does not appear to have
been a writer likely to use magic purely for spectacle, without
some deeper purpose. He was a scholar, widely read in neoplatonic philosophy—especially in the works of Ficino—and
in occult writings. He is one playwright, in fact, of whom we
can confidently say that he had firsthand knowledge of neoplatonic magical theories.[4]

Chapman's knowledge of aspects of hermetic and occult
philosophy is most clearly indicated by the complex intellectual puzzles of his "Shadow of Night" and by the glosses he
provided for readers of that work.[5] In fact, Chapman's dedication to "The Shadow of Night"—which scorns ordinary
men who expect to gain knowledge easily—indicates his familiarity with the neoplatonic conception of knowledge as
something acquired through a series of carefully executed pu-
rifications and rituals aimed at contacting heavenly spirits:

> Now what a supererogation in wit this is, to thinke skil so migh-
> tilie pierst with their loues, that she should prostitutely shew
> them [passion-driven men] her secrets, when she will scarcely be
> lookt vpon by others but with inuocation, fasting, watching; yea
> not without hauing drops of their soules like an heauenly famil-
> iar.[6]

Such evidence of Chapman's interest in the esoteric and in
neoplatonism affects our understanding of *Bussy* because it
suggests that his abrupt and apparently unnecessary intrusion
of magic into the play probably had a purpose beyond mere
spectacle.

When Bussy decides to employ magic to learn more about
the plots against him, he has already tried, and triumphed
over, almost every challenge his world has to offer. Brought by

---

4. Chapman's occult and neoplatonic learning is discussed at some length
by Millar MacLure in *George Chapman: A Critical Study*, pp. 32–82, and
mentioned with specific regard to *Bussy D'Ambois* by Eugene M. Waith in
The Herculean Hero in Marlowe, Chapman, Shakespeare and Dryden, pp.
98–100. Raymond B. Waddington also suggests Chapman's familiarity with
neoplatonic and occult thought in *The Mind's Empire: Myth and Form in
George Chapman's Poems*, pp. 8–10.

5. "The Shadow of Night," in *The Poems of George Chapman*, ed. Phyllis
B. Bartlett, pp. 19–45. Roy Battenhouse, "Chapman's *The Shadow of Night*:
An Interpretation," provides a convincing argument for the neoplatonic backgrounds of this poem. See also K. W. Schrickx, *Shakespeare's Early Contemporaries: The Background of the Harvey-Nashe Polemic and "Love's Labour's Lost,"* pp. 43–60.

6. "The Shadow of Night," p. 19.

Monsieur from his "green retreat" to court, Bussy first tries his hand in battle with some mocking courtiers and wins a triple duel, which is inflated by the Nuntius who reports it into a battle of heroic proportions (2.1.25–137).

His second major success comes in the realm of love. Tamyra, who has sternly rejected the advances of the powerful Monsieur, actually initiates a relationship with Bussy; her passion for him sweeps aside her usual self-control.[7] Chapman takes pains to keep their love—its adulterous nature notwithstanding—out of reach of his audience's condemnation. He portrays it as the only warm and human relationship in the play, except, of course, for Tamyra's deep bond with her spiritual father—and pander—the Friar. Presenting Bussy and Tamyra's relationship in terms of courtly love (mistress-servant), Chapman keeps all overt displays of physical passion offstage. Even the spying maid reports only that she saw the lovers reading a letter in the privacy of Tamyra's bedroom. Moreover, Chapman destroys an audience's sympathy for the wronged husband by allowing Montsurry, Tamyra's husband, to judge assaults on his wife's virtue according to the rank of the perpetrator. He encourages Tamyra at least to listen politely to Monsieur's sexual advances but rages out of control when he hears that she is involved with Bussy. Any remaining sympathy for Montsurry runs dry after his cruel torture of Tamyra in act 5.[8] But while Bussy is successful in love (even where others have failed), it remains true that the deception and lies necessary to the maintenance of a courtly love relationship are at odds with the honesty that Bussy advocates in the rest of his actions, assuring us of some final crisis when he will have to face the paradoxes of his situation.

Finally, Bussy is also successful in the court itself. Though Bussy speaks roughly of court and courtiers and has killed three of the king's best soldiers, Henry chooses him as his principal adviser, calling him his "eagle" and praising him for

7. Some critics read Tamyra as a loose, worldly woman, merely another mistake in Bussy's fall from virtue. See, for example, Linwood E. Orange, "*Bussy D'Ambois*: The Web of Pretense." A more tenable view of the ambiguity of Tamyra's character and her struggle between passion and conscience is well expressed by both Parrott (p. 545) and Brooke (p. xlvii) in their editions of the play.

8. Albert H. Tricomi has argued that Chapman's 1641 revision of the play works to create a far more sympathetic audience reaction to Montsurry's behavior than was permitted by the 1607 text; see his "The Revised Version of Chapman's *Bussy D'Ambois*: A Shift in Point of View," p. 291.

his outspoken honesty. Though Henry is not well developed
as a character, he does appear to be gifted with good sense,
keen observation, and a certain fairness. His is almost a choral
role: in effect, he is a neutral spokesman and adjudicator
(much like Prince Escalus in *Romeo and Juliet*). Though he
apparently has little power to reform the general moral bank-
ruptcy of his court, he himself does not share in the corruption except by association. Thus, his swift elevation of Bussy,
apparently an instinctive grasp by Henry for naturalness and
honesty amid the general corruption, offers additional evidence of Bussy's exceptional nature. Worldly success is his on
every front.

By the end of act 3, little remains for Bussy to accomplish.
He has triumphed on the dueling ground, in the bedchamber,
and at the court. But, despite his success and the support of
the king, Bussy senses plots against him: Monsieur and Montsurry begin to behave suspiciously, and Guise has never been
friendly. As the ostensible favorite in the world he inhabits,
Bussy has almost nowhere to go with his suspicions. Monsieur, brother to the king, is after all his patron, and Montsurry may justly accuse him of adultery. In the midst of all
the intriguing and double-dealing, it is not surprising that
Bussy seeks for information outside the corrupt world with
which he is entangled. He requests Friar Comolet to call up
spirits:[9]

> And therefore [I] have entreated your deep skill
> In the command of good aërial spirits,
> To assume these magic rites, and call up one
> To know if any have reveal'd unto him
> Anything touching my dear love and me. (4.2.8–12)

The nature of the spirits that Bussy requests the Friar to
summon is ambiguous, like much else in Chapman's play.
Bussy asks for "good aerial spirits"; the Friar raises Behemoth, the "great Prince of Darkness."[10] Normally this would

9. In the 1607 text Bussy does not suggest the magic. The Friar volunteers
his assistance, indicating that Tamyra has suggested consultation with the
spirits. The 1641 text retains a trace of this arrangement ("honour'd daughter,
at your motion," 4.2.43).

10. Chapman's choice of Behemoth as his principle demon is not easy to
understand. The name comes from Job 40:15–24, where behemoth is described as a great land beast, a parallel to leviathan in the sea. Both Leviathan
and Behemoth are occasionally included in Renaissance demonologies. Maxmilian Rudwin, *The Devil in Legend and Literature*, reports two different

be an unquestionably negative spirit. But elsewhere Chapman values shadows and darkness as positive, as the sources of true knowledge.[11] In addition, the Friar (much like Friar Bacon in *John of Bordeaux*) claims heavenly support for what he does "by my power of learned holiness / Vouchsaf'd me from above" (4.2.45–46), and his invocation of the spirits stresses the beauty of the darkness they rule more than any horror:

> Veni, per Noctis & tenebrarum abdita profundissima;
> per labentia sidera; per ipsos motus horarum
> furtivos, Hecatesque altum silentium! Appare
> in forma spiritali, lucente, splendida & amabili. (4.2.56–59)

> By the secret depths of Night and Darkness, by the
> wandering stars, by the stealthy march of the hours
> and Hecate's deep silence, come! Appear in spiritual
> form, gleaming, resplendent, lovely.[12]

Chapman's use of light and dark imagery is extremely complex throughout his work. Nowhere is it more riddlingly complex than in this first conjuring scene where our expectations about the value of light and dark images are frustrated and overturned. Reflecting on their need to know what is in the secret paper held by Monsieur, the Friar remarks to Bussy, "We soon will take the darkness from his face / That did that deed of darkness" (4.2.39–40). Clearly, the *betrayal* of the adulterous relationship is what the Friar sees as "that deed of darkness," a reversal of the conventional moral code and of

---

associations for Behemoth: "Johannes Wierus has presented us with a partial list of the demons attached to the royal court of Gehenna . . . Behemoth fulfills the function of grand cup-bearer" (p. 80), and "Behemoth, in the French medieval mysteries, is the demon of despair" (p. 84). A nineteenth-century illustration of Behemoth reprinted from Colin de Plancy, *Dictionnaire infernal* (1863), in Rossell Hope Robbins, *The Encyclopedia of Witchcraft and Demonology* (New York: Crown Publishers, 1959), p. 128, shows a potbellied elephantlike figure and is labeled by Robbins, "Behemoth, demon of the delights of the belly." None of this seems to fit with Chapman's "Prince of Shades," guardian of secret knowledge and wisdom, unless Chapman is being deliberately ironic in permitting a creature associated with bestial indulgence in food and drink to claim guardianship of esoteric secrets.

11. Battenhouse, in "Chapman's *The Shadow of Night*," pp. 596–97, commented on Chapman's use of night in that poem: "Day's beauty promotes all sorts of abuse, while Night offers freedom, succor, and sweet dreams of comfort and of prophecy. Visions of the future vouchsafed to Night's devotees are 'virtue's share,' and such esoteric knowledge is not a vanity." Peter Bement, however, argued that the conception of night in the last four acts of *Bussy D'Ambois* is of an evil "shadow night" (see below, n. 21).

12. Translated by Parrott in his notes: *Plays and Poems*, 2:557–58.

conventional language, in both of which "the deed of darkness" ordinarily refers to the sex act, not its revelation. When
Behemoth arrives, he puns on the associations of light and
dark:

> Why call'dst thou me to this accursed light,
> To these light purposes? I am Emperor
> Of that inscrutable darkness where are hid
> All deepest truths, and secrets never seen. (4.2.66–69)

For Behemoth, light is trivial, while darkness is associated not
with evil so much as with deep profundities that must be hidden from the world at large. Perhaps ironically, Behemoth's
companion spirits are represented by "blue fires," and when
Cartophylax departs on his vain errand, "a torch removes."

The stage directions regarding the torch suggest that staging itself probably served as a partial indicator of Chapman's
concern with light and dark. Chapman's play seems to have
been written for the boys of St. Paul's and therefore would
have received an indoor staging where torches would have had
a marked effect.[13] Behemoth "ascendit," presumably through
the same stage trap through which the Friar led Bussy on his
first visit to Tamyra. The remaining spirits enter—perhaps
from the ordinary entrances—while audience attention is
fixed on the thunder-heralded appearance of Behemoth. The
spirits are not clearly distinguished; perhaps they looked
something like the "shapes" whom Ariel directed in *The
Tempest*. If darkly garbed, the spirits would have been chiefly
recognized by the torches they carried, and the removal and
return of "a torch"—Cartophylax—would have been theatri-
cally effective. To have the demonic spirits represented by
light is an interesting reversal of expectation, as is Behemoth's
promise to "rise, / Shining in greater light, and show him
[Bussy] all / That will betide ye all" (4.2.155–56). We remember that the spirit who speaks this line has been called "Prince
of Shades" by the Friar. Just as Chapman uses two nights, he
uses two lights: one the superficial light of day, of the everyday
world; the other the light of knowledge that shines brightest
in the profoundest dark. Light and dark are not clearly demarcated in this scene as good and evil, but somehow each
partakes of both good and evil.

13. See Lordi's discussion of the play's early stage history in his edition of
Bussy D'Ambois, pp. xv–xvii.

Obviously, Chapman's use of magic is of a piece with the
rest of his play. Just as Bussy's words and actions do not
match,[14] so do mismatched elements compose the magic of
the play. For example, the dramatic and overtly evil magic that
seems promised when Comolet summons the Prince of
Shades turns out to be disappointingly innocuous. The spirits
are called not for an evil purpose or for impressive magical
feats but only for the information they can provide about the
intentions of Bussy's enemies. However, even their information is limited. Cartophylax reports:

> He hath prevented me, and got a spirit
> Rais'd by another great in our command,
> To take the guard of it [the papers which will betray
>   the lovers] before I came. (4.2.92–94)

There are problems here. If Behemoth is indeed the Prince of
Shades, why is he so easily foiled? The "He" who prevents
Behemoth, having no antecedent, is unidentified, but the passage implies that "He" (apparently an enemy of Bussy's) has
also been employing spirits and doing so more successfully
than Friar Comolet. From knowledge of other magical dramas, we suspect that a magical context lies behind these lines
(Friar Bacon's spirits stymied the spirits of Vandermast in a
similar way), but Chapman never clears up the puzzle. We do
not know for sure who Behemoth's opposition is.

A later passage, when Behemoth reappears to Bussy, suggests the identity of Friar Comolet's earlier opponents. When
Bussy asks whom Tamyra will send to summon him, Behemoth cannot answer.

> Bussy: Who lets thee?
> Behemoth: Fate.
> Bussy: Who are Fate's ministers?
> Behemoth: The Guise and Monsieur. (5.3.62–64)

If these two prevent Behemoth's answer in act 5, they probably were also to blame for Cartophylax's earlier failure to get
the letters. Chapman seems deliberately vague about reasons
for the limitations on the spirits who appear in his play.
Whether or not the Guise and Monsieur employ their own
countermagic, the success of their plot and the failures of Cartophylax and Behemoth evidence the strictly limited powers

14. Waith, *The Herculean Hero*, p. 93; Bement, *George Chapman*, p. 129.

of magic in *Bussy D'Ambois*—limitations characteristic of most stage magic, including that of Faustus and Friar Bacon.

Though Chapman clearly wished to emphasize these restrictions on magic, he also seems to have seen magic as a positive influence within the world of the play. Friar Comolet's magic looks good when set beside the hypocrisy and conspiracy of the Guise and Monsieur, just as Bussy's adulterous love for Tamyra looks good when compared to Monsieur's lust for her. Friar Comolet's intentions are excellent, and Behemoth's advice is ultimately sound, though Bussy chooses to ignore it. Chapman's play presents a world where all values are relative and where even the demonic magic that summons the Prince of Shades offers relief from a corrupt world.

Another peculiar feature of the first magic scene is Behemoth's offer to reappear to Bussy and to reveal more. Traditionally, spirits appear only to the initiated, to those skilled in the arcane arts. Bussy has not been so initiated, as he is clearly aware:

[Behemoth] told me that by any invocation
I should have power to raise him, *though it wanted
The powerful words and decent rites of art.* (5.3.25–27; my
    italics)

What explains Behemoth's gratuitous offer seems to be Bussy's greatness—obvious even to the inhabitants of the spirit world—which permits him to bypass the ordinary routes to extraterrestrial communication, just as he earlier bypassed the traditional steps to power in court and success in love.[15]

Less easy to understand in this scene is Chapman's use of the dumb show, in which Bussy and his friends witness the meeting of Monsieur, the Guise, and Montsurry but are unable to hear what is said, while the audience both sees and hears. Greene had earlier utilized this device, in *Friar Bacon*, where the audience's special privilege had some point. In Chapman's play, the audience learns nothing from the dia-

15. Though I agree with Waith in seeing positive elements in the magic scenes, I do not agree that Bussy "has been initiated into these mysteries by the Friar" (*The Herculean Hero*, p. 102). Such initiation into magic requires self-discipline and long preparation (such as is suggested by Chapman in the dedication to "The Shadow of Night," quoted above), not simply word-of-mouth instruction. It is appropriate in this play for Bussy simply to be exempt from the preparations normally requisite for consultation with the spirits.

logue that is not pretty obvious from what is seen: the three
courtiers are plotting; Monsieur makes Montsurry very angry,
and he stabs Tamyra's maid when she enters with a message.
The characters' inability to hear the conspirators' conversation perhaps further emphasizes the restrictions on magic,
but the emphasis is unnecessary. In this instance Chapman
seems to follow a tradition of stage magic without wholly
integrating it into his own construction.

The final peculiarity of the scene comes when Behemoth,
preparing to descend, offers one last word of advice: "mean-
time be wise, / And curb his [Bussy's] valour with your poli-
cies" (4.2.157–58). Though Behemoth does not directly urge
Bussy to be politic, Bussy promises, at Tamyra's insistence,
that he will use policy; yet it was policy of which he was once
bitterly critical:

> But his unsweating thrift is policy,
> And learning-hating policy is ignorant
> To fit his seed-land soil; a smooth plain ground
> Will never nourish any politic seed. (1.1.124–27)

We never see a politic Bussy, for events from this moment
move too quickly. But surely one of Chapman's intentions in
introducing the subject is to remind the audience that Bussy
has now succumbed to all those courtly temptations he had
scorned in his opening speech. Asked by Monsieur to come
to court, "the well-head," Bussy had sneered:

> At the well-head? Alas, what should I do
> With that enchanted glass? See devils there?
> Or, like a strumpet, learn to set my looks
> In an eternal brake, or practise juggling,
> To keep my face still fast, my heart still loose;
> Or bear (like dame schoolmistresses their riddles)
> Two tongues, and be good only for a shift. (1.1.84–90)

By act 4, Bussy in his short time at court has dissembled,
become involved in adultery, and quite literally seen demons.
As in all else he does, Bussy seems to violate his own code on
a larger scale than most mortals. Richard Ide, writing about
Bussy within the context of heroic drama, has suggested that
Bussy's difficulty is his inability to assimilate his heroic self-

image to life in a tragic world.[16] Within this context Bussy's ugly promise to use policy against his enemies may be seen as his misguided and, as Ide said, "unnatural" attempt to come to terms with a world with which he has no natural affinity. This emphasis on Bussy's inability to reconcile life in society with his heroic code fits with Chapman's concern in the play with what it means and how important it is to be a man. Early on, Bussy had remarked in defense of his quarrel over his reputation, "When I am wrong'd . . . / Let me be king myself (as man was made)" (2.1.197–98). The king describes Bussy as "a man so good, that only would uphold / Man in his native noblesse" (3.2.90–91). And Tamyra, questioned about why she calls Bussy "the man" instead of by his name, replies, "Man is a name of honour for a king" (4.1.49). Montsurry, in contrast, breaks the "bounds of manhood" (5.1.127) and is "not manly" (5.1.14) as he "manlessly" (5.4.160) tortures Tamyra to discover the name of her go-between. Even Guise and Monsieur, discussing Bussy as they wait for his murder, call him "this whole man" (5.2.41), and the Umbra Friar's final eulogy emphasizes the same theme: "Farewell, brave relics of a complete man" (5.4.147). "The complete man," it seems, cannot find a place in a flawed society.

But the limited view Chapman offers of the supernatural, of the world of "deepest truths and secrets never seen," suggests nothing better. Behemoth gives, finally, valid advice to Bussy, but the limitations on his revelations and the riddling indirection of his answers suggest that the world of the spirits will not, or cannot, provide a clear solution to Bussy's dilemma. Behemoth's words do not seem rational. If they are to be accepted, they must be accepted with faith. His advice cannot be analyzed rationally or compared with other courses of action. Thus, when he reappears in 5.3, fulfilling his promise to state exactly what Bussy must do (or not do) to avoid being trapped, Bussy refuses to accept his counsel. Eugene Waith has remarked quite justly that Bussy "suffers not for involving himself with the powers of darkness but for not believing in them."[17] Having conquered the world pretty much on his own terms, and then sought beyond that limited "girdled" earth

16. Richard S. Ide, *Possessed with Greatness: The Heroic Tragedies of Chapman and Shakespeare*, pp. 75–101.
17. *The Herculean Hero*, p. 104.

for greater knowledge, Bussy finally refuses to accept blindly the suprarational, to cut himself off from love and from those worldly ties that neoplatonists found most cloying and burdensome in their climb to wisdom.

Nicholas Brooke read the Behemoth scenes as Chapman's expression of the futility of spiritual assistance and of the trapped condition of man:

> The responsibility [for not having called Behemoth earlier] remains with man. The cumulative effect of points like this, together with the oracular futility of the foreknowledge Behemoth *does* provide, gives the scene a central place as an image of necessity: the devil's foreknowledge makes man's will anything but free, whilst the devil's own impotence makes his foreknowledge ridiculous.[18]

Such a reading would better suit Chapman's use of astrology in his later play, *Byron's Conspiracy*. There an astrologer, after predicting that the hour to come will be dangerous to himself, goes on to meditate the very issues that Brooke mentions with regard to magic in Bussy:

> How hapless is our knowledge to foretell,
> And not be able to prevent a mischief:
> O the strange difference 'twixt us and the stars;
> They work with inclinations strong and fatal,
> And nothing know; and we know all their working,
> And nought can do, or nothing can prevent![19]

When Chapman chose, he could clearly articulate man's trapped position in a deterministic universe. There is no such statement in *Bussy*, for Bussy never perceives himself as a victim of any suprarational power. He dies because of the choices he has made, not because some external force has decreed his death.

A second telling contrast between the two plays is found in the heroes' responses to messages from suprahuman sources. Byron's reaction to the astrologer's prediction is almost fatalistic rebellion:

> I have a will and faculties of choice,
> To do, or not to do: and reason why
> I do, or not do this: the stars have none;
> They know not why they shine, more than this taper,

18. "Introduction," *Bussy D'Ambois*, p. xlvii.
19. *Byron's Conspiracy*, 3.3.3–8, in *Plays and Poems*, ed. Parrott.

Nor how they work, nor what: I'll change my course,
I'll piece-meal pull the frame of all my thoughts,
And cast my will into another mould.[20]

Byron's refusal is an outright defiance of the stars. Even he
does not doubt that the stars do control; his rebellion against
them is a futile gesture, and their prediction, of course, comes
true. Bussy's situation is similar but differs in a crucial detail.
The spirit world provides him with information, not fiat, and
Bussy is free to accept or reject that information. On the evidence of his senses, Bussy rejects Behemoth's advice:[21] "Oh,
lying Spirit, / To say the Friar was dead! I'll now believe /
Nothing of all his forg'd predictions" (5.3.86–88). His response is not the quixotic defiance of Byron but rather a rational decision between two conflicting stories.[22]

Tamyra's summons, against which he has clearly been
warned by Behemoth, comes written in blood, a symbol
throughout the play of human fallibility and loss of control
(see 1.1.222; 2.2.140–41; 5.1.176–77). Persuaded by the appearance of the Friar (the disguised Montsurry) and by the
blood, which he interprets as the "sacred witness of her love,"
Bussy turns his back on Behemoth's warnings. He prefers to
rely on his own sensory perceptions rather than on Behemoth's assurance that the Friar is dead. He rejects the assistance of the spirits and trusts instead to his own judgment and
strength.

In the final act, the natural imagery by which Bussy has
been described throughout the play (seed, laurel, eagle) gives
way to images of celestial brilliance (star and thunderbolt).
Like the philosophical magician, Bussy is here associated
with the cosmos, not the "girdled" earth. But Bussy's worldly
achievements and undaunted human courage, not his spiritual contacts, put him into the firmament as a star. The stel-

20. Ibid., 3.3.112–18.
21. Waith, The Herculean Hero, p. 104. A different view of Behemoth's
advice is argued by Peter Bement: "Despite Behemoth's claims to mysterious
knowledge, he offers to Bussy not truth, but the perversion of truth; not
knowledge, but the perversion of knowledge; his 'secrets never seen' seem in
fact to be the foul 'secrets' shown 'most harlot-like' by the 'Stepdame Night'
of Hymnus in Noctem" (George Chapman, pp. 122–23).
22. Waddington, The Mind's Empire, p. 30, also emphasizes Bussy's
choice: "Adam and Bussy in this situation decide in favor of their human
rather than their suprahuman tendencies, and this choice, of course, is the
essence of the tragic dilemma." For further discussion of Bussy's choice, see
Irving Ribner, Jacobean Tragedy: The Quest for Moral Order, p. 32.

lification of Bussy, though not an uncommon motif in the final scenes of tragedies, seems particularly appropriate in a play that introduces magic, for the philosophic magician was promised a rise to heavenly realms (whether literally or figuratively depended on the writer making the claim). At least one sixteenth-century engraving shows a magician stepping from star to star (see Frontispiece). Chapman's use of the stellification motif is ironic, of course, for the neoplatonic belief in magic as a way to transcend the world and its corruption is neatly sidestepped by Bussy, who prefers to earn his place in the heavens by remaining in the world and fighting until he is killed.

Thus, though the magical scenes in *Bussy D'Ambois* make no difference to the plot, they make a good deal of difference to our understanding of Bussy. Were magic either clearly good or clearly evil, then Bussy would have been either clearly justified or wrong in employing it. Instead, the ambiguities associated with magic permit us to see Bussy perched as usual on the margin of absolute risk as he chooses first to employ magic and later to disregard it.

About Chapman himself we may feel a similar uncertainty. Brooke suggested that Chapman "seems gradually to have lost confidence in the Neo-platonic synthesis."[23] Perhaps Bussy's refusal of otherworldly knowledge and his failure to rise above physical passion are indications of some disillusionment with neoplatonic theory. But they may also merely suggest its practical ineffectiveness, especially for a character of Bussy's active temperament, a "manly man."

23. "Introduction," *Bussy D'Ambois*, p. xxii.

Hendrick Goltzius, *The Magician or Allegory of Time and Nature*, circa 1585–1590 (courtesy Davison Art Center, Wesleyan University).

6

Prospero

Master of Self-knowledge

Unlike the magic of plays discussed in earlier chapters, the nature of the magic in *The Tempest* has received a good deal of critical attention and persuasive explication. Critics have frequently identified Prospero's art as theurgy and often related it to neoplatonic theories of magic.[1] The intellectual quality of his magic, his command over Ariel (who is clearly daemon, not demon), his concern for astrological guidance, and his use of music in his magic have all been cited to prove his theurgistic and neoplatonic associations. Yet beneath this general chorus of agreement a good deal of disharmony is present. To cite only one example, C. S. Lewis has contended that Prospero's magic is realistic and contemporary, what "might be going on in the next street," while C. J. Sisson asserted in flat contradiction that Prospero's magic is classical and bears little resemblance "to the powers and feats claimed by the professional magicians in contemporary practice."[2] Both observations contain elements of truth: the hybrid nature of Prospero's magic makes it at home in the mysteriously musical and constantly shifting landscape of the island and allows Shakespeare much versatility in its use in the play.

1. See, for example, *The Tempest*, ed. Frank Kermode, pp. xl–xli; D. G. James, *The Dream of Prospero*; Walter Clyde Curry, *Shakespeare's Philosophical Patterns*, pp. 163–99; C. J. Sisson, "The Magic of Prospero"; W. Stacy Johnson, "The Genesis of Ariel"; Karol Berger, "Prospero's Art."
2. Lewis, *English Literature in the Sixteenth Century, Excluding Drama*, p. 8; Sisson, "The Magic of Prospero," p. 75.

But earlier magical plays have led us to expect hybrid magic; indeed, the most surprising feature of this acknowledged masterpiece among magical plays is how much it shares with and derives from its dramatic forebears. The only unusual features of Prospero as dramatic magician are the success of his magic and his total dominance of the play in which he participates; otherwise he is a rather conventional figure. Far more than Faustus, who captures our attention partly because of his failure to play stereotypical "magician's roles," Prospero displays familiar magical attributes. He is the victor in a magical contest; he commands spirits; he is the director of numerous shows and spectacles; and he assists young love.

I.

The magical contest between Prospero and Sycorax is presented with great care, even though it is narrated by Prospero and Ariel and not witnessed by the audience. The "arts" of Sycorax and Prospero competed, not the characters themselves. Indeed, Sycorax was dead before Prospero arrived on the island, so he bears no responsibility for killing or punishing her. His competitive act is thus totally positive: he has freed Ariel from the hollow tree where Sycorax had imprisoned him, a release Sycorax herself had apparently been unable to accomplish. A reminder of the earlier competition (and a grudging admission by an enemy of Prospero's power) is Caliban's testimony that Prospero's "Art is of such pow'r, / It would control my dam's god, Setebos, / And make a vassal of him" (1.2.372–74).[3] In *The Tempest*, as in most plays involving magical competition,[4] the triumph of a given side proves its moral superiority to the magic of the loser, thereby justifying the winner's magic. After all, only Prospero's more powerful "good" magic can counteract the "bad" magic of Sycorax. Shakespeare clearly included this account of Prospero's indirect competition with Sycorax to strengthen Prospero's credentials as a "good" magician.

Another common magical accomplishment is Prospero's ability to command spirits who actually implement his

3. *The Riverside Shakespeare*, ed. G. Blakemore Evans. All other references to Shakespeare's plays are to this edition.

4. Greene's *Friar Bacon* is something of an exception, since Vandermast's magic is not bad or evil; Bacon's victory is nationalistic, not moral.

magic. As early as *The Old Wives Tale* and *John a Kent*, spirits aided the magician; Kent's Shrimp is a near relative of Ariel, invisible to all but his magician master and the audience, responsible for shows, for mysterious music, and for leading certain characters astray. Spirits offer evidence of a magician's power and usually suggest the moral value of that power. Shrimp and Ariel, associated with the air and with nature, are morally neutral or even good, while Bacon's spirits and those who pretend to serve Faustus are demonic, servants of the underworld who indicate that the magic they assist is morally dubious or at least dangerous.

Shakespeare carefully depicted the relationship between Ariel and Prospero. Prospero never conjures or ritually summons Ariel onstage; all his bonds of control over the spirit were forged before the play began; onstage a simple command brings Ariel to serve his magician (occasionally with some protest).[5] Ariel's nature and the details by which he is presented make clear that he is drawn in the image of the daemons of neoplatonic theory, as various critics have pointed out.[6] But his dramatic function is traditional. A beautifully particularized representative of a long line of spirits who serve magicians, Ariel provides spectacle, proof of Prospero's power, and helps explain how the play's magic is performed. Prospero alone is not capable, if he is human, of raising a tempest or of making unearthly music. Only by gaining control of the spirits who manage the functioning of the natural world can a man accomplish what Prospero does; Ariel is a necessary intermediary. As such, he leaves Prospero's humanity intact.[7]

Another traditional role of the magician, one that has tremendous importance in *The Tempest*, is Prospero's function as producer and director of shows. "For what is the magician but, as always in the old plays, a stage manager of shows, with his wand and his magic inscribed 'book'—what is this but a sublimated Master of the Revels?"[8] In fact, virtually the entire *Tempest* is Prospero's production, from the opening storm to the final command to Ariel to provide calm seas and auspicious gales. In no other play is so much of the action pre-

5. James, *The Dream of Prospero*, p. 63.

6. See especially Johnson, "The Genesis of Ariel," p. 210.

7. Stanley Wells, "Shakespeare and Romance," in *Later Shakespeare*, ed. John Russell Brown and Bernard Harris, p. 71.

8. Muriel Bradbrook, "Shakespeare's Primitive Art," p. 233.

planned and controlled by a magician. So controlled is Prospero's production that it has led Enid Welsford, for one, to
claim that *The Tempest* is more masquelike than *Comus* and
to compare Prospero to a masque-presenter.[9]

Within the large structure that Prospero manages, a number
of small, self-contained scenes, almost plays-within-the-play,
are also directed by Prospero. Such scenes are familiar products of magicians. But, despite the surface conventionality of
such "shows" as part of *The Tempest*, their number and their
contribution to the thematic movement of the play they
adorn are unusual. They differ from John a Kent and John a
Cumber's little shows of "antiques" and Friar Bacon's banquet and transportations largely in their thematic integration
with the play that contains them. In earlier magical plays, the
magician's shows were primarily extraneous entertainments
that displayed his magical power. *The Tempest* needs no such
demonstration of Prospero's power, but Prospero uses spectacle anyway, for didactic purposes: each little show is especially selected for its audience, and each overturns the initial
expectations of that audience in some way. *The Tempest* may
be closer to masque than any other Jacobean drama, but its
masque elements—used primarily for diversion in many Jacobean plays—are integral to the action and theme of the play
as a whole.

Five separate shows appear in *The Tempest*. The first and
most spectacular is the opening storm itself, prepared for us
all, audience and characters alike. Only Ariel, Prospero, and
apparently Caliban are immune to its terror. This is the only
show during which Prospero himself does not appear onstage,
the only one that the audience does not immediately perceive
to be his controlled creation. Like all the other shows, it is
designed to surprise, to be other than what it first appears. We
discover its illusory nature with Miranda in the second scene;
the other characters have yet to hear at the play's end what
the tempest was. Prospero's magic in the storm is pure illusion, rearrangement of appearances to play tricks on men's
senses,[10] and this is largely the extent of his magic throughout
the play. Excepting Ariel's reported release from the tree and

9. *The Court Masque: A Study in the Relationship between Poetry and
the Revels*, pp. 339–40.

10. Robert Egan, *Drama within Drama: Shakespeare's Sense of His Art*,
p. 93.

Caliban's alleged bruises, Prospero's magic leaves no perma-
nent physical changes. The storm leaves ship, men, and garments all "fresher than before" (1.2.219).

Prospero's next three shows are companion pieces,[11] following one another closely in the play and almost inviting comparison. The first such display is the banquet-and-harpy se-
quence presented to the Neapolitan courtiers as they wander
forlornly around the island. Prospero, very much the director
of this performance, is "on the top" overseeing both Ariel's
performance and his audience's reactions.[12] The beginning of
the show is disarmingly pleasant. A banquet is brought on by
shapes moving with "gentle actions of salutations" (3.3.18,
s.d.), inviting the men to eat. The banquet gives the illusion
of well-being, suggesting what might have been—the joy of
friendly communion—had these not been "three men of sin"
(3.3.53).[13] But this friendly and gentle beginning is suddenly
reversed by the arrival of Ariel as harpy. Immediately the banquet disappears, for these men are not worthy to partake of it.
As the tempest was apparently destructive and only later
shown to have a good purpose, so the banquet appears wel-
coming only to be changed abruptly into a scene of warning.
Perhaps the whole show figures in little the feast that the
three sinners thought they had secured in seizing Prospero's
Duchy, a feast that has turned to nothing in their present
helpless and powerless position on the island. In any case,

11. Catherine M. Shaw, "*Some Vanity of Mine Art*": The Masque in Renaissance Drama, believes that the banquet-harpy scene represents "antimasque disharmony and confusion designed to contrast the harmony and
order of the main masque which follows immediately after" (1:160). Unfortunately, Shaw does not convincingly prove this relationship between the two
shows, nor does she even mention the third show that Prospero puts on for
the clowns.

12. J. C. Adams, "The Staging of *The Tempest*, III, iii," provides an excellent discussion of the scene and a practical explanation for Prospero's presence onstage.

13. The exact significance of the banquet remains a mystery. Kermode, in
his edition of *The Tempest*, suggests that it presents some sort of temptation
(p. 86, n. 17); Northrop Frye in his Penguin edition of the play (Baltimore,
1959) argues that it is "symbolic of deceitful desires" (p. 1369); John Armstrong, *The Paradise Myth*, says that the banquet "celebrates the rightness of
the *status quo*" (p. 84); Robert Grams Hunter, *Shakespeare and the Comedy
of Forgiveness*, claims, "Prospero's banquet . . . is a type, not of Satan's temptations, but of the commonest of all symbolic banquets: the Communion
table" (p. 234); and Jacqueline E. M. Latham, "The Magic Banquet in *The
Tempest*," stresses the multiple and ambiguous associations of the magical
banquet.

Prospero here mixes verbal warning and remonstrance with visible action. The abrupt disappearance of the inviting banquet underlines Ariel's speech, offering evidence that the island brings punishment rather than hospitality to these men.

The care with which Prospero has planned each of his shows is evident when we put beside the banquet-harpy scene the betrothal masque he prepares for Ferdinand and Miranda. Prospero, again onstage directing and supervising the performance of his spirits, calls attention to the close relation between his shows: "I must use you in such another trick," he informs Ariel (4.1.36). The wedding masque differs from its predecessor, however, in emphasizing verbal message over visual spectacle. Ferdinand and Miranda, best of the characters Prospero controls, can respond to poetry and to verbal education as the sin-clogged courtiers cannot. Though visually lovely, the masque conveys its lessons primarily through its verse.

However, its apparent order and beauty are partially qualified, this time, perhaps, against Prospero's own expectation. Just as the horror of the storm and the pleasant invitation of the banquet prove in need of qualification, so the betrothal masque—where "temperate nymphs" and "sunburn'd sicklemen" frolic in perfect harmony together—cannot be allowed a perfect conclusion. Prospero remembers Caliban, who could never have a place in such an ordered vision, and speaks; the spell is "marr'd."[14] Prospero himself cuts short the most perfect and ideal of all the shows he creates, perhaps because he realizes anew that such perfection is only illusion. Clearly, he does not personally fear Caliban's revolt, but recollecting it reminds him that the masque is "baseless fabric" without correspondence to reality. The "show" prepared for the play's two most promising people must be qualified just like all the other shows—even if against Prospero's will—for Ferdinand and Miranda inhabit a world containing Calibans and Antonios as well as kindly Gonzalos.

However beautiful the wedding masque—however realistic any of Prospero's presentations—it is only a show. Prospero

14. For some critics the masque is flawed in other ways. Egan, *Drama within Drama*, p. 107, states that the masque world is "not simply ordered and controlled but pruned and gelded of all that is spontaneous and primal, leaving only that which is cold, hard, and sterile." See also Ernest B. Gilman, "'All Eyes': Prospero's Inverted Masque," p. 224.

makes no pretense to the lovers that the masque is anything but his own creation, "my present fancies," no pretense that goddesses have actually descended to bless their match. The production is simply Prospero's most impressive way of giving Ferdinand and Miranda his blessing and of conveying to them the proper ideals of love and marriage. It is another of Prospero's didactic messages.

The show for Caliban, Trinculo, and Sebastian immediately follows the masque. It is the simplest and least interesting show in the play, hardly deserving comparison with its predecessors. But it fits the intellectual capabilities of its intended audience. Like the banquet-harpy scene, it has two parts. The first merely displays ornate clothes strung on a line. These gaudy things suit Stephano and Trinculo as the more sophisticated banquet suited the nobles. The clowns seize the clothing and are accosted, in the second part of the show, by Prospero's spirits in the shapes of hunting dogs, set on by Prospero and Ariel. No verbal warning or lesson accompanies this scene, for its audience will not respond to mere words, as Prospero has proved in his experience with Caliban. The thieves, caught red-handed, are punished, immediately and physically. Their lesson must come in the form of pinches and pains—physical discomforts are the only punishment they understand.[15]

Prospero has planned well: he gives each group the show it most deserves and is best able to understand. In each case, the apparent harmony or attractiveness of the opening vision is qualified or negated by what follows. The vision of perfection proffered the lovers is left incomplete. The apparent benevolence of the island toward the nobles is turned to punishment because of their past and present sins. For the clowns, the attractiveness of the glittering clothes they find and seize is quickly shown to be illusory, for their greed leads directly to their deserved punishment. In all these scenes Prospero is present: they are, in effect, his messages to the various groups, made more effective by their dramatic form.

Prospero's final show differs greatly from his earlier ones. Yet its differences help measure the changes that have occurred during the play. Those characters who can repent have

15. In his edition of *The Tempest*, Frye makes a similar point about the appropriateness of ordeal to character and details somewhat more fully the parallels between the three shows (p. 1369).

done so, and Prospero no longer needs to create didactic illusion. In this final show, Ferdinand and Miranda play chess.
Prospero's actors are no longer spirits engaged in pretense but
real characters. Prospero presents the lovers with true theat-
rical flourish. A little like Paulina in *The Winter's Tale*, he
builds suspense in his audience. Promising that he will "bring
forth a wonder," Prospero steps up to the opening of his cell
and, drawing a curtain, reveals the two lovers. His audience
expects another magical vision: Alonso, accustomed by now
to the illusions and confusions of the place, is not sure
whether he sees appearance or reality—"If this prove / A vision of the island, one dear son / Shall I twice lose" (5.1.175–
77). Despite Alonso's mistrust, the lovers are real; magic has
been abandoned. Its usefulness is over. Magic provided the
climate necessary to promote inner changes in Alonso and to
control the impulses of the wicked characters. But it is limited in its power to rectify the past and to control the present.
It has had and will have no effect on the inner state of those
characters who refuse to feel guilt, just as magic has been
ineffective in changing human nature in plays previously examined. Ferdinand and Miranda embody Prospero's vision of
the future, a future to be shaped by them and by others without the assistance of magic.

Prospero's role as presenter is important, partly because his
shows, unlike most magicians' presentations, exist more for
their message than for spectacle. Chasing clowns with hunting dogs may appear comparable to Friar Bacon's transportation of Vandermast back to Germany or to Faustus's horning
of Benvolio as a rather spectacular and not particularly pro-
found trick. But Prospero is never guilty of purposeless cheap
magic, as Bacon and Faustus sometimes are. His understanding of the characters he controls only persuades us more
firmly of his wisdom and of the credibility of his magic.

In one other conventional magician's role, Prospero assists,
indeed actively promotes, the love affair between his daughter
and Ferdinand. Though he has received a good deal of knuc-
kle-rapping from critics for his engineering of the match, Prospero no more controls the inner lives of Ferdinand and Miranda than he controls those of Sebastian and Antonio. He
can provide a promising environment, an occasional hurdle or
delay, but he has no power to make them love. Prospero is far

more personally involved in this match than Peter Fabell, Friar Bungay, or John a Kent are with the affairs in which they interest themselves, but, as in those earlier plays, the magician only facilitates—not creates—the love that brings the play to its happy conclusion.

II.

One other aspect of Prospero's magic is often assumed to be traditional, his abjuration of magic and promise to drown his book and break his staff. C. S. Lewis, for example, suggested that a sixteenth-century audience would expect some sort of abjuration: "[Prospero's] speech of renunciation, sometimes taken as an autobiographical confidence by the poet, was to them necessary in order that the ending might be unambiguously happy."[16] Of all the magicians examined, however, only Friar Bacon in *Friar Bacon*, the magicians in *A Looking Glass for London*, Pope Alexander VI in *The Devil's Charter*, and Cyprian in the post-*Tempest* play *The Two Noble Ladies* repent or abjure their magic. Of these, all but Friar Bacon have used magic for clearly evil purposes. Contrarily, benevolent magicians who do not repent or renounce magic include Bomelio in *The Rare Triumphs of Love & Fortune*, John a Kent, Friar Bacon in *John of Bordeaux*, and Peter Fabell in *The Merry Devil of Edmonton*. Abjuration was clearly not essential for magicians, although enough precedents in magical literature exist to make abjuration something an audience might rather expect than not.[17] Yet Prospero's abjuration does not appear to be merely a pro forma bow to audience expectation, even though, of all the magicians I have surveyed, he seems to have the least reason to renounce magic. He has made no errors with his "art" (as Bacon had), nor has he overtly challenged the power of God (as had other repentant magicians). His obvious mistake in emphasizing his studies

16. *English Literature in the Sixteenth Century*, p. 8.

17. Barbara A. Mowat, "Prospero, Agrippa, and Hocus Pocus," argues, "The renunciation of magic, the return to the conventional world, and the concern with his own mortality . . . most clearly link Prospero to the wizard tradition" (p. 292), in which abjuration of magic was virtually mandatory. Mowat's article emphasizes, as I do, the ambiguities and complexities of Prospero's magic but accounts for them by arguing that Prospero is a pastiche of different magical traditions—commedia dell'arte magicians, wizards, classical enchanters, hermetic magi, and stage jugglers, practitioners of legerdemain.

to the neglect of his civic responsibilities lies outside the play, but only through his magic is he now able to begin to rectify that earlier error.

To understand Prospero's decision to abandon the magic that apparently serves him well, we must recognize his abjuration as a vital part of his overall plan. It is not an impulse of the moment. From the first act he has promised Ariel his freedom within two days, and for Prospero to continue to practice magic without Ariel is unimaginable. A number of critics, however, searching for dramatic tension in the play, locate the conflict within Prospero himself and believe that the drama's principal action is his change from an initial desire for revenge to his later forgiveness of his enemies. For that forgiveness, Ariel's speech at the beginning of act 5 is frequently taken as the catalyst. D. G. James, for example, wrote, "In place of magic forgiveness comes now. Prospero's forgiveness does not come easily or readily. He needed to be instigated to it, we remark, by Ariel; and when he expresses it, he does so not without a touch of priggishness."[18] Since, moreover, Prospero's soliloquy abjuring magic follows immediately after Ariel's speech, critics frequently assume a cause-and-effect relationship between the two speeches. Thus Norman Rabkin commented that Prospero's "movement to the benign and charitable renunciation of the last act is a spiritual revolution that we watch on stage."[19] But surely Prospero's benevolence toward his enemies has been obvious from the first act. Not only his promise to free Ariel but also his concern not to harm the courtiers in any way and to keep their ship in good condition suggest that Prospero's intentions go far beyond sterile revenge and that he has planned from the beginning to give up his magic, forgive his enemies, and return with them to Milan. For what other reason would he have hoped for the marriage of Ferdinand and Miranda even before their first meeting?[20] The only uncertainty about Prospero's intentions is how long he will let the courtiers suffer before releasing them from their madness, and Ariel's report of their condition

18. *The Dream of Prospero*, p. 140. On this point, see also Harry Epstein, "The Divine Comedy of *The Tempest*," pp. 282–83.

19. *Shakespeare and the Common Understanding*, p. 224.

20. F. D. Hoeniger, "Prospero's Storm and Miracle," and Rose Abdelnour Zimbardo, "Form and Disorder in *The Tempest*," p. 52, ask the same question.

and near pity for them prompts Prospero to release them at once.

Prospero's renunciation of magic is a well-considered choice, consonant with his other actions in the play, for Prospero knows the limits of his power. His decision to abandon magic is part of a primary theme of *The Tempest*: the limits to which man is subject and how he may best work within them.[21] Limits upon men, or, more precisely, on magicians, have been a theme of nearly all the magical plays here considered: Sacrapant could not control himself, though he could control others; Greene's Bacon overstepped the bounds of proper magic by the egocentricity of his magical ambitions; Pope Alexander's magic allowed him to view events but not to control them; Faustus's grand desires were much curbed by the limits Mephistophilis imposed. At first glance, Prospero seems unfettered by the restrictions that other magicians encountered, for everything (except, perhaps, the wedding masque) goes as he has planned. Yet he is successful primarily because he knows his limitations and works productively within them. Prospero cooperates with nature, as Northrop Frye has pointed out: "Prospero's magic is an identification with nature as a power rather than as an order or harmony, and is expressed in images of time rather than space, music rather than architecture. Like all magicians, he observes time closely . . . and his charms are effective only if he follows the rhythm of time."[22] Close observation of time is certainly characteristic of Prospero, though perhaps not of "all" magicians. His reiterated concern with time (see, for example, in 1.2 alone, lines 23, 37, 50, 237–40, and so on), his expressed need to accomplish his entire scheme within four hours, is not simply a gratuitous whim. The moment most propitious to his action is at hand, and he must use it well:

> By accident most strange, bountiful Fortune
> (Now my dear lady) hath mine enemies
> Brought to this shore; and by my prescience
> I find my zenith doth depend upon
> A most auspicious star, whose influence

21. In many respects my emphasis on the play's concern with limits parallels Zimbardo's in "Form and Disorder."

22. *A Natural Perspective: The Development of Shakespearian Comedy and Romance*, p. 152.

If now I court not, but omit, my fortunes
Will ever after droop. (1.2.178–84)

Working with auspicious astrological signs, anxious to complete his work before those signs change,[23] Prospero has to be
time-conscious; his power depends on utilizing time properly.

Though Prospero has prepared carefully for the moment, he
finds magical control hard to sustain, and the possibility of
failure is always present. Robert West claimed that Prospero
is "tense with doubts that he alone among the characters can
feel and that a modern audience probably appreciates much
less than a Jacobean one did."[24] Though his doubts do not
seem to weigh upon him all that heavily, Prospero's concern
that his spells are working well explains why he questions
Ariel so carefully about the success of the tempest, why he is
so delighted to see Ferdinand and Miranda falling in love, and
why he reiterates that everything is going according to plan:

My high charms work,
And these, mine enemies, are all knit up
In their distractions. (3.3.88–90)

Now does my project gather to a head:
My charms crack not; my spirits obey; and Time
Goes upright with his carriage. (5.1.1–3)

Perhaps the best way to emphasize how wrong things could
have gone is to remember Faustus, who paid no attention to
the proper time but hurried his attempts at magic, whose spirits did not obey, or rather obeyed only under certain conditions, and whose initial projects were never carried out. Unlike Faustus, Prospero knows how to admit and accept
limitations, even such a limitation as Caliban exemplifies.
For Prospero is limited by more than time and the possibility
of his magic going awry. Even at its most potent, magic has
no power to alter men's souls, to civilize a Caliban or to bring
an Antonio to repentance. This limitation, too, is familiar
from other magical plays; usually it occurs in cases where love
potions are ineffective because no magic can force a woman's
love (as in *John of Bordeaux*, *The Wars of Cyrus*, and *Two*

23. Wayne Shumaker, *The Occult Sciences in the Renaissance: A Study
in Intellectual Patterns*, p. 2, in his discussion of casting horoscopes, asserts
the importance of single hours in astrological calculations.
24. *Shakespeare and the Outer Mystery*, p. 85.

Noble Ladies). This limitation, especially with regard to Caliban, Prospero accepts with much less grace than other restrictions. He is angry that Caliban cannot be reformed, cannot be molded according to Prospero's own notion of goodness. But by the play's end he is willing to acknowledge Caliban and to take responsibility for him as he is: "This thing of darkness I / Acknowledge mine" (5.1.275–76). The hardest of all limitations to bear, the impossibility of improving those unwilling to be improved, is finally accepted by Prospero.

But he has not always understood about limitations. He committed errors in the past, as he admits to Miranda when he narrates to her their history:

> I, thus neglecting worldly ends, all dedicated
> To closeness and the bettering of my mind
> With that which, but by being so retir'd,
> O'er-priz'd all popular rate, in my false brother
> Awak'd an evil nature, and my trust,
> Like a good parent, did beget of him
> A falsehood in its contrary, as great
> As my trust was, which had indeed no limit,
> A confidence sans bound. (1.2.89–97)

Prospero reveals himself twice guilty in recounting his tale. First, he "neglect[ed] . . . worldly ends." By throwing himself into his studies, being "rapt" and "transported," Prospero was guilty of upsetting the proper balance between contemplation and action. His second mistake was also one of excess, of trusting without limits, which in turn produced Antonio's betrayal "sans bound." Clearly, Prospero was partly to blame for his own deposition, and he has learned much about control and balance in twelve years on the island. Much of the play's interest lies in the way Prospero uses power: once before he used it badly; now the questions are whether he can keep it within bounds and whether he will use it wisely for general good instead of for selfish ends. Power corrupts; it corrupted Antonio and Alonso twelve years before their island sojourn; it corrupts Sebastian and Trinculo and Stephano before our eyes. Magicians in other plays have been ruined by a desire for power: Bacon's magic becomes dangerous when he tries to use it to enhance his own reputation, and Faustus is corrupted by his longing to be a demigod. We are fascinated to watch Prospero, who has more power than any of the others, to see if he can hold to his benevolent purpose. We note his occasional irritation, the desire he naturally has, and once or twice expresses, for revenge, and wait to see if he will falter. But he never does. Obviously, Prospero has changed from the naively trusting and "rapt" scholar of Milan. But his change took place before the shipwreck, and the play unfolds as a perfect example of that control and balance, that proper use of magic and its results, however precariously maintained, which Prospero has learned in his exile.[25]

The play's concern with the limits and boundaries to which man is subject explains, without resorting to allegory, several of the problems critics have raised about the play. The emphasis on chastity that Prospero reiterates to the lovers, for example, has earned him such labels as *busybody* and *prig*, but he is simply admonishing Ferdinand about the importance of self-control—"do not give dalliance / Too much the rein" (4.1.51–52)—and of observing the rules of the marriage ritual in which he is soon to participate. Nothing shows more clearly Prospero's rage for order than the betrothal masque he creates: measured, harmonious, and to be completed by a dance. Prospero's didactic attitude toward the young lovers may offend some critics, but he is merely trying to teach the lessons of controls and limits less harshly than he himself has been forced to learn them.[26] One indication that he has been effective (or perhaps that his lesson was unnecessary) is the lovers' choice, in the final scene, of a game of chess, highly structured with many rules and, according to Kermode, an accepted pastime for noble lovers.[27] Even here, Miranda's protestations that no matter what Ferdinand does she will call it "fair play" suggest that she still has much to learn about the world.

The references to innocence and naiveté that permeate the play take on some negative connotations once we learn in scene 2 that it was his confidence "sans bound" that lost Prospero his Duchy. Miranda is the most positive of the naive characters, fully willing to see everyone and everything from

25. For a similar argument about Prospero's stance in the play, see Leland Ryken, "The Temptation Theme in *The Tempest* and the Question of Dramatic Suspense."

26. Zimbardo, "Form and Disorder," p. 53.

27 *The Tempest*, ed. Kermode, pp. 122–23, n. 171 s.d.

the civilized world as wonderful. Only about Caliban, the one being besides her father whom she knows well, does Miranda have negative opinions: "Abhorred slave! / Which any print of goodness will not take" (1.2.351–52). This appraisal of Caliban suggests that Miranda is educable about the evil to be found in the world, and despite her naive outburst at the sight of the less than noble courtiers—"O brave new world / That has such people in it" (5.1.183–84)—we respond positively to her enthusiasm, knowing that she has as protectors people more knowledgeable about the world than she.

The other chief "innocent" of the play is Gonzalo, the unfailing optimist, forever ready to find good in all people and events. But though he is clearly one of the play's good characters, his judgment is not to be trusted. Unlike Miranda, Gonzalo has had plenty of opportunity to witness the world's evil—it was he, after all, who supervised the banishment of Prospero—and still he has not learned. Gonzalo's optimism is balanced perfectly by the cynicism and pessimism of Sebastian and Antonio. Though Gonzalo is a far better person than they, his unqualified exuberance is as much an excess as their materialistic cynicism. Nowhere is this excess more evident than in Gonzalo's utopian fantasy of a world where, as he stresses, there are to be no boundaries, no limits:

> . . . for no kind of traffic
> Would I admit; no name of magistrate;
> Letters should not be known; riches, poverty,
> And use of service, none; contract, succession,
> Bourn, bound of land, tilth, vineyard, none. (2.1.149–53)

The response of the play's various characters to the apparent lack of control on the island—Sebastian and Antonio's plot of fratricide and regicide; Stephano and Trinculo's mounting ambition to rule; Caliban's murderous plans—immediately negates Gonzalo's vision. Such innocence as his is dangerous, no matter how appealing. Trusting to Providence completely and doing nothing for oneself is a kind of sloth of which one increasingly suspects Gonzalo to be guilty.[28] Prospero, once trusting like Gonzalo, but now active and no longer "rapt," understands the need to be alert to evil.

28. For a far more positive response than I can muster to Gonzalo and his optimism, see David C. Brailow, "Prospero's 'Old Brain': The Old Man as Metaphor in *The Tempest*," pp. 297–99.

The delicate set of balances on which *The Tempest* is poised has been noted repeatedly. But the balance most crucial to an understanding of Prospero's renunciation of magic is the balance in the play between the human and the nonhuman.

Just as *The Tempest* examines the limits of innocence, so does it treat the limits of humanity. Several times in the play Shakespeare calls attention to the problem of defining the human. Miranda mistakes Ferdinand for a spirit; he mistakes her for a goddess (1.2). Caliban thinks Stephano and Trinculo are Prospero's spirits come to punish him, while they mistake him for a fish and a monster (2.2). Gonzalo assumes the spirits who serve the banquet are "people of the island" (3.3). All of these mistakes draw attention to the need to identify what is human.

Moreover, several characters embody in themselves a duality. Caliban—"man-monster," "servant-monster," "misshapen knave," and "demi-devil"[29]—has no certain place on the scale of being; no one can decide whether he is man or beast. His animal instincts are always foremost, but he is human enough to have learned language and, by the play's end, to despise his drunken companions and resolve to sue for grace. In some ways Ariel, too, is almost human. Unlike the largely silent spirits over whom he has charge, Ariel delights in language. He has long talks with Prospero, arguing with him or complimenting him very much as a human being might. This element of Ariel's character is made clearest, of course, at the beginning of act 5, when he describes the pitiful condition of the courtiers and avers that he would pity them "were I human" (5.1.19).

But Prospero himself provides the most crucial test in the play of what it is to be human. Throughout, he acts much like

29. Shakespeare has rejected in his portrait of Caliban a tradition that would have made Caliban, too, a possessor of magical power. Merlin and a number of other medieval romance magicians were the offspring of a human woman and a devil. Because his mother, Sycorax, was a witch, Caliban is a natural candidate for inheriting special powers. This tradition would probably have been familiar to Shakespeare, for *The Birth of Merlin*, Rowley's(?) 1608 play, makes much of Merlin's birth. But Shakespeare chose to make Caliban powerless, though he described him in terms of the freakish, not-quite-human appearance that was a sign of such parentage. Perhaps also explained by this tradition are the elaborate but ineffective curses Caliban calls down on Prospero. Had Caliban magical power, these would be evil incantations, but Prospero's power is so great as to neutralize any other magic on the island, and Caliban curses fruitlessly.

a god while at the same time maintaining his human roles as father to Miranda and as the wronged ruler of Milan. Onstage, the duality of Prospero's nature is signaled clearly by the donning and doffing of his magician's cloak. Whenever Prospero is acting as a magician—immediately after the tempest, in his conversations with Ariel, when he produces his magical shows—he is dressed in the cloak. When he is involved in human relationships—the talk with Miranda, probably when he gives the lovers his blessing before their masque, and at the play's end when he forgives his enemies—Prospero is without the cloak.[30] In the last scene, he wears his ducal clothing, symbolic of the role of governor that he lost and now is to reassume. It is this final change of clothes that signals once and for all that Prospero has tipped the delicate balance he has maintained throughout the play; he has chosen to be human and not godlike.

In neoplatonic theory, of course, the aim of the magician was to gain knowledge, to strip himself of the concerns of the world, and, in effect, to abandon his flawed and earthbound humanity. Walter Clyde Curry described this process:

> Mere man may control irrational daemons in the practice of goetical art; but when his soul has been elevated to the point where he commands aerial daemons, then he is able to control mundane natures, not as man but as theurgist. He now makes use of greater mandates than pertain to himself as man. As his soul passes further through the spheres of ethereal and celestial daemons, his mystic powers become greater and more god-like. And finally, when he is completely assimilated to the gods, he becomes impassive like them and is able to exercise all the powers of the gods themselves. . . . Theurgical practices . . . represent no more than a means of preparation for the intellectual soul in its upward progress; union with the intelligible gods is the theurgist's ultimate aim.[31]

In this scheme of things, there is no place for a return to worldly affairs or to humanity. Impassivity suggests remoteness; Curry felt that this is the state that Prospero achieved. Other critics also have seen Prospero achieving perfect harmony by the play's end so that "rough magic" is no longer necessary for him. Hardin Craig, for example, commented,

30. Robert Egan, *Drama within Drama*, p. 93, thinks this removal of his cloak indicates Prospero's "separation of his artistic function from his identity as a man."

31. *Shakespeare's Philosophical Patterns*, pp. 182, 196.

"Prospero can burn his book and drown his staff, for they are no longer needed, for he has become perfect in himself as a single, separate, completely powerful and educated man."[32] But things are hardly so perfect at the play's end: Sebastian and Antonio show no evidence of reform, and Prospero silences them only by threatening to reveal their plot to Alonso; Caliban, though he says he will sue for grace, is still Caliban; and Prospero is going back to wrestle with a job in which he once failed miserably.

Prospero's choice—to return to Milan, to resume his worldly position, and to abjure magic—is a choice to remain human, despite all the weakness and danger human beings are subject to. He will use the wisdom gained from his books and from his experience on the island in the world of flux where he has human ties. To have retained his magic and continued on the path to wisdom mapped out by the neoplatonists would have been to become the impassive, godlike figure of Curry's description. But Prospero is acutely aware of his human responsibilities and of his human limits, his susceptibility to time, and chooses to remain where "Every third thought shall be my grave."[33]

In some ways his decision resembles Bussy D'Ambois's refusal to reach beyond the world for knowledge. He resembles, too, one neoplatonist magician who did not subscribe to the impassivity and aloofness expected of the philosopher-magician. In his "Preface" to Henry Billingsley's translation of Euclid's *Elements*, John Dee described the natural philosopher (and hence the theurgistic magician, though Dee would not have dared to use those words):

> Thus, can the Mathematicall minde, deal Speculatiuely in his own Arte: and by good meanes, Mount aboue the cloudes and sterres; and thirdly, he can, by order, Descend, to frame Naturall thinges, to wonderfull vses: and when he list, retire home into his

32. "Magic in *The Tempest*," p. 10.
33. West, *Shakespeare and the Outer Mystery*, sees the necessity for Prospero's abjuration somewhat more pessimistically than I do: "Prospero parts with . . .[his magic] and with mysterious Ariel in a way that suggests that whatever the glories and enlargements of such excursions as his into outerness, he must in the end, short of utter destruction, turn back to the world of pathos and the grave. . . . In the always alluring and always blighted theory of magic . . . the dubiety of the means and the infection of the ends is inescapable, for no man reaches with real power into outerness" (p. 93). It strikes me that the grim necessity in Prospero's abjuration that West's reading insists on seriously violates the tone of act 5.

owne Centre: and there, prepare more Meanes, to Ascend or Descend by: and, all, to the glory of God and our honest delectation
in earth.[34]

Much as Dee described the duty of "the Mathematicall
minde," so Prospero has learned to control the extraterrestrial
world for the benefit of humanity. As Dee urged, he not only
ascends to wisdom but also descends again to apply it. Thus
he is unlike the neoplatonic theorizers for whom magic was
a means of escape to other worlds of knowledge and resembles
rather the earnest English scientist and magician who tried to
put theory into practice to "the end of well doing, and not of
well knowing only."[35] For his efforts at practical magic, Dee
earned a reputation as a quack. But perhaps, to Shakespeare
and his contemporaries, Dee appeared more like Prospero, a
man of wisdom and power who devoted his talents to better-
ing his world.

Thus, Prospero knows from the play's beginning the boundaries of his art and knows, too, that at a certain point he must
renounce it. Having learned both magical and self-control, he
halts his progress upward, refusing to climb further, to become more than man, for he is "one of their kind" (5.1.23).

III.

Prospero's decision to limit his magic, confining it to a certain sphere of action, is echoed by the structure of The Tempest itself. The play has long been recognized as metadramatic, chiefly because of Prospero's "revels" speech and the
epilogue, both of which force metadramatic recognitions.

34. "Mathematicall Preface," The Elements of Geometrie of the most auncient Philosopher Evclide of Megara, sig. C3ᵛ.

35. Sir Philip Sidney, A Defence of Poetry, in Miscellaneous Prose of Sir
Philip Sidney, ed. Katherine Duncan-Jones and Jan Van Dorsten, p. 83. The
general argument of this part of Sidney's Defence seems almost a refutation
of the neoplatonic theory of removal from worldly concerns and concentra-
tion on knowledge. Sidney wrote, "For some that thought this felicity prin-
cipally to be gotten by knowledge, and no knowledge to be so high or heavenly as acquaintance with the stars, gave themselves to astronomy; others,
persuading themselves to be demigods if they knew the causes of things,
became natural and supernatural philosophers. . . . When by the balance of
experience it was found that the astronomer, looking to the stars, might fall
in a ditch, that the inquiring philosopher might be blind in himself" (p. 82).
It is not surprising to remember that Sidney was one of Dee's pupils and may
have studied neoplatonism with him (see Frances A. Yates, Giordano Bruno
and the Hermetic Tradition, pp. 187–89).

And, of course, the identification of Prospero with Shakespeare, of one's magic with the other's drama, is still tempting to many. Apart from reference to Shakespeare's biography, however, the play calls attention to itself as play in a number of ways.

Among its most important metadramatic elements is the similarity between the limits that Prospero imposes on his magic and those the playwright places on his play. Though most critics comment on the play's observance of the three unities, no one has offered a convincing dramatic explanation for their presence.[36] L. G. Salingar has spoken of "the sense of difficulty overcome," and Bernard Knox has remarked that "the fantasy and originality of the setting must be balanced and disciplined by a rigid adherence to tradition."[37] But such comments are inadequate. In this play about a creative magician who works within the limits of his magic and his humanity, Shakespeare has undertaken to demonstrate that he, too, can work within limits traditionally prescribed for drama by classical theory. Magic and dramatic creation are similar; form matches content; magician and dramatist both work gracefully within the boundaries of their art.

A concern with limits is not the only similarity between the playwright and Prospero, between drama and magic. Prospero functions for Shakespeare to give the play its comic structure. He plans his action carefully so that gradually the three groups of characters he controls approach a common spot, the area in front of his cell. Ferdinand is admitted there almost at once, as the suitor of Miranda, but the courtiers come only after much trial and wandering. The clowns—who first come too soon and with intent to murder Prospero—are driven away, only to be summoned again for judgment in the last moments of the play. Like any good comic dramatist, Prospero gathers his entire cast onstage for the finale so that proper rewards and punishments may be meted out. Shakespeare used Prospero to accomplish his own purposes, for he

36. A biographical explanation for the observance of the unities has frequently been offered: *The Tempest* is Shakespeare's answer to Ben Jonson's repeated criticism of drama that did not observe the unities. See, for example, R. G. Howarth, *Shakespeare's "Tempest,"* pp. 34–35.

37. Salingar, "Time and Art in Shakespeare's Romances," p. 34; Knox, "*The Tempest* and the Ancient Comic Tradition," in *English Stage Comedy*, p. 54.

too needed all present in order to end *The Tempest*. Prospero thus makes plausible within the fiction of the play the mechanical manipulation necessary to end it. The dramatist and his chief character function together as smoothly as Prospero and Ariel.

Finally, of course, the language and imagery of the play continually insist upon its metadramatic implications. Like drama, magic is always a temporary illusion in *The Tempest*—an "insubstantial pageant." This is true of magic in most of the plays previously examined; the illusion that magic provides and the magician's frequent provision of shows have almost always had metadramatic undertones. In *The Tempest*, however, the associations with drama, always latent in the conventions of Renaissance stage magic, are fully developed. The art of magic and the art of dramaturgy are inextricably entwined, their similarities highly developed. Prospero's magic is primarily illusion; so is theater.[38] Yet each has possibilities for educating, for momentarily so altering perceptible reality that audiences may, like Alonso, be impelled toward self-examination. In *The Tempest*, magic has the power to frighten, to instruct, to delight—all powers possessed by drama, as well. Though its metadramatic association is not the only function of magic in Shakespeare's play, or necessarily its primary one, magic's dramatic potential—present but incompletely realized in many earlier magical plays—is here given full development and adds a good deal to the richness of Shakespeare's play.

The Tempest is the culminating treatment not only of magic's metadramatic possibilities but of other of its thematic associations as well. The play presents the most complete picture of the positive potential of magic we have seen. While *Faustus* shows magic at its lowest, as a trick the devil uses to ensnare a human soul by deceptive promises of power, *The Tempest* reveals magic at its most powerful, used carefully by a man who understands its limits and does not twist it for his own egotistical satisfactions. Greene's *Friar Bacon* implies

38. The most complete exploration of the poet/dramatist parallel is Alvin B. Kernan's *The Playwright as Magician: Shakespeare's Image of the Poet in the English Public Theater*, which emphasizes the exigencies of writing drama for a public theater, which require that a playwright (like a magician) be "at once a mere trickster or sleight-of-hand artist and a philosopher" (p. 155).

that such magic is possible, but in Greene's play magic is skewed by Bacon's pride and his misunderstanding of the proper use of his power.

Concomitant with its careful presentation of magic (purposefully kept vague as to details so that there might be nothing concrete to criticize) is *The Tempest*'s examination of the man who practices it. Prospero makes no mistakes as a magician, has no flaws in his magic that might explain why magic does not make him forever omnipotent. Thus Prospero becomes the supreme embodiment on the English stage of the paradoxical figure of the magician: a man of great power who can force or influence nature to alter her course for him, but a man nonetheless limited who is, finally, not a god, only human, and thus faces boundaries beyond which he must not pass. Such limitations characterize almost all dramatic magicians from Sacrapant and Bomelio to Bacon and Faustus (a few minor exceptions, such as Bacon in *John of Bordeaux* and Merlin in *The Birth of Merlin*, apparently have no restrictions whatsoever). Yet always some extraneous reason prevents the magician from reaching the full development one might expect from his powers: he is a minor character and not fully realized in the play; he stands in opposition to God and thus cannot achieve anything significant; he has a flaw—pride, lust, haste—that makes him pervert his magic to unworthy ends. None of these excuses for limitation characterizes Prospero. Yet he embodies the paradox of superhuman power that is humanly limited.

This very paradox, I suspect, made the magician an attractive figure for some English dramatists. The emphasis on the humanity of the magicians created for the stage is, after all, the feature that most distinguishes them from the freakish caricatures who are the magicians in medieval narrative romances. Knowing that some of their contemporaries regarded magic as dangerous, unholy, or the work of the devil and that others—including some of Europe's leading intellectuals—saw it as a positive means of attaining wisdom and power with which to better the world, dramatists may have fastened upon magic, perhaps unconsciously, as an ideal image for conveying one view of man's place in the universe. The dominant thrust of Renaissance thought emphasized that man had great power to shape and change himself and his world; he was "the great Amphibian" or the "chameleon" who could rise almost to the height of the angels or fall almost to the level of the beasts. What better way to express man's potential than through the image of magic, as Pico did in his *Oration*? And what better way to express the frustrating fact that, however, great his powers, man could never escape the weakness and fallibility of his humanity than by emphasizing the limitations on those magical powers, which promise much but can be carried only to the limits of mortality?

IV.

Prospero is the last important magician in English drama before the closing of the theaters in 1642. Aside from the two weak and stereotyped plays already discussed—*The Two Merry Milkmaids* and *The Two Noble Ladies*—no other post-*Tempest* plays extant make use of serious magic. Popular though *The Tempest* must have been, it evidently found no real imitators until its heavily rewritten and operatic versions appeared in the Restoration.[39] Belief in magic as a potential source of power and wisdom was on the wane, even before Shakespeare created Prospero. Agrippa, Bruno, and John Dee were dead; their English successors were largely almanac-makers and creators of love potions. Perhaps Shakespeare dared to present a benevolent magician before the magic-fearing king only because magic no longer compelled even James's serious belief.[40] Increasingly the property of the lower classes, magic was no longer the pastime of intellectuals, as neoplatonic magic surely had been to some degree in sixteenth-century England.[41] Plays like Jonson's *The Alchemist* and *The Devil Is an Ass* ridiculed magic and its associated occupations as frauds; Simon Baylie's *The Wizard* (1638) is a somewhat later play of the same sort. This tradition of debunking magic reached back in English literature—long before the resurgence of serious magic—at least as far as Chaucer's "Canon Yeoman's Tale."

39. Four such Restoration versions appear in *After "The Tempest,"* intro. George Robert Guffey.

40. David Harris Willson, *King James VI & I*, discusses James's changing attitudes toward magic and witchcraft (pp. 308–12).

41. In the mid-seventeenth century, mystic poets like Vaughan and Traherne used magic for other purposes than those examined here. Primarily, their mysticism and hermeticism gave them an esoteric language and system of beliefs in which to express man's relationship to the cosmos. For them, magic was a means and not an end to be seriously pursued.

In England, magic and science—those fascinating and dangerous Siamese twins of the middle ages and early Renaissance—had apparently been separated successfully. John Dee
was one of the last Englishmen who balanced overt belief in
magic with an active interest in experimental science. Increasingly, practical men like Francis Bacon, who wished to
bring about changes in the world they lived in, emphasized
science. But the separation between magic and science was
more evident in language than in actual practice and belief.
Even those who have reputations as scientists—people such
as Bacon and Sir Isaac Newton—retained considerable involvement with magic through the seventeenth and into the
eighteenth century. But most of this magical activity was carried on under the label *science* (much as science had, in the
middle ages, been subsumed by the label *magic*).[42] "Magic,"
on the other hand, became by default the province of mys-
tics—such as Thomas Vaughan—who had no practical aims
for it. More frequently still, it was the resort of the supersti-
tious and gullible who wished to solve problems through easy,
supernatural means.[43]

On the English stage, magic survived only in a highly styl-

42. Lester H. Brune, "Magic's Relation to the Intellectual History of Western Civilization," remarks, "From 1600 to 1900, nourished by technological
innovations resulting from scientific discoveries, science gained dominance
as the proper form of human knowledge. . . . In the Age of Science, magical
concepts could continue to be a lesser, if not primitive form of knowledge, or
they could seek to be accepted as scientific principles" (p. 61). Much work
has been done in the last decade on the magical and hermetic elements in
the work of men like Francis Bacon and Sir Isaac Newton: see, for example,
Paolo Rossi, *Francis Bacon: From Magic to Science*, trans. Sacha Rabinovitch; Richard S. Westfall, "Newton and the Hermetic Tradition," in *Science,
Medicine and Society in the Renaissance: Essays to Honor Walter Pagel*, ed.
Allen G. Debus, 2:183–98; P. M. Rattansi, "Newton's Alchemical Studies,"
in the same volume, pp. 167–82; and David Kubrin, "Newton's Inside Out!
Magic, Class Struggle, and the Rise of Mechanism in the West," in *The Analytic Spirit: Essays in the History of Science in Honor of Henry Guerlac*, ed.
Harry Woolf, pp. 96–121, who argues that Newton withheld much of his occult writing because he "realized the dangerous social, political, economic,
and religious implications that would be associated with him should he dare
reveal his true thoughts" (p. 97). For a more general perspective on magic's
continuation into the seventeenth and eighteenth centuries, see Allen G. Debus, *Man and Nature in the Renaissance*, esp. pp. 101–41.

43. Though belief in intellectual magic declined early in the seventeenth
century, witchcraft and popular magic provided by local wizards and wise
men lived on, declining only on a wave of skepticism in the later part of the
century. See Keith Thomas, *Religion and the Decline of Magic: Studies in
Popular Beliefs in Sixteenth and Seventeenth Century England*, esp. pp. 253–
63, 570–83.

ized form, one that had traditionally employed the figurative and patently unreal—allegorical abstractions and gods and goddesses—to figure forth its message. Indeed, it was probably because he no longer compelled belief, was no longer a human figure, that the magician was given a place in Stuart court masques.

Writing fifty years after *The Tempest*, Dryden offered an indication of the climate of belief that permitted the magician to exist only in court masque. Patronizing and full of the scorn of a generation newly liberated from belief in magic, these lines—from the prologue of his and D'Avenant's revision of *The Tempest*—summarize Dryden's view of the magic in Shakespeare's play:

> But Shakespear's Magick could not copy'd be,
> Within that Circle none durst walk but he.
> I must confess 'twas bold, nor would you now,
> That liberty to vulgar Wits allow,
> Which works by magick supernatural things:
> But Shakespear's pow'r is sacred as a King's.
> Those Legends from old Priest-hood were receiv'd,
> And he then writ, as people then believ'd.[44]

Serious magic had obviously left the English public stage. The only refuge for such "Legends" were the intentionally unrealistic forms of court masque and, later, of opera—where Dryden himself frequently employed magic.

44. "Prologue to the Tempest or the Enchanted Island," in *After "The Tempest,"* sig. A4ʳ, lines 19–26.

Aery spirit   Scogã Scolton   A Brother of the
                                Rosicros.

Inigo Jones, costume sketches for Ben Jonson's *The Fortunate Isles and Their Union*, 1624 (courtesy Devonshire Collections, Chatsworth, England).

7

The Magician in Masque

In ancient times, when any man sought to shadowe or heighten his Invention, he had store of feyned persons readie for his purpose, as *Satyres*, *Nymphes*, and their like: such were then in request and beliefe among the vulgar. But in our dayes, although they have not utterly lost their use, yet finde they so litle credit, that our moderne writers have rather transfered their fictions to the persons of Enchaunters and Commaunders of Spirits, as that excellent Poet *Torquato Tasso* hath done, and many others.

In imitation of them (having a presentation in hand for Persons of high State) I grounded my whole Invention upon Inchauntments and several transformations.

So Thomas Campion explained his use of magic in his masque celebrating the 1614 wedding of Robert Carr, Earl of Somerset, and Lady Frances Howard. His explanation is both direct and candid.[1] Enchanters and Commanders of Spirits were fashionable: they were found in his most respected literary models.

In addition, although Campion neglected to say so, magicians are exceptionally well qualified for a role in masque. "The masque deals, not with the last phase of a conflict, but with a moment of transformation," wrote Enid Welsford.[2] And what character can more appropriately perform transformations than the magician: shape-changer, controller of spirits, prophet of the future? In Stuart masques, marvelous changes

1. Thomas Campion, *A Masque at the Marriage of Somerset and Howard*, in *The Works of Thomas Campion*, ed. Walter R. Davis, p. 268. Further references to Campion's work in my text are to this edition.
2. *The Court Masque: A Study in the Relationship between Poetry and the Revels*, p. 339.

are commonplace: trees become men; men become animals and vice versa; visions appear and fade away; mountains emerge and vanish. Sometimes—though perhaps not as often as might be expected—figures with magical powers are responsible for these transformations.

As Campion suggested, the level of public sophistication about stage magic had clearly changed since John Dee's mechanical beetle provoked rumors about his magical powers. By comparing the current use of enchanters to the former use of satyrs and nymphs, Campion implied that a belief in the existence of "real" magic was on the verge of disappearing altogether. By 1614, magicians had evidently become "feyned persons" in the eyes of the sophisticated court audience, even if such characters still commanded a modicum of belief among "the vulgar." Their credibility was recent enough, as my examination of magicians in drama attests, to command an audience's attention, if not its belief. The date of Campion's prologue corresponds almost too neatly with the waning of the magician as a character on the popular stage. The climate that had permitted serious consideration of magic in England at the turn of the century had changed, and magicians appeared now only in "fictions."

The subject matter of masques, their apparently magical stage effects (for which, had Inigo Jones staged them half a century earlier, he would surely have been labeled a magician), and their peculiar transitoriness all contributed to the aura of enchantment surrounding their production. The Elizabethans had repeated opportunities to watch the destruction of Bacon's brazen head or to see Faustus hauled off to hell. But Merlin spoke only once in *Prince Henries Barriers*, and the witches danced but a single night in Jonson's *Masque of Queenes*. Such fleeting spectacle may not seem unusual to a generation weaned on television specials. But that so much beauty, ingenuity, and expense were finally so transitory apparently impressed the inhabitants of Stuart England, if Prospero and Ben Jonson can be taken as reliable commentators on the subject.[3]

3. See *The Tempest*, 4.1.147–56, for Prospero's famous speech on dissolution and transitoriness. Ben Jonson commented on the insubstantiality of masque several times, most notably in the introduction to his masque *Hymenaei*, in *Ben Jonson*, ed. C. H. Herford and Percy and Evelyn Simpson, 8:209–10. References to all Jonsonian masques are to this edition.

With magic and enchantment so much a part of all aspects of the masque, it is something of a surprise to discover how few magicians and enchanters actually appeared on the masquing stage. Angus Fletcher, commenting that most of masque's "methods can be subsumed under the category of magic," described "a mystagogical Renaissance, with its hermetic magic, its memory theatres, its Egyptian theomancy, its Cabala, its wild fascination with inconceivable devices of order-in-chaos."[4] In fact, very little specific or coherent magic appeared in individual masques. Perhaps the general magical flavor that characterized the genre required few characters to explain or provide a rationale for magic (as more realistic drama did require: there, magicians as spectacle presenters often provided a rational link between the supposedly realistic world of the plot and the patently unrealistic, often allegorical, spectacle the magicians introduced).

Even when they did appear, masque enchanters were far more like medieval magicians and wizards than like the magicians who had performed just a few years earlier on the stages of the public theaters. Dramatic magicians have at least rudimentary personalities. Possessed of some human features and traits, they interact with other characters and can only rarely be summed up as representative of some particular abstraction like Envy or Lust. Masque magicians, on the other hand, have no human features. They resemble the deformed, freakish wizards of medieval romance. Unlike wizards, however, the one-dimensional masque magician usually personifies some abstract quality like Error, Suspicion, or Desire. The distinction in drama between male and female enchanters is not found in masque (as it was not found in medieval narratives). If anything, women enchantresses outnumber their male counterparts in masques, and no apparent distinction differentiates the magic the two sexes perform. In short, masque magicians are of a piece with the other allegorical and one-dimensional figures of masque. They show little resemblance to the more realistic and humane magicians portrayed in some Tudor-Stuart drama. Instead, they are sophisticated, consciously allegorical versions of characters who had earlier appeared in narrative romances or classical literature. Merlin finds a new home in masque, as do Circe and all her col-

4. *The Transcendental Masque: An Essay on Milton's "Comus,"* pp. 38, 105–6.

leagues who possess magic wands and the power to shape-change.

Like most masque characters, masque magicians are emblematic. They figure the emotional or psychological conditions of man or of a commonwealth rather than attempting to imitate real people. As Rosemond Tuve commented, masque

> is characterized by subtleties of idea, conveyable by images; . . . [drama] by subtleties of psychological motivation and personality, conveyable by characterization. . . . But in a masque psychological refinements are implicit in the meaning of the great images, not inter-acting before us in complete people.[5]

Very often, masque stages an essentially internal conflict. The action may, for example, occur within a human heart and represent the conflict between worldly love and chaste love, the debate between pleasure and virtue, and so forth. More often than not, magicians represent negative qualities in masques. Almost invariably villains, they must be defeated in order for harmony to be restored.

I.

In Tudor masques, in which some sort of magical change was necessary, the sovereign, merely by his presence, usually brought about the transformation. Magicians were rarely required. One early example occurs in Gascoigne's *The Princely Pleasures at Kenilworth Castle* (1575), in which the Lady of the Lake, imprisoned by Sir Brute, can be released only when "a worthier maide then she, / her cause do take in hand."[6] Speaking directly to Queen Elizabeth on behalf of the imprisoned Lady, Triton assures her: "Your presence onely shall suffice, / her enemies to convince" (2:103). And of course, the Lady of the Lake immediately appears, freed magically by the sovereign. With the possible exception of the lost masque of Astronomers (1559),[7] in fact, no surviving evidence suggests

5. *Images and Themes in Five Poems by Milton*, p. 154.
6. *The Complete Works of George Gascoigne*, 2:103. Further references in my text are to this edition. See Stephen Orgel's description of the occasion in *The Jonsonian Masque*, pp. 39–41.
7. Included in the list compiled by Mary Steele, *Plays and Masques at Court during the Reigns of Elizabeth, James and Charles*, p. 5, the masque is undescribed. My conjecture that it may have dealt with magic is based simply on the fact that magicians and astronomers were often assumed to be the same in sixteenth-century England.

that magicians or their close relatives had much importance in Tudor entertainments. Only in 1604, in a meager description of another lost masque, does the trickle of enchanters and magicians in masques begin:

> On New Yeares Night we had a play of Robin goode-fellow and a maske brought in by a magicien of China. There was a heaven built at the lower end of the hall, owt of which our magicien came downe and after he had made a long sleepy speech to the King of the nature of the cuntry from whence he came comparing it with owrs for strength and plenty, he sayde he had broughte in cloudes certain Indian and China Knights to see the magnificency of this court. . . . the magicien dissolved his enchantment, and made the maskers appear in theyr likenes.[8]

Apparently this Chinese magician functioned much as the magicians in drama examined earlier: he provided the rationale for the appearance of the spectacle.

Writing of the development of the induction in Tudor drama, Welsford has suggested, "Dramatists were expected to divert their audiences with interludes of music and dancing, and their use of the induction was a clumsy attempt to prevent these interludes from confusing the dramatic action, while giving them at the same time some more or less rational connection with the plot."[9] In many plays, like *Doctor Dodypoll* and *John a Kent*, the magician apparently became another solution to the same problem by providing an excuse for the introduction of spectacle. Although the lost masque of 1604 apparently followed this model, a somewhat different situation usually obtained with respect to masque. For masque had to be integrated not with a dramatic world but with the real court world, and masque writers had far better means than a magician to connect their two worlds. The masquers, themselves courtiers, provided the same sort of bridge between worlds that the magician offered in drama. Involved in the worlds both of the masque and of the court, they opened a broad path for audience involvement:

> [Masque] attempted from the beginning to breach the barrier between spectators and actors, so that in effect the viewer became part of the spectacle. The end toward which the masque moved was to destroy any sense of theater and to include the whole court

8. Quoted in Welsford, *The Court Masque*, p. 170.
9. Ibid., p. 280.

in the mimesis—in a sense, what the spectator watched he ultimately became.[10]

Instead of preserving the fiction of the play world, as the magician presenter does in drama—keeping the distance between spectator and play intact, insuring that the illusion created in the theater will not be broken—the traditional
masque presenter, only infrequently a magician, calls attention to the symbolic or ceremonial fiction that his audience
is about to witness and join in as participants. Thus the
masque presenter, as well as the masquing courtiers, bridges
the gap between spectator and masque and initiates the court
audience into the world of the masque.

The masque presenter is common in Elizabethan masques.
He nearly always makes long set speeches to explain the
meaning of the show he is introducing. As masques grew
more dramatic during the reign of James, however, the presenter became less important. Though the noble masquers themselves still rarely spoke in Jacobean productions, the expla-
nations of the masque emerged more and more frequently
through dialogue rather than in a long introductory speech by
the presenter. Partly for this reason, few of the magicians in
Jacobean masques can be called presenters. The magician of
China in the lost 1604 masque described above obviously
served as his masque's presenter; so did the old Enchantress
in Marston's *Entertainment of the Dowager-Countess of
Derby* (1607). Of the other Jacobean masques containing magicians or enchanters that I have examined, only in two, Jonson's *Masque of Queenes* (1609) and D'Avenant's *Salmacida
Spolia* (1640), do magic-wielding characters introduce the
masque. In the masques of Jonson and D'Avenant, however,
the magical characters actually introduce the antimasque,
which in both productions precedes the main masque (for the
connection between magicians and the antimasque, see below, p. 158). Thus, the magician-as-presenter is found primarily in drama and not in masque. Instead of linking masque
and court, masque magicians most often function simply as
characters within the masque, usually completely oblivious—as many masque characters are not—of the court world
before which they appear.[11]

10. Orgel, *The Jonsonian Masque*, pp. 6–7.
11. Ibid., p. 14, notes that the convention of having heroes occupy the main
masque and villains the antimasque helped to establish "distinctions of sen-

Most often the magical figure is identified with the anti-
masque and is somehow the villain of the piece. Merlin's ap-
pearance in the *Speeches at Prince Henries Barriers* (1610) is
exceptional in its benevolence. The English magician praises
Henry, prophesies the Prince's glorious future, and arouses
Chivalry to do knightly combat with the Prince.[12] Jonson's
Merlin is a very traditional and patriotic character. Campion's
The Lords' Masque (1613) contains another exception.
Through his musical magic, Orpheus releases Entheus, poetic
furor, from his imprisonment in the cave of madness. Both
Orpheus and Merlin are, of course, traditionally benevolent
figures. To have portrayed either of them as a villain (as D'A-
venant later portrayed Merlin in *Britannia Triumphans*)
would have been highly unusual. William Browne, however,
did the unusual in his *Ulysses and Circe* (1615). Completely
ignoring the standard moral implications of the Circe myth,[13]
Browne created a third benevolent enchanter. His good Circe
is devoted to Ulysses and has not transformed Ulysses's men
but merely induced them to fall into a deep sleep. Apart from
these three important exceptions, all other masque magicians
I know of are evil, villainous characters, associated with the
disruption and disturbances of the antimasque. The three
masques with benevolent magicians share fairly close dates
of performance (1610, 1613, 1615) and do not particularly emphasize the necessity of the sovereign's intervention in the
masque's action. (Jonson lavishly praised King James as a worthy successor to King Arthur in *Prince Henries Barriers*, but
the king does not appear in the masque. Prince Henry does
not function in quite the same way as would his father, for
Prince Henries Barriers primarily demonstrates his personal
charm, chivalry, and promise; it does not assert his royal
power to preserve order and harmony in the court world.)
    The role of the sovereign or noble patron has a great deal to
do, I think, with the infrequency of good magicians in the

sibility and morality. Thus, the characters in Jonsonian anti masques, played
by professional actors, are nearly always unaware that there are spectators."
    12. *Ben Jonson*, 7:323–36. Mary C. Williams, "Merlin and the Prince: *The
Speeches at Prince Henry's Barriers*," argues convincingly that Jonson took
Merlin very seriously indeed in this masque and made him its most important character, the poet-magician who advises the prospective monarch.
    13. See R. F. Hill's introduction to *Ulysses and Circe* in *A Book of
Masques in Honour of Allardyce Nicoll*, ed. T. J. B. Spencer, p. 183; and Rosemond Tuve, *Allegorical Imagery: Some Medieval Books and Their Posterity*,
pp. 33, 225–26.

court masque. No supernatural power could be granted to an even vaguely human character who might rival or dim the power of the monarch. In a genre capable of portraying the king of the gods reforming his court on Olympus after the ideal model provided by England's king and queen (in Carew's *Coelum Britannicum*), there could be no benevolent power greater than the sovereign's. Rather, magicians provided an opposing force for the monarch's power to overcome. (So did the defeat of wicked magicians in such didactic dramas as *A Looking Glass for London* demonstrate the superior powers of God.) Summarizing the most common situation represented in the Jacobean court masque, David Woodman commented,

> Chaos, in several court masques, is due to the willful use of black magic by such enchanters as Circe. Almost invariably, a mythological god or royal personage to whom the masque pays compliment functions as the victorious adversary of the enchanter and, as an agent in the plot, has the potency of a deus ex machina.[14]

Because of the peculiar demands of the masque, the magician frequently links the main masque and the antimasque. Sometimes magical figures even dance the antimasque. In such a production as Jonson's *Masque of Queenes*, for example, the witches provide a long, introductory antimasque; and in D'Avenant's *Salmacida Spolia* the Furies, who clearly have magical powers, perform the antimasque. In two of D'Avenant's other masques, *The Temple of Love* (1634) and *Britannia Triumphans* (1637), evil magicians call up spirits who perform the antimasque. Because of their involvement with the antimasque, the magicians themselves usually are grotesque characters or, at least, creators of chaos and disharmony. This view of the magician is especially common in later Caroline masques, in which antimasques grew increasingly frequent and extreme.[15]

Two masques exemplify the frequently grotesque portrayal of the magician in Stuart masque: Campion's 1614 *Masque*

14. *White Magic and English Renaissance Drama*, p. 89.
15. Fletcher, *The Transcendental Masque*, p. 21, explains this increase in antimasque activity: "Dionysus gets into the late masques with almost neurotic frenzy, in a cancerous proliferation of anti-masque dances—but for good reason, since politics outside the court is getting closer to the court, and misrule is becoming a genuine political threat to the protected sacred space, the *coelum britannicum*." Though this is clearly not the only reason for the growth of the antimasque, it is an interesting suggestion.

at the Marriage of Somerset and Howard (a marriage more appropriately characterized by evil magic than any spectator or participant perhaps realized),[16] and D'Avenant's much later masque, *The Temple of Love*, written for Queen Henrietta Maria in 1634.

In Campion's masque, a number of squires, coming to court to celebrate the marriage, have been transformed into golden pillars by:

Deformed *Errour* that enchaunting fiend,
And wing-tongu'd *Rumor*, his infernall freind,
With *Curiositie* and *Credulitie*,
Both Sorceresses. (P. 269)

Each of the four is then described: Errour, for example, is scaled like a serpent, with hair of snakes, and a "deformed visard." The four begin to dance and are soon joined by the four winds, the four elements, and the "four parts of the earth" (Europe, Asia, Africa, and America). All dance together "in a strange kind of confusion" and then "past away, by foure and foure." They are replaced onstage by Eternity, the three Destinies, Harmony, and nine musicians. These new characters explain that the enchantment of the squires can be dissolved only by the Queen: "For she, she, only she / Can all Knotted spels unty" (p. 272). By plucking a branch from the "Tree of Grace and Bountie," the Queen changes the pillars back into squires, and the masque's "plot" is over. All that remain are elaborate dances and complimentary songs. The enchanters never appear again; the masque presents no real contest between the opposing powers of magicians and sovereign. The early disorder simply dissolves into harmony. The political and moral allegory is clear; only the Queen can dissolve the chaos and distrust created in the kingdom.

D'Avenant also created deformed magicians, though with-

16. For discussions of the intricate poisoning attempts and intrigues perpetrated in order to bring about the Carr-Howard wedding, see G. P. V. Akrigg, *Jacobean Pageant or the Court of King James*, pp. 190–204. Detailed and spicy accounts are found in William McElwee, *The Murder of Sir Thomas Overbury*, and Edward Le Comte, *The Notorious Lady Essex*, although one wonders if historical veracity does not sometimes take a backseat to entertaining narrative in both these versions. In any case, the rumors and scandal that accompanied this tainted marriage, along with Queen Anne's known opposition to the match, suggest that this is one of the most pointed of all the court masques. Only Anne can release those wedding guests immobilized by the sorcery of error, rumor, and suspicion.

out the specific allegorical labels of Campion's masque. Divine Poesy opens the masque by prophesying to a group of
poets Indamora's arrival to release youths long imprisoned by
magicians in a false temple of love. Then the magicians enter
from an underground cave, "their habits of strange fashions,
denoting their qualities; and their persons deformed."[17] They
worry awhile about Indamora's imminent arrival. She has already begun to dry the mists in which they had hidden Love's
true temple. Finally, the magicians decide to try their powers
"to hinder destiny" and call up spirits from the four elements.
The spirits enter separately, each accompanied by several un-
pleasant types of people: "quarreling men with a loose wench
amongst them," alchemists, "drunken Dutch skippers," and
"witches, usurers, and fools." After they dance the antimasque, this odd collection of spirits and people is immediately replaced onstage by Indamora's Indian and Persian pages,
followed by a ship carrying Orpheus and another bearing Indamora (Henrietta Maria) and her ladies. Indamora's presence,
of course, dispels the mists that still obscure the Temple of
True Love, and Chaste Love descends from heaven to join in
the final song. As in Campion's masque, the magicians—
their deformities signaling their nonhuman nature and "evil"
role—are confined to their own section of the masque and are
defeated without any confrontation. The monarch, merely by
virtue of his presence, has the power to defeat dissension and
disorder.

A note of rising hysteria seems to characterize the later
masques written for Charles. The number of antimasques in
each masque increases while simultaneously the power of the
sovereign to wrest order from chaos becomes increasingly
sweeping and arbitrary. No benevolent magicians appear in
the later masques. Even a character such as Merlin, traditionally identified with prophecy and support of the English monarchy, performs bad magic and is responsible for disorder. In
fact, D'Avenant's portrayal of Merlin in *Britannia Triumphans*, in which his traditional function is deliberately reversed, offers a good final example of how magicians are portrayed in many masques. Here Merlin is more like an
antimasque magician (and is indeed responsible for both an-

---

17. *The Temple of Love*, in *The Dramatic Works of William D'Avenant*,
ed. James Maidment and W. H. Logan, 1:291. All further references to D'A-
venant's masques are to this edition.

timasques in the work) than he is like earlier versions of himself.

The masque opens with a debate between Imposture and
Action over the nature of man. Claiming that "all / Delight
still to be cosen'd," Imposture concludes that every man
might as well give himself up to a life of voluptuous pleasure.
Action declares, however, that it is possible (despite puritanical opinion to the contrary) to enjoy moderate pleasure as long
as "every act be squared by virtue's rule."[18] Imposture calls
on Merlin, fortuitously risen from his grave for the occasion,
to conjure a vision of hell that will show Action all those who
chose to live according to Imposture's ethic while they were
alive. Into a scene "transformed into a horrid hell" come six
antimasque entries, including musicians, tradesmen, baboons, mountebanks, courtiers, and—last—leaders of previous English rebellions. After they have danced the antimasque, Bellerophon (Heroic Virtue) enters riding Pegasus,
and he and Action dismiss "These airy mimic apparitions,
which / This cosening prophet would present" (2:275). After
more conversation, Imposture asks Merlin to call up one more
vision for Bellerophon to see, a medieval knight and his lady.
The "Mock Romanza" that ensues is pure farce, as a dwarf,
squire, knight, and giant all battle over a very aggressive
maiden. Merlin ultimately turns the combat into a dance, and
when it is over the antimasque disappears. Bellerophon is dis-
gusted (as is the reader, since this antimasque has no apparent
connection to the concerns of the rest of the masque). He
cries out to Merlin, "Blow thine own dust about! until we find
/ No small remainder of ill gather'd thee / And like to it; so
waste thy memorie" (2:282). Shortly thereafter, Merlin and
Imposture exit to make way for Fame ("'Tis fit you vanish
quite when they [Fame and 'Those that in this Isle / The old
with modern virtues reconcile'] appear," says Bellerophon).
The two characters never reappear. Fame sings the praises of
Britanocles (Charles); the masquers dance; a chorus of poets
sings praise to the queen; the sea nymph Galatea appears on
a dolphin claiming that Britanocles rules so well that even the
sea nymphs come to visit him. The masque ends with a val-
ediction praising the royal marriage and recommending the
king and queen as models to all lovers:

18. *Dramatic Works*, 2:271.

To bed, to bed! may every lady dream
From that chief beauty she hath stolen a beam,
  Which will amaze her lover's curious eyes!
Each lawful lover, to advance his youth,
Dream he hath stolen his vigour, love, and truth;
  Then all will haste to bed but none to rise! (2:290)

D'Avenant's masque, exceptionally disjointed, contains no clear central focus. It is thus, from one point of view, not a significant guide to other contemporary practice in masque. But D'Avenant's apparent rejection both of British history and tradition and of the common, lower-class English citizens who enter in the first antimasque does, in fact, suggest an important characteristic of late Caroline masque. Sea nymphs are worthy and hence welcome to visit Britanocles, but the masquemaker implies that the ancient legends and the general populace are worthy only of parody and antimasque status: neither the common people nor Merlin, the traditional British prophet, but rather the sea nymphs are allowed to sing Charles's praises. Merlin, the usual upholder of monarchy and of traditions, is transformed into a "cosening" purveyor of cheap visions. Only Britanocles, who knows how fitly to mix virtue and pleasure, is worthy of imitation—a pattern for everything from ruling to carrying out the duties of the marriage bed. By making Merlin responsible for baboons and a burlesque romance, D'Avenant turned his back on the past in order more fully to glorify the present. The repeated insistence upon the king's complete omnipotence, here and in other late masques, is at least partially responsible, I think, for the very negative portrayal of magicians in most Caroline masques. Charles's power eclipses all magical power, including that usually employed to glorify British history and tradition.

Both Campion's and D'Avenant's masques reveal the almost total neglect in the Stuart masques generally of philosophical magic, the learned, daemonic magic that influenced much of the drama. Most masques show no awareness that characters like Faustus, Friar Bacon, and Prospero had ever been created, or that Ficino, Agrippa, and Dee had ever lived and worked. Instead they present magicians like those of narrative romance: deformed, often malevolent creatures who have only to wave a wand to bring about transformations, and whose chief importance is to figure some particular abstraction. In creating magicians, masque writers apparently went for models to medieval romance and classical myth. They almost completely ignored the popular drama written between 1580 and 1612.

II.

One exception to these generalizations is Ben Jonson, most prolific of the masque writers. Jonson's *Alchemist* suggests that he was not disposed to take magic seriously. His use of magic in masque confirms this suspicion. Jonson's portrayal of Merlin has been mentioned above: in the *Speeches at Prince Henries Barriers*, he depicted a traditional Merlin, prophesying optimistically about the future of the English prince. In two other masques, however, Jonson came closer than any other masque writer to describing the magical beliefs current in Stuart England.

Thus, he portrayed the witches in *The Masque of Queenes* (1608) not as "enchantresses" interchangeable with magicians in their function but as real witches. Jonson based their depiction—he is quick to tell us—upon the most authoritative books on the subject.[19] The witches do not call up spirits or daemons—for witches have no summoning power over spirits—but repeat instead charms intended to affect the natural world. They do not present the antimasque; they perform it. The witches work together, almost as a coven, deriving much of their power from their collective presence. Their behavior differs greatly from that of the magician, who usually works independently. In other words, Jonson's masque presents witches who are not simply displaced romance figures but who reflect the conception of their nature current in seventeenth-century England (though much of that conception is based on classical literary models).

Similarly, Jonson dealt with philosophical magic in a later masque, *The Fortunate Isles and Their Union* (1624). As we might expect, Jonson ridiculed such magic, but he did introduce the subject into his masque, even if only to discount it. The masque opens as Iophiel, "an aery spirit, and (according to the *Magi*) the *Intelligence* of *Iupiters* sphere," enters "running."[20] (The initial irony of opening a masque—the genre

19. See *Ben Jonson*, 7:283.
20. Ibid., 7:707.

that most abounds in descents from heaven—with an "aery" spirit who enters conventionally on his own feet suggests immediately that magic and its effects will be discredited in the action that follows.) Though he clearly has come to earth on some errand, Iophiel is immediately distracted by the appearance of Mere-Foole, a melancholy student of magic and a recent convert to Rosicrucianism. Mere-Foole has undergone all the purification rituals described by the order. But he has not yet been granted any contact with a spirit or an Intelligence, and he is upset. Iophiel determines to have some fun with Mere-Foole: he introduces himself as Jupiter's Intelligence and makes Mere-Foole elaborate promises that parody the intellectual aspirations of the philosophical magicians.

> When you haue penetrated hills like ayre,
> Diu'd to the bottome of the Sea, like lead,
> And riss' againe like corke; walk't in the fire
> As 'twere a *Salamander*, past through all
> The winding orbes, like an Intelligence,
> Vp to the *Empyreum*, when you haue made
> The World your gallery, can dispatch a businesse
> In some three minuts, with the *Antipodes*,
> And in fiue more, negotiate the *Globe* ouer;
> You must be poore still.
> . . . I will but touch your temples,
> The corners of your eyes, and tinct the tip,
> The very tip o' your nose, with this *Collyrium*,
> And you shall see i'the aire all the *Ideas*,
> Spirits, and *Atomes*, Flies, that buz about
> This way, and that way, and are rather admirable,
> Then any way intelligible. (7:713, lines 171–92)

Mere-Foole believes Iophiel completely. When asked whom he would like Iophiel to call before him, the befuddled scholar first chooses Zoroaster, "Because he's said to be the Father of coniurers / And a cunning man i'the starres" (7:714, lines 217–18). He asks next for Hermes Trismegistus, Pythagoras, Plato, and Archimedes. His list is composed of authorities to whom neoplatonic magicians turned for wisdom. Iophiel has no intention of producing these philosophers (each of them, he claims, is busy at some ridiculous task and cannot come). Instead he calls up the English poets Skelton and Scogan,[21]

21. See ibid., 10:672, n. 279–80, for discussion of the apparent confusion

who respond to Mere-Foole's request for "Ellen of Troy" with a group of English literary and dramatic characters (some their own creations) who come tumbling onstage to dance an antimasque. After they vanish, Iophiel disabuses Mere-Foole of his illusions, telling him that he has seen not "The company o' the *Rosie-Crosse*! you wigion" but rather "The company of *Players*" (7:722, lines 431–32). Mere-Foole exits, and Iophiel, recalling his original purpose, turns to King James to deliver a message from Jupiter concerning the union of the Fortunate Isles. He also introduces the main masquers who have come to pay homage to the ruler of the united isles. After their traditional compliments to the King, predictions for his prosperous future, and dances, the masquers withdraw.

The Fortunate Isles clearly falls into two parts joined only by Iophiel's presence in both. In the first part, Iophiel dupes Mere-Foole and debunks the philosophical magic in which Mere-Foole believes. In the second, Iophiel serves as a messenger from Jupiter, complimenting the King on his ability to rule the united and "fortunate" isles successfully. Iophiel is, in many ways, the key to this apparently disjointed masque: their varying perceptions of him characterize both the masque participants and the audience.

The court and King, conditioned by the usual forms and ritual compliments of court masque, understand Iophiel and his message from Jupiter as compliments to the ruler and his court, an elegant and lively means of saying that the heavens bless and approve the order James has established in England. The spectators and the King have the sophistication necessary to interpret the masque metaphorically, to see Iophiel as representative of abstract qualities. Mere-Foole, on the other hand, is a literalist. With the limited awareness of most antimasque characters, the weak-headed scholar sees Iophiel as a real daemon and believes implicitly in the reality of the stage performance in which he unknowingly acts. Mere-Foole never doubts that Iophiel really inhabits Jupiter, and thus has all sorts of wonderful powers, until Iophiel finally tells him that the lively antimasque characters he has seen are not spirits but a company of players. Only then does Mere-Foole recognize his error.

One of the masque's functions, then, is to explore different

---

over Scogan's identity. Jonson's editors suggest that he confused John Scogan, court fool to Edward IV, with Henry Scogan, a poet and friend of Chaucer.

ways of interpreting and understanding the same phenomenon. To the audience and the main masquers, Jonson attri-
buted the imagination necessary to think on more than one
level. These are the true audience for whom the poet wrote.[22]
But he portrayed Mere-Foole, a would-be magician and a fool
for wanting to explain the mysteries of the universe by magic,
as lacking any ability to see beyond the literal level and as
completely without imagination. Far from the peak of human
achievement and creativity, which Prospero represented and
Faustus wanted to, Mere-Foole—the most limited character
in Jonson's masque—is completely unable to understand the
world he inhabits. As David Woodman commented, "Any belief here that the magus and his Neoplatonic spirits could con-
duct effective magical experiments becomes completely
laughable."[23]

By portraying an aspiring magician as his gull, Jonson
clearly intended to satirize magic and magicians. But magic
functions in the masque as more than a target for satire.
Magic is traditionally associated with the creation of illusion.
But Jonson discredited the magician's ability to create illusion
and therefore had to find another source for the apparently
"magical" illusions of his masque. His alternative, that the
poet and player create the "magical" illusion of the masque,
in effect "demetaphorizes" the analogy between magician and
creative artist that stands behind so many magical characters.
If what Mere-Foole sees is not a company of spirits but the
players themselves, then the poet and players are the true magicians. The characters whom Skelton and Scogan bring onstage to dance the antimasque, literary creations borrowed by
Jonson from earlier English literature, unite poets and fictional characters in providing the "magic" of the antimasque.
Just so have Jonson and his scene designer provided the
"magic" of the masque itself.

Not only is the poet responsible for the provision of illusion
for his audience; each illusion must also be suited to the person for whom it is intended (much as Prospero provided three

22. Stephen Orgel, "The Poetics of Spectacle," p. 387, urges the need for
the audience's understanding of the artistic illusion: "We need a better word
than magic to describe what Jones' theater was doing. It was not magic precisely because it required so completely the collusion of the observer; his wit
and understanding made the miracles and metamorphoses possible. If anyone
is *deceived*, the effect has failed."
23. *White Magic*, p. 101.

different sorts of illusions for the three groups he controlled on his island). Iophiel does not pretend to call up Plato or Zoroaster for Mere-Foole. Instead he summons old court entertainers and a number of bawdy, lowlife characters. It would breach decorum to allow Mere-Foole to see Helen of Troy, just as it would to present the King with the compliments of Elinor Rumming. Only the formal and classical masque of the sea gods and the harmonious dances are ostensibly intended for the King and his court (though of course they watch and are entertained by the whole masque); the jigging rimes and dances are intended for Mere-Foole. Both halves of the masque present illusions: Mere-Foole, a believer in magic, accepts the illusion he sees as reality; the King interprets his illusion correctly, as a transitory emblem of harmony. Like those of magicians in other plays and masques, Jonson's illusions are appropriate to their recipients.

In *The Fortunate Isles*, Jonson used magic in the context of a concern for literary creation, as did many of the dramatists discussed in earlier chapters. Unlike them, he did not make magical and literary creation analogous, nor was magic a metaphor by which he spoke of artistic creation. Instead, Jonson deflated magical pretensions by suggesting that all magic is illusion and that a magician who assumes he has special powers is deluded. Jonson regarded the literary artist, not the magician, as the appropriate master and controller of illusion. Not content, as were some other masque writers, to use magic purely as spectacle or as a foil to the more powerful magic of the monarch, Jonson debunked magic in order to talk about the power of the poet. Angus Fletcher may well have been thinking of *The Fortunate Isles* when he wrote of Jonson,

> The virtuoso self-consciously projects his awareness that he is a virtuoso, that he is playing the role of the godlike creator, that he is mediating the imaginative process and in fact is "performing" his creation. On this ground a number of Jonson's masques make the defense of artistic genius their "device."[24]

III.

The Fortunate Isles is the only masque other than *Comus* concerned in any way with philosophical magic. Jonson's

24. *The Transcendental Masque*, p. 133.

broad parody of neoplatonic magic and its belief in daemons is very different from Milton's more subtle and qualified treatment of it. But the conclusions the two masques draw about the validity of such magic are strangely similar. Milton's masque, like Jonson's earlier one, discredits the magician's pretensions. Comus does not control daemons, and it is not he who mounts toward extraterrestrial wisdom and knowledge in Milton's vision.

Like *The Fortunate Isles*, *Comus* opens with an address by a daemonic spirit sent to earth by Jove to perform an assigned task. The Attendant Spirit, however, shows little of Iophiel's mirth. The different tone of his opening speech reflects an outlook very different from Iophiel's: the Spirit is more serious and attentive to duty than Jupiter's Intelligence. Jonson's masque begins with parody and concludes with a gratifying but light compliment. Milton's masque is concerned with the spiritual condition of those who inhabit a "Sin-worn mould." While its final moments, like Jonson's masques, are gratifying compliment, their lightness of tone derives partly from relief that serious dangers have been successfully avoided.

The neoplatonic elements of *Comus* have long been recognized by critics.[25] Many of these elements are associated with the Attendant Spirit: his epilogue and prologue are filled with images of the soul rising (or falling) in relation to the "pinfold" earth; moreover, the Trinity College MS attaches the label *daemon* to him.[26] But critics have made little or nothing of the combined presence in the masque of a daemon *and* a magician. David Woodman remarked in passing, "The beneficent Attendant Spirit, who is from Jove's court, is a spirit such as the white magician might try to attract to the sublunary world."[27] But he said nothing more about the daemon's traditional relationship to magic. *The Fortunate Isles*, with both a daemon and a would-be magician as characters, is partly concerned with the subject of philosophical magic. So is *Comus*, which ironically overturns the relationship neoplatonists assumed to exist between magician and daemon. In-

25. See, for example, Sears Jayne, "The Subject of Milton's Ludlow Mask," *PMLA* 74 (1959): 533–43, rpt. in *Milton: Modern Essays in Criticism*, ed. Arthur E. Barker, pp. 88–111; G. F. Sensabaugh, "The Milieu of *Comus*"; John Arthos, *On "A Mask Presented at Ludlow Castle*," pp. 33–40.

26. Rosemond Tuve, *Images and Themes*, p. 135, n. 19, finds the platonic associations of the Attendant Spirit "confirmed" by the name *Daemon*.

27. *White Magic*, p. 107.

stead, Milton juxtaposed the two characters in a struggle for the allegiance of the Lady and her brothers.

The presence of the daemon in masque—especially this masque, with its pastoral elements[28]—is no surprise. Interaction between heavenly and earthly realms is an accepted part of the pastoral world.[29] And in masque, noted for descents of heavenly messengers, daemons or daemonlike figures are common (Iophiel in *The Fortunate Isles* and Euphemus in Jonson's *Love's Triumph through Callipolis* are only two examples). What is unusual, however, is the presence of a magician in a world even partially pastoral in nature. This combination of daemon, magician, and neoplatonic ideas can hardly be accidental in a writer so widely acquainted with neoplatonic writings as Milton.[30] His decision to make Comus the "son of Circe," rather than to write of Circe herself or of Circe's daughter, may have been made with the neoplatonic magician in mind. Ordinarily masques present more female than male enchanters, and Milton would have found a good deal of literary precedent in other forms, as well, for a female embodiment of lust and sensual temptation (Circe, Acrasia, Armida). The partly sexual nature of Comus's temptation of the Lady may be Milton's chief reason for switching the sex of the usually female magical representative of lust and desire.[31] But his wish to suggest other associations (with Jonson's belly god, for example, as well as with neoplatonic magic) is also likely to have determined how he shaped the character of Comus.

Normally, of course, magician and daemon were associated in a more or less voluntary partnership. A magician desired to remove himself from the taints of worldly affairs and to gain celestial wisdom and power. He therefore entreated—or com-

28. Tuve, *Images and Themes*, p. 124, remarks, "An Attendant Daemon is no stranger to pastoral."

29. Peter Saccio, *The Court Comedies of John Lyly: A Study in Dramaturgical Allegory*, p. 216, says, "The world of pastoral has always mingled deities and mortals. The divine and the human tend to exist there with less rigid separation than elsewhere. We really experience no sense of ontological confusion, no sense of violation of the human level by intrusion of the divine."

30. Irene Samuel, *Plato and Milton*, pp. 35–40, discusses Milton's neoplatonism and concludes that he knew of "hermetic mysticism" and was probably familiar with much of Ficino's work and translations.

31. John Arthos, *On "A Mask,"* p. 7, offers this explanation for Comus's sex.

manded, depending on the interpreter of the theory—daemons to grant him special knowledge and power in order to assist his intellectual and spiritual ascent. To accomplish his initial connection with a daemon, a magician was expected to perform certain rituals, often using sensory allurement or bait to attract the daemon's attention. Comus employs many of the sensual lures appropriate to the neoplatonic magician—music and dance, food and drink, astrological consultations—but his purpose is to lure human beings down the platonic scale toward animality rather than to lure a daemon to assist in elevating the magician "higher than the Sphery chime."

Comus's first appearance, bearing his cup and charming rod, attests that he sees himself as a special, "purer" creature:

> We that are of purer fire
> Imitate the Starry Choir,
> Who in their nightly watchful Spheres,
> Lead in swift round the Months and Years. (Lines 111–14)[32]

More than human, Comus has a particular ritual to perform. The midnight "rites" in which he and his "herd" participate have as much dark purpose as those performed by Faustus on another late night. Comus is not simply a representative of evil or of sensuality. He is also a deliberate planner and plotter of magical chaos, aware of his special nonhuman powers and how best to use them. He is the opposite of a neoplatonic magician; he is a creature determined to use his powers not to elevate man but to lower him.

In some senses, theories inherent in neoplatonic magic are reaffirmed in *Comus*. Daemons do, in fact, descend to aid humans who "by due steps aspire / To lay their just hands on that Golden Key / That opes the Palace of Eternity" (lines 12–14). But they do not come to the tune of magic rituals or to the demands of a magician. Rather they come unasked, impelled by virtue and by nothing else. Milton's Attendant Spirit functions much as neoplatonists believed daemons, planetary intelligences, would function. But, ironically, a magician is also present, working not with and as the master of the daemon, but rather directly against him. Comus uses his magical powers of self-aggrandizement to gather a "herd" as large as

---

32. John Milton, *Comus*, in *Complete Poems and Major Prose*, ed. Merritt Y. Hughes, p. 92. All further references to Milton's works in my text are to this edition.

his mother's,[33] while the daemon attempts to aid the virtuous in their climb away from Comus's sensuality.

Conflict in the masque does not occur primarily between Comus and the Lady (who as a human being is unfairly matched with the nonhuman Comus) but rather between the Attendant Spirit (aided by Sabrina) and Comus.[34] The parallels between the Attendant Spirit and Comus make their opposition hard to ignore. They open the masque with long introductory speeches. First the Attendant Spirit, who knows all about Comus and who has arrived from Jove's court for the express purpose of protecting the siblings from Comus, speaks. Then Comus, about whom the Attendant Spirit has warned us, takes over the stage. Like most antimasque characters, he has little knowledge outside his immediate world. He does not know, for example, about the Attendant Spirit or of the presence of the three young people in the wood. The perspectives of these two inhuman characters are thus immediately contrasted, not only in their relative breadth of knowledge but also in their interpretations of the cosmos. The Attendant Spirit has the perspective of a sky-dweller. He sees the earth as a "pinfold" and the islands of Great Britain as jewels adorning the ocean. Comus, on the other hand, looks up from his wood to heavenly lights that, according to him, exist mainly to regulate affairs on earth: to tell the shepherd to pen his sheep, to regulate days and seasons, and to mark the end—too soon for Comus and his crew—of nocturnal rituals.

Milton establishes another contrast between the two when the Attendant Spirit chooses to change his "sky robes" for the clothes and appearance of a shepherd, just as Comus chooses to appear as a shepherd to the Lady. Onstage, the Attendant Spirit actually changes his appearance by changing clothes. Comus, however, remains the same and merely alters the Lady's perception of him by means of magic dust. Comus uses

33. Arthos, On "A Mask," p. 41, thus summarizes Comus: "What is certain is that he is an immortal magician, interested in the pleasure of the revels and in converting as many mortals to brutelike forms as he can, ambitious and a proselyte."

34. Fletcher, The Transcendental Masque, pp. 20–21, 167, also finds the masque's conflict to be between the Attendant Spirit and Comus, describing it as "the overthrow of one magician by another" (p. xiii). A. E. Dyson, Between Two Worlds: Aspects of Literary Form, p. 16, and Arthos, On "A Mask," p. 50, are among the many critics who find the masque's central opposition to be between Comus and the Lady.

deceptive illusion, while the Attendant Spirit "really" changes. The Spirit's adoption of a shepherd's role is legitimate metaphorically: he will be the good shepherd who guides his charges out of the dangerous wood; and, as Henry Lawes, he is literally guide and teacher to the Egerton children.

While Comus attempts to enthrall the Lady, the Attendant Spirit is occupied with her two brothers, who have separated from her. Though not endangered like their sister, they have made the mistake of wandering away from her. In the darkness, standing still and no longer wandering, they fruitlessly debate their sister's condition. Though the masque clearly emphasizes the Lady's temptation, the brothers are also important, for nothing positive can happen until the three are reunited. Thus, Comus's confrontation and deception of the Lady are balanced by the Attendant Spirit's encounter with and enlightenment of the brothers. While the Lady follows Comus, the brothers have remained immobile, debating. When, later, the Lady is immobilized, only her power of speech remaining, the brothers regain their direction and arrive to help. Milton's masque is almost perfectly balanced to this point.

The balance remains even after Comus has been driven away, for his enchantment persists. The Attendant Spirit can balance and counteract Comus himself, for the Attendant Spirit has his own magical power in the form of haemony. But Sabrina and her magical rituals are necessary to counteract the enchantment that binds the Lady even after Comus has fled.[35] Comus claims to be both a magician and a spokesman for nature—which he represents as sensual, fertile, even overproductive, unless humans fully indulge themselves in her products and thus take care of the surplus. The Attendant Spirit is an appropriate foil to Comus the magician, for he has haemony and his commission from Jove. But Sabrina, a water nymph and a true representative of nature, is necessary to correct Comus's distorted picture of nature. Her ability to break Comus's enchantment and her history of chastity prove the accuracy of the Lady's view of the natural world as providing sufficiency rather than superfluity:

35. See Fletcher, *The Transcendental Masque*, p. 167.

Nature's full blessing would be well dispens't
In unsuperfluous even proportion,
And she no whit encumber'd with her store. (Lines 772–74)

Milton carefully arranged the nonhuman characters in the masque to balance and contrast with one another as they test their powers against each other for the control of the children.

But the nonhuman characters do not wield all the power in the masque. The stances adopted by the children themselves are most crucial, for it is on the children that the attention of the nonhuman characters is focused and for them that the nonhumans practice their various forms of magic. Each child makes an initial, though not terribly serious, error. He then redeems that error by the wisdom of his next choice. The brothers err by abandoning their sister and becoming immersed in an endless debate on the power of chastity. Their sister's initial mistake is to allow herself to be deceived into following Comus. But the brothers choose to trust and take the advice of the Spirit (except when it comes to handling Comus's wand properly), while the Lady eventually perceives the true nature of her "shepherd" and resists his advice and temptation. The children are responsible for making wise choices within the masque. Though they need help—the brothers to find and successfully drive away Comus, the Lady to be released from immobility—they help themselves a good deal, too.

In some respects, the masque figures portray the situation of earthbound humanity hoping to make its way to "the starry threshold of *Jove's* Court." Man must do much for himself— hold to virtue, make wise choices, resist temptations—but he is incapable of being entirely self-sufficient and of reaching his goal without help. He requires some supernatural aid. For this reason, perhaps, Milton denied the possibility of neoplatonic magic in his masque. Ficino and Agrippa implied that man is able to raise himself to worlds beyond, that he may become powerful and virtuous enough to transcend earth through his own efforts. Daemons come from above to serve him when *he* calls *them*. In *Comus*, however, the heavens decide when humans need and deserve assistance. The Spirit's final lines, spoken while he rises back to heaven, affirm the essential mutuality of human ascent to the heavens:

Love virtue, she alone is free,
She can teach ye how to climb
Higher than the Sphery chime;
Or if Virtue feeble were,
Heav'n itself would stoop to her. (Lines 1019–23)

The balance and cooperation necessary to get the children through the dark wood safely image the mutuality necessary for human salvation. *Comus* contains no solely individual achievement. Even the Lady's strong resistance to Comus cannot prevent her body's immobilization. The Attendant Spirit cannot cure this part of Comus's charm by himself; he must enlist the aid of Sabrina.

In presenting its theme of human and supernatural cooperation, *Comus* utilizes many of the traditions associated with evil magicians in drama, though Milton slightly alters some in order to accommodate them to the masque form. First, of course, is the opposing magic of Comus on one side and the Attendant Spirit on the other.[36] Milton did not treat this opposition as a contest, as is usual in drama.[37] In plays such as *Friar Bacon* or *A Looking Glass for London*, opposing magicians or a magician and some godly power attempt to best one another by spectacular tricks. But Comus and the Attendant Spirit do not compete; in fact, Comus apparently never learns of the Attendant Spirit's presence. *Comus* resembles other masques in deemphasizing the contest. Milton did not throw good and evil magic together onstage. As in *The Temple of Love*, or Campion's masque for Carr and Frances Howard, evil magic is displayed and then displaced by powerful good. Though the Lady complicates the basic pattern by her need to choose between virtue and Comus's temptation, there is no agony in the choice for her. Comus's temptation never tempts her. From the first, no one can doubt her allegiance. She simply exemplifies the proper choice for rational and virtuous people. Thus, while *Comus* surely presents two

36. Ibid., p. 39, sees these opposed magics as the focus of the masque: "*Comus* . . . hinges upon a drama of conflicting magics, not, as is commonly said, upon a moral debate."

37. Nils Erik Enkvist, "The Functions of Magic in Milton's *Comus*," p. 312, argues, in contrast, that the use of magic "did not endanger dramatic conventions; in literature magic had often been associated with the academic disputation, the *débat*; and, since the works of a magician can be suddenly undone by more powerful magic, it provided the author with an admirable means of achieving a dramatic *dénouement*."

opposing magics, it portrays no dramatic contest. Good magic (here a combination of human virtue aided by a stooping heaven) overcomes evil without a battle, just as in earlier masques.

Another familiar aspect of Milton's portrayal of magic is his emphasis on magic as illusion. When Comus transforms himself into a shepherd, as was noted above, he does not actually change his shape; rather, he changes the Lady's perception of him. Similarly, a drink from his cup not only changes the drinker's physical appearance (his head becomes that of a beast) but also alters the drinker's perception of himself and the world around him:

> . . . they, so perfect is their misery,
> Not once perceive their foul disfigurement,
> But boast themselves more comely than before,
> And all their friends and native home forget,
> To roll with pleasure in a sensual sty. (Lines 73–77)

Comus adds to the punishment of his victim's deformation the illusion that all is well.

The limitations of Comus's magic are similar to those of the magic of many evil magicians in drama. The Lady's response to Comus's immobilization of her body echoes speeches from a number of magical dramas:

> Thou canst not touch the freedom of my mind
> With all thy charms, although this corporal rind
> Thou has immanacl'd, while Heav'n sees good. (Lines 663–65)

The same limitation characterizes magic in such diverse earlier plays as *The Wars of Cyrus*, *John of Bordeaux*, and *Two Noble Ladies*. It is also true of the magic in other masques—such as Aurelian Townshend's *Tempe Restored*, in which the Fugitive Favorite who has escaped from Circe explains:

> 'Tis not her Rod, her Philters, nor her Herbes,
> (Though strong in Magicke) that can bound mens
>   minds,
> And make them Prisoners, where there is no wall.
> It is consent that makes a perfect slave.[38]

Milton gave life to the conventional statement about magic having power over the body but not the soul by making it

38. *Tempe Restored*, p. 5.

literal onstage. The Lady's body is immobilized (for magic has power over the senses), but her mind remains free to counter Comus's persuasions.

Much of Comus's magic simply makes literal and explicit conventional metaphors. Just as he shows magic controlling the body but not the mind, he makes beasts of men who have themselves wrought their bestial transformation, for, by drinking from his cup and displaying their intemperance, they have shown themselves sensually inclined and animalistic. Milton used the technique of literalizing an abstract idea on-stage throughout his masque. The characters in *Comus* ex-emplify the various gradations of the platonic ladder: the At-tendant Spirit has completed the spiritual ascent, while Comus's herd, at the other extreme, has sunk below the level of human beings into brutish degradation. In some senses, Comus is one of the most limited magicians we have exam-ined, for his magic brings about few changes; it merely makes visible the inner state of his victims. At the very most he can affect one's body, but never one's unwilling mind.

Readers have long been reluctant to condemn Comus to-tally. Their response may be caused in part by the limited range of his magic (no one joins his herd who is not willing) and in part because of the general atmosphere of ambiguity that characterizes Milton's masque. Few clear norms or mea-sures inhabit the world of *Comus*. Most masques very clearly separate good from evil by their structures: the main masque is often almost entirely separate from the one or more anti-masques. A similar distinction between good and evil is often effected by staging; in *The Temple of Love*, for example, the magicians enter from a dark cave, while Indamora and her ladies sail grandly onstage in ships. Costuming and physical features also help to make distinctions: deformed magicians or witches dressed in outlandish costumes are often con-trasted with the regal, gorgeously dressed main masquers. In *Comus*, many of these easy distinctions are absent. Comus interacts with the Lady, a chief figure in the main masque, and he alters her vision so that she sees him as a simple shep-herd (though his beast-headed herd remains to give her some true information about his nature). All characters share the dark woods as their main locale. The audience recognizes the Attendant Spirit as a good character, for it has seen him de-scend from heaven, and it understands Comus to be bad, for it has heard the Attendant Spirit's description of him and seen the revel of his crew. But the dichotomy between good and evil is less clearly visible than in most masques, and the characters within the masque, the children, find no visible distinctions. This ambiguity in the masque serves to emphasize the difficulty of recognizing evil in this "dim" world and makes the children's final emergence from the wood a real triumph. In Milton's masque, evil may be chased away, but it does not dissolve or change as in some other masques. Comus lives on to tempt future wanderers in his wood.

The image patterns of the masque add to its ambiguity. It is not possible confidently to assign values to the various images prominent in the world of the masque. Most prominent of all is its imagery of light and dark. Each character except Sabrina uses star, moon, or sun imagery when speaking, but the image assumes different values according to the speaker. Both the Attendant Spirit and Comus, for example, compare themselves to stars. The brothers and their sister wish for stars to guide them. Comus uses a star to mark the beginning of his revels. Light at night is thus connected with both good and evil. If the coming of night is responsible for the children's troubles and if Comus romps only at night, then perhaps the sun is the positive light image of the masque.[39] The Lady speaks, after all, of "the Sun-clad power of Chastity" (line 782). But Comus's mother, Circe, is "the daughter of the Sun" (line 51), and it is "to quench the drought of *Phoebus*" (line 66) that Comus persuades his victims to drink from his cup. The sun is no more dependably positive than were the moon and stars.

Light imagery also occurs when the brothers, completely lost in the darkness, beg for the light of human hospitality:

> . . . some gentle taper,
> Though a rush Candle from the wicker hole
> Of some clay habitation, visit us
> With thy long levell'd rule of streaming light,
> And thou shalt be our star of *Arcady*,
> Or *Tyrian* Cynosure. (Lines 337–42)

But a lighted dwelling is not necessarily a safe place either. In the next scene, the Lady has found a habitation, Comus's pal-

39. Arthos, *On "A Mask,"* p. 29, seems to suggest this positive value to light: "The poem expresses in many ways the idea that evil flourishes in the dark, and that the light of reason guides a virtuous life."

ace. This scene is more brightly lighted than any other in the
masque, except perhaps the reunion scene at the masque's
end. In the palace, she is tempted with a drink "that flames
and dances in his crystal bounds" (line 673).

The masque thus presents no consistent way to interpret
light. The Elder brother suggests:

> He that has light within his own clear breast
> May sit i'th'center, and enjoy bright day,
> But he that hides a dark soul and foul thoughts
> Benighted walks under the midday Sun;
> Himself is his own dungeon. (Lines 381–84)

Interior light, virtue, is the only light that can safely be relied
upon in this "dim spot."

Other images—jewels, liquors, nature itself—have similarly ambivalent connotations within the masque. Comus's
ability to create "blear illusion" (line 155) casts doubt and
ambiguity over the poem's whole landscape. Nothing but
one's own integrity is certain on the "pinfold earth." Unlike
the black-and-white world created in most other masques,
where good and evil contrast starkly, Comus's world is best
described as "dim." Only the Attendant Spirit can claim to
have attained a world "Where day never shuts his eye" (line
978), and that is a world beyond the range of Milton's masque.

In *Comus*, as in many other plays and masques, the association of magic and illusion helps to define the world in
which the action takes place. Occasionally, as in *The Tempest*, magic's illusion is positive and it helps to teach characters important lessons. Sometimes magic itself is an illusion,
deceiving those who hoped to use it, as it deceives Mere-Foole
and Faustus. More frequently, however, magical illusion results in ambiguity, making distinctions and judgments difficult to arrive at, as in *Friar Bacon* or in *Comus*. Whatever its
use, the illusionistic nature of magic remains important for
magic's treatment in both drama and masque.

Though masque magicians resemble medieval romance
magicians far more than they do Faustus or Prospero, themes
and situations developed by the popular stage's portrayal of
magicians were available to masque writers who chose to use
them. Indeed, masque writers could employ ideas traditionally associated with magic—such as its illusionistic nature—
in a perfunctory and undeveloped way because popular drama

had so thoroughly explored them. The magical contest in drama, for example, where good always triumphs over evil magic, prepares for our acceptance of the masque version, where good triumphs over evil by fiat, with no contest. Popular drama also prepares us to understand that magic has power over the body but not over the mind and spirit, and that magic is associated with spectacle and often with artistic creativity. The availability of these associations suggests one reason masque magicians carry allegorical significance, in marked contrast to their counterparts in medieval romance—counterparts whom they otherwise much resemble.

In a period when belief in philosophical magic was waning and almost gone, magic found its strongest use as extended metaphor. No longer was belief sufficient to sustain a realistic dramatic contest between good and evil magic or to allow magic to accomplish wonders or to damn a man forever. But enough intellectual understanding of the respect and power previously accorded magic remained so that it could be used figuratively or allegorically.[40] To compliment a monarch's power, one might show him overcoming magicians, and a Lady's chastity was praised as she successfully resisted the evil magic of Comus.

When the theaters closed, and as rationalism and skepticism came to dominate the minds of English intellectuals, magic lost most of its power as metaphor as well. Its associations with neoplatonism and historical philosophers nearly forgotten, magic was limited in the Restoration theater almost solely to opera, as in Dryden's *King Arthur*, in which it provided fantastic ornamentation and little else. Whatever intellectual respectability magic had ever acquired waned early in the seventeenth century. Late in that century, Dryden could speak of its serious use only with amazement and condescension:

> . . . nor would you now,
> That liberty to vulgar Wits allow,
> Which works by Magick supernatural things.[41]

40. Enkvist, "The Functions of Magic," p. 317, claims of *Comus*: "The great skill with which the magic of *Comus* is integrated with the many other elements and rivets them seamlessly together suggests that to Milton, at the time of the composition and revision, magic was an intellectual rather than emotional issue."

41. "Prologue to the Tempest or the Enchanted Island," in *After "The Tempest,"* sig. A4ʳ, lines 21–23.

Yet in his brief hour upon the stage, the magician displayed a surprising versatility. In addition to such largely mechanical achievements as providing variety and spectacle in the dramas he inhabited, he was often an exemplum: a man who arrogated too much power to himself; a man who blindly believed in what proved to be illusion; a man who set himself against God and the right; a creator or an artist. In his finest and most complex moments, the magician was a dignified alternative to the "great amphibian" as an emblem of mankind. Caught between two worlds, he was gifted with great power and at the same time limited by his humanity.

In many ways the magician figure comes full circle, from the nonhuman freakish characters of medieval narrative romances to the nonhuman freakish figures of masque. But in the process he plays a central role in some of the Renaissance theater's most sensitive explorations of the nature of man and of his place in a world he comes painfully near to controlling.

Bibliography

Primary Sources

After "The Tempest." Introduction by George Robert Guffey. Augustan Reprint Society. Special Series, no. 4. Los Angeles: William Andrews Clark Memorial Library, 1969.

Agrippa, Henry Cornelius. *De occulta philosophia libri tres.* Cologne, 1533.

————. *Of the Vanitie and Vncertaintie of Artes and Sciences.* Translated by Ja[mes] Sa[nford]. London, 1569.

The Apocryphal New Testament. Translated by Montague Rhodes James. Oxford: Oxford University Press, 1926.

Aquinas, Thomas. *Quaestiones quodlibetales.* Edited by P. Fr. Raymundi Spiazzi. Rome: Marietti, 1956.

Ariosto, Ludovico. *Orlando Furioso.* Translated by William Stewart Rose. Edited by Stewart A. Baker and A. Bartlett Giamatti. Indianapolis: Bobbs-Merrill, 1968.

Of Arthour and of Merlin. Edited by O. D. Macrae-Gibson. 2 vols. Early English Text Society, no. 268. London: Oxford University Press, 1973.

Augustine. *The City of God.* Translated by Marcus Dods. New York: Modern Library, 1950.

Bacon, Roger. "Epistola Fratris Rogerii Baconis de secretis operibus artis et naturae et de nullitate magiae." In *Opera quaedam hactenus inedita,* edited by J. S. Brewer, pp. 523–45. London: Longman Green, 1859.

Barnes, Barnabe. *The Devil's Charter: A Tragedie Containing the Life and Death of Pope Alexander the Sixt.* Edited by R. B. McKerrow. 1904; rpt. Vaduz: Kraus Reprint, 1963.

A Book of Masques in Honour of Allardyce Nicoll. Edited by T. J. B. Spencer. Cambridge: Cambridge University Press, 1967.

Bruno, Giordano. *Giordano Bruno: His Life and Thought.* Edited and translated by Dorothea Waley Singer. New York: Abelard-Schulman, 1950.

Campion, Thomas. *The Works of Thomas Campion.* Edited by Walter B. Davis. New York: W. W. Norton, 1970.

Casaubon, Meric. *A True and Faithful Relation of What Passed Between Dr. John Dee and Some Spirits.* London, 1659.

Chapman, George. *Bussy D'Ambois*. Edited by Nicholas Brooke. The Revels Plays. Cambridge: Harvard University Press, 1964.

———. *Bussy D'Ambois*. Edited by Robert J. Lordi. Regents Renaissance Drama Series. Lincoln: University of Nebraska Press, 1964.

———. *The Plays and Poems of George Chapman*. Edited by T. M. Parrott. 2 vols. 1910–1914; rpt. New York: Russell and Russell, 1961.

———. *The Poems of George Chapman*. Edited by Phyllis B. Bartlett. New York: Modern Language Association, 1941.

Chaucer, Geoffrey. *Works*. Edited by F. N. Robinson, 2d ed. Boston: Houghton Mifflin, 1957.

Clyomon and Clamydes. Edited by Betty J. Littleton. The Hague: Mouton, 1968.

D'Avenant, William. *The Dramatic Works of Sir William D'Avenant*. Edited by James Maidment and W. H. Logan. 5 vols. 1872; rpt. New York: Russell and Russell, 1964.

Dee, John. *General and Rare Memorials Pertayning to the Perfecte Arte of Navigation*. London, 1577.

———. *A Letter, Containing a Most Brief Discourse Apologeticall*. London, 1599.

———. "Mathematicall Preface." In *The Elements of Geometrie of the most auncient Philosopher Evclide of Megara*, translated by Sir Henry Billingsley. London, 1570.

———. *The Private Diary of Dr. John Dee and the Catalogue of His Library of Manuscripts*. Edited by James Orchard Halliwell. 1842; rpt. New York: Johnson Reprint, 1968.

Early English Prose Romances. Edited by William J. Thoms. 3 vols. 1858; rpt. New York: AMS Press, 1970.

Eschenbach, Wolfram von. *Parzival*. Translated by Helen M. Mustard and Charles E. Passage. New York: Vintage, 1961.

Gascoigne, George. *The Complete Works of George Gascoigne*. 2 vols. Cambridge: Cambridge University Press, 1907.

Gawain and the Green Knight. Edited by J. R. R. Tolkien and E. V. Gordon. Oxford: Clarendon Press, 1930.

Geoffrey of Monmouth. *Vita Merlini*. Edited by Basil Clarke. Cardiff: University of Wales Press, 1973.

Greene, Robert. *Friar Bacon and Friar Bungay*. Edited by J. A. Lavin. The New Mermaids. London: Ernest Benn, 1969.

———. *Friar Bacon and Friar Bungay*. Edited by Daniel Seltzer. Regents Renaissance Drama Series. Lincoln: University of Nebraska Press, 1963.

———. *The Plays and Poems of Robert Greene*. Edited by J. Churton Collins, 2 vols. Oxford: Clarendon Press, 1905.

John of Bordeaux or the Second Part of Friar Bacon. Malone Society Reprints. Oxford: Oxford University Press, 1935.

Jonson, Ben. *Ben Jonson*. Edited by C. H. Herford and Percy and Evelyn Simpson. 11 vols. Oxford: Clarendon Press, 1925–1952.

Lovelich, Henry. *Merlin: A Middle-English Metrical Version of a French Romance*. Edited by Ernst A. Kock. London: Truebner, 1904.

The Lumley Library: The Catalogue of 1609. Edited by Sears Jayne and Francis R. Johnson. London: The Trustees of The British Museum, 1956.

Malory, Thomas. *The Works of Sir Thomas Malory*. Edited by Eugène Vinaver. London: Oxford University Press, 1954.

Map, Walter. *De Nugis Curialium*. Translated by Montague R. James. Cymmrodorion Record Series. no. 60. London: n.p., 1923.

Marlowe, Christopher. *The Complete Plays*. Edited by Irving Ribner. New York: Odyssey, 1963.

———. *Doctor Faustus*. Edited by John D. Jump. The Revels Plays. Cambridge: Harvard University Press, 1962.

———. *Marlowe's "Doctor Faustus" 1604–1616: Parallel Texts*. Edited by W. W. Greg. Oxford: Clarendon Press, 1950.

Merlin or the Early History of King Arthur. Edited by Henry B. Wheatley. London: K. Paul, Trench, Truebner, 1899.

Milton, John. *Complete Poems and Major Prose*. Edited by Merritt Y. Hughes. New York: Odyssey, 1957.

The Mirror for Magistrates. Edited by Lily B. Campbell. New York: Barnes and Noble, 1960.

Munday, Anthony. *John a Kent and John a Cumber*. The Malone Society Reprints. Oxford: Oxford University Press, 1923.

Nashe, Thomas. *The Works of Thomas Nashe*. Edited by Ronald B. McKerrow. 5 vols. Oxford: Basil Blackwell, 1966.

Paracelsus: Selected Writings. Edited by Jolande Jacobi. Translated by Norman Guterman. Bollingen Series 28. New York: Pantheon, 1958.

Peele, George. *The Life and Works of George Peele*. Edited by Charles Tyler Prouty. 3 vols. New Haven: Yale University Press, 1952–1970.

Plato. *The Dialogue of Plato*. Translated by B. Jowett. 4th ed. 4 vols. Oxford: Oxford University Press, 1953.

Porta, Giambattista della. *Natural Magick in XX Bookes*. Anonymous translator. London: T. Young and S. Speed, 1658.

The Rare Triumphs of Love and Fortune. The Malone Society Reprints. Oxford: Oxford University Press, 1930.

Renaissance Philosophy I: The Italian Philosophers. Edited and translated by Arturo B. Fallico and Herman Shapiro. New York: Modern Library, 1967.

Scot, Reginald. *The Discoverie of Witchcraft*. 1584; rpt. Carbondale: Southern Illinois University Press, 1964.

Shakespeare, William. *The Riverside Shakespeare*. Edited by G. Blakemore Evans. Boston: Houghton Mifflin, 1974.

———. *The Tempest*. Edited by Frank Kermode. The Arden Shakespeare. 6th ed. Cambridge: Harvard University Press, 1958.

The Shakespeare Apocrypha. Edited by C. F. Tucker Brooke. 1908; rpt. Oxford: Oxford University Press, 1967.

Sidney, Philip. *A Defense of Poetry*. Edited by J. A. Van Dorsten. Oxford: Oxford University Press, 1966.

———. *Miscellaneous Prose of Sir Philip Sidney*. Edited by Katherine Duncan-Jones and Jan Van Dorsten. Oxford: Clarendon Press, 1973.

The Sources of the Faust Tradition from Simon Magus to Lessing.

Edited by Philip Mason Palmer and Robert Pattison More. 1952; rpt. New York: Haskell House, 1965.

Spenser, Edmund. *The Poetical Works*. Edited by J. C. Smith and Ernest de Selincourt. 1909; rpt. Oxford: Clarendon Press, 1964.

Tasso, Torquato. *Jerusalem Delivered*. Translated by Edward Fairfax. 1600; rpt. New York: Capricorn, n.d.

Townshend, Aurelian. *Tempe Restored*. London: A. M. for R. Allet and G. Bakek, 1631.

The Two Merry Milkmaids. Tudor Facsimile Texts. London, 1914.

The Two Noble Ladies and the Converted Conjurer. The Malone Society Reprints. Oxford: University Press, 1930.

The Wars of Cyrus. Edited by James Paul Brawner. Illinois Studies in Language and Literature 28, no. 3–4. Urbana: University of Illinois Press, 1942.

Webster, John. *The White Devil*. Edited by John Russell Brown. The Revels Plays. London: Methuen, 1966.

The Wisdom of Doctor Dodypoll. The Malone Society Reprints. Oxford: Oxford University Press, 1964.

Secondary Sources

Adams, J. C. "The Staging of *The Tempest*, III, iii." *Review of English Studies* 14 (1938):404–19.

Adams, Robert P. "Critical Myths and Chapman's Original Bussy D'Ambois." *Renaissance Drama* 9 (1966):141–61.

Akrigg, G. P. V. *Jacobean Pageant or the Court of King James*. 1962; rpt. New York: Atheneum, 1967.

Alpers, Paul J. *The Poetry of "The Faerie Queene."* Princeton: Princeton University Press, 1967.

The Analytic Spirit: Essays in the History of Science in Honor of Henry Guerlac. Edited by Harry Woolf. Ithaca: Cornell University Press, 1981.

Annals of English Drama 975–1700. Edited by Alfred Harbage; revised by Samuel Schoenbaum. Philadelphia: University of Pennsylvania Press, 1964.

Armstrong, John. *The Paradise Myth*. London: Oxford University Press, 1969.

Arthos, John. *On "A Mask Presented at Ludlow Castle."* University of Michigan Contributions in Modern Philology 20. Ann Arbor: University of Michigan Press, 1954.

Barkan, Leonard. *Nature's Work of Art: The Human Body as Image of the World*. New Haven: Yale University Press, 1975.

Battenhouse, Roy. "Chapman's *The Shadow of Night*: An Interpretation." *Studies in Philology* 38 (1941):584–608.

Bement, Peter. *George Chapman: Action and Contemplation in His Tragedies*. Salzburg Studies in English Literature: Jacobean Drama Studies 8. Salzburg: Institut für Englische Sprache, 1974.

———. "The Imagery of Darkness and of Light in Chapman's *Bussy D'Ambois*." *Studies in Philology* 64 (1967):187–98.

Berger, Harry, Jr. "Busirane and the War between the Sexes: An Interpretation of *The Faerie Queene*, III, xi–xii." *English Literary Renaissance* 1 (1971):99–121.

———. "The Structure of Merlin's Chronicle in *The Faerie Queene* III. iii." *Studies in English Literature* 9 (1969):39–51.

Berger, Karol. "Prospero's Art." *Shakespeare Studies* 10 (1977):211–39.

Bevington, David M. *From "Mankind" to Marlowe: Growth of Structure in the Popular Drama of Tudor England.* Cambridge: Harvard University Press, 1962.

Bhattacherje, Mohinimohan. *Platonic Ideas in Spenser.* London: Longmans, 1935.

Blackburn, William. "'Heavenly Words': Marlowe's Faustus as a Renaissance Magician." *English Studies in Canada* 4 (1978):1–14.

Boas, Marie. *The Scientific Renaissance 1450–1630.* New York: Harper Torchbooks, 1962.

Bradbrook, Muriel C. *The Growth and Structure of Elizabethan Comedy*, 1955; rpt. Baltimore: Penguin, 1963.

———. "Shakespeare's Primitive Art." *Proceedings of the British Academy* 51 (1965):215–34.

Brailow, David C. "Prospero's 'Old Brain': The Old Man as Metaphor in *The Tempest*." *Shakespeare Survey* 14 (1981):285–303.

Brown, Beatrice Daw. "Marlowe, Faustus, and Simon Magus." *PMLA* 54 (1939):82–121.

Brune, Lester H. "Magic's Relation to the Intellectual History of Western Civilization." *Journal of Thought* 18 (1983):55–63.

Bushnell, N. S. "Natural Supernaturalism in *The Tempest*." *PMLA* 47 (1932):684–98.

Calder, I. R. F. "John Dee Studied as an English Neoplatonist." Ph.D. Diss., University of London, 1952.

Campbell, Lily B. *Scenes and Machines on the English Stage during the Renaissance.* 1923; rpt. New York: Barnes and Noble, 1960.

Chambers, E. K. *Arthur of Britain.* New York: October House, 1967.

Cheney, Donald. *Spenser's Image of Nature: Wild Man and Shepherd in "The Faerie Queene."* New Haven: Yale University Press, 1966.

Christopher Marlowe. Edited by Brian Morris. Mermaid Critical Commentaries. London: Ernest Benn, 1968.

Christopher Marlowe's "Doctor Faustus": The Text and Major Criticism. Edited by Irving Ribner. New York: Odyssey, 1966.

Coursen, Herbert R., Jr. "Prospero and the Drama of the Soul." *Shakespeare Studies* 4 (1968):316–33.

Craig, Hardin. "Magic in *The Tempest*." *Philological Quarterly* 47 (1968):8–15.

Craik, T. W. "Faustus' Damnation Reconsidered." *Renaissance Drama*, n.s. 2 (1969):189–96.

Critical Studies of "Sir Gawain and the Green Knight." Edited by Donald Howard and Christian Zacher. Notre Dame: University of Notre Dame Press, 1968.

Comparetti, Domenico. *Vergil in the Middle Ages.* London: Swan Sonnenschein, 1895.

Curry, Walter Clyde. *Shakespeare's Philosophical Patterns*. Baton Rouge: Louisiana State University Press, 1959.

Cutts, John P. *Rich and Strange: A Study of Shakespeare's Last Plays*. Pullman: Washington State University Press, 1968.

Davidson, Clifford. "Doctor Faustus of Wittenberg." *Studies in Philology* 59 (1962):514–23.

Deacon, Richard. *John Dee*. London: Frederick Muller, 1968.

Debus, Allen G. *Man and Nature in the Renaissance*. Cambridge History of Science. Cambridge: Cambridge University Press, 1978.

Distler, Paul F. *Vergil and Vergiliana*. Chicago: Loyola University Press, 1966.

Dobrée, Bonamy. "The Tempest." *Essays & Studies* (1952):13–25.

Duthie, G. I. "Some Observations on Marlowe's *Doctor Faustus*." *Archiv* 203 (1966):81–96.

Dyson, A. E. *Between Two Worlds: Aspects of Literary Form*. London: Macmillan, 1972.

Eagleton, Terence. *Shakespeare and Society: Critical Studies in Shakespearian Drama*. New York: Schocken, 1967.

Ebner, Dean. "*The Tempest*: Rebellion and the Ideal State." *Shakespeare Quarterly* 16 (1965):161–73.

Egan, Robert. *Drama within Drama: Shakespeare's Sense of His Art*. New York: Columbia University Press, 1975.

Elizabethan Drama: Modern Essays in Criticism. Edited by Ralph J. Kaufmann. New York: Oxford University Press, 1961.

Elizabethan Poetry: Modern Essays in Criticism. Edited by Paul J. Alpers. New York: Oxford University Press, 1967.

Elizabethan Theatre. Edited by John Russell Brown and Bernard Harris. Stratford-upon-Avon Studies 9. London: Edward Arnold, 1966.

Ellrodt, Robert. *Neoplatonism in the Poetry of Spenser*. Geneva: Librairie E. Droz, 1960.

Empson, William. *Some Versions of Pastoral*. 1935; rpt. Norfolk, Conn.: New Directions, 1960.

English Stage Comedy. Edited by William K. Wimsatt. English Institute Essays. New York: Columbia University Press, 1955.

Enkvist, Nils Erik. "The Functions of Magic in Milton's *Comus*." *Neuphilologische Mitteilungen* 54 (1953):310–18.

Epstein, Harry. "The Divine Comedy of *The Tempest*." *Shakespeare Studies* 8 (1975):279–96.

Essays on Shakespeare and Elizabethan Drama in Honor of Hardin Craig. Edited by Richard Hosley. Columbia: University of Missouri Press, 1962.

Evans, Maurice. "Platonic Allegory in *The Faerie Queene*." *Review of English Studies*, n.s. 12 (1961):132–43.

———. *Spenser's Anatomy of Heroism: A Commentary on "The Faerie Queene."* Cambridge: Cambridge University Press, 1970.

Evans, R. J. W. *Rudolph II and His World: A Study in Intellectual History, 1576–1612*. Oxford: Clarendon Press, 1973.

Festugière, R. P. *La Révélation D'Hermès Trismégiste*. Paris: Librairie Lecoffre, 1950.

Fieberling, Evelyn Bess. "The Magician in Italian and English Renaissance Drama." Ph.D. Diss., Johns Hopkins University, 1975.

Fletcher, Angus. *The Transcendental Masque: An Essay on Milton's "Comus."* Ithaca: Cornell University Press, 1971.

French, A. L. "The Philosophy of *Dr. Faustus.*" *Essays in Criticism* 20 (1970):123–41.

French, Peter J. *John Dee: The World of an Elizabethan Magus.* London: Routledge and Kegan Paul, 1972.

Frye, Northrop. *A Natural Perspective: The Development of Shakespearian Comedy and Romance.* New York: Columbia University Press, 1965.

Garin, Eugenio. *Science and Civic Life in the Italian Renaissance.* Translated by Peter Munz. New York: Anchor, 1969.

Giamatti, A. Bartlett. "Marlowe: The Arts of Illusion." *Yale Review* 61 (1972):530–43.

Gilman, Ernest B. "'All Eyes': Prospero's Inverted Masque." *Renaissance Quarterly* 33 (1980):214–30.

———. *The Curious Perspective: Literary and Pictorial Wit in the Seventeenth Century.* New Haven: Yale University Press, 1978.

Greene, Thomas M. *The Descent from Heaven: A Study in Epic Continuity.* New Haven: Yale University Press, 1963.

Greg, W. W. *A Bibliography of the English Printed Drama to the Restoration.* 4 vols. Oxford: University Press, 1939–1959.

Habicht, Werner. *Studien zur Dramenform vor Shakespeare: Moralitat, Interlude, romaneskes Drama.* Heidelberg: Carl Winter, 1968.

Hamilton, A. C. "Sidney and Agrippa." *Review of English Studies,* n.s. 7 (1956):151–57.

Harris, Anthony. *Night's Black Agents: Witchcraft and Magic in Seventeenth-Century English Drama.* Totowa, N.J.: Rowman and Littlefield, 1980.

Hattaway, Michael. "The Theology of Marlowe's *Doctor Faustus.*" *Renaissance Drama,* n.s. 3 (1970):51–78.

Hoeniger, F. D. "Prospero's Storm and Miracle." *Shakespeare Quarterly* 7 (1956):33–38.

Homan, Sidney R. "Chapman and Marlowe: The Paradoxical Hero and the Divided Response." *Journal of English and Germanic Philology* 68 (1969):391–406.

Howarth, R. G. *Shakespeare's "Tempest."* N.p.: Australian English Association, 1936.

Howe, James Robinson. *Marlowe, Tamburlaine and Magic.* Athens: Ohio University Press, 1976.

Huizinga, J. *The Waning of the Middle Ages.* 1924; rpt. New York: Anchor, n.d.

Hunter, G. K. "Five-Act Structure in *Doctor Faustus.*" *Tulane Drama Review* 8 (1964):77–91.

Hunter, Robert Grams. *Shakespeare and the Comedy of Forgiveness.* New York: Columbia University Press, 1965.

Hyman, Stanley Edgar. *Iago: Some Approaches to the Illusion of His Motivation.* New York: Atheneum, 1970.

Ide, Richard S. *Possessed with Greatness: The Heroic Tragedies of*

Chapman and Shakespeare. Chapel Hill: University of North Carolina Press, 1980.

James, D. G. *The Dream of Prospero*. Oxford: Clarendon Press, 1967.

Jayne, Sears. "Ficino and the Platonism of the English Renaissance." *Comparative Literature* 4 (1952):214–38.

Johnson, F. R. *Astronomical Thought in Renaissance England: A Study of English Scientific Writings from 1500 to 1645*. Baltimore: Johns Hopkins University Press, 1937.

————. "Marlowe's Astronomy and Renaissance Scepticism." *ELH* 13 (1946):241–54.

Johnson, W. Stacy. "The Genesis of Ariel." *Shakespeare Quarterly* 2 (1951):205–10.

Kernan, Alvin B. *The Playwright as Magician: Shakespeare's Image of the Poet in the English Public Theater*. New Haven: Yale University Press, 1979.

Kirschbaum, Leo. "Comedy in Doctor Faustus." In *The Plays of Christopher Marlowe*, pp. 114–22. Cleveland: World, 1962.

————. *Two Lectures on Shakespeare*. London: Clover Press, 1961.

Kocher, Paul H. *Christopher Marlowe: A Study of His Thought, Learning, and Character*. Chapel Hill: University of North Carolina Press, 1946.

Later Shakespeare. Edited by John Russell Brown and Bernard Harris. Stratford-upon-Avon Studies 8. London: Edward Arnold, 1966.

Latham, Jacqueline E. M. "The Magic Banquet in *The Tempest*." *Shakespeare Studies* 12 (1979):215–27.

Le Comte, Edward. *The Notorious Lady Essex*. New York: Dial Press, 1969.

Leech, Clifford. *Shakespeare's Tragedies and Other Studies in Seventeenth Century Drama*. London: Chatto and Windus, 1950.

Lewis, C. S. *The Allegory of Love*. Oxford: Oxford University Press, 1938.

————. *English Literature in the Sixteenth Century, Excluding Drama*. Oxford History of English Literature. Oxford: Clarendon Press, 1954.

————. *Studies in Medieval and Renaissance Literature*. Cambridge: Cambridge University Press, 1966.

McAlindon, T. "Magic, Fate, and Providence in Medieval Narrative and *Sir Gawain and the Green Knight*." *Review of English Studies* 16 (1965):121–39.

McCallum, J. D. "Greene's *Friar Bacon and Friar Bungay*." *Modern Language Notes* 35 (1920):212–17.

McElwee, William. *The Murder of Sir Thomas Overbury*. London: Faber and Faber, 1952.

MacLure, Millar. *George Chapman: A Critical Study*. Toronto: University of Toronto Press, 1966.

McNeir, Waldo F. "Robert Greene and *John of Bordeaux*." *PMLA* 64 (1949):781–801.

————. "Traditional Elements in the Character of Greene's Friar Bacon." *Studies in Philology* 45 (1948):172–79.

Malory's Originality. Edited by R. M. Lumiansky. Baltimore: Johns Hopkins University Press, 1964.

Manley, Frank. "The Nature of Faustus." *Modern Philology* 66 (1969):218–23.

Marlowe's "Doctor Faustus": A Casebook. Edited by John D. Jump. London: Macmillan, 1969.

Marsh, D. R. C. *The Recurring Miracle: A Study of "Cymbeline" and the Last Plays.* Lincoln: University of Nebraska Press, 1962.

Mehl, Dieter. *The Elizabethan Dumb Show: The History of a Dramatic Convention.* Cambridge: Harvard University Press, 1966.

Milton: Modern Essays in Criticism. Edited by Arthur E. Barker. New York: Oxford University Press, 1965.

Mortensen, Peter. "*Friar Bacon and Friar Bungay*: Festive Comedy and 'Three-Form'd Luna.'" *English Literary Renaissance* 2 (1972):194–207.

Mowat, Barbara A. "Prospero, Agrippa, and Hocus Pocus." *English Literary Renaissance* 11 (1981):281–303.

Nauert, Charles G. *Agrippa and the Crisis of Renaissance Thought.* Illinois Studies in the Social Sciences, no. 55. Urbana: University of Illinois Press, 1965.

Orange, Linwood E. "*Bussy D'Ambois*: The Web of Pretense." *Southern Quarterly* 8 (1969):37–56.

Orgel, Stephen. *The Jonsonian Masque.* Cambridge: Harvard University Press, 1965.

———. "The Poetics of Spectacle." *New Literary History* 2 (1971):367–89.

Ornstein, Robert. "Marlowe and God: The Tragic Theology of *Doctor Faustus*." *PMLA* 83 (1968):1378–85.

Panofsky, Erwin. *The Life and Art of Albrecht Dürer.* Princeton: Princeton University Press, 1955.

Parker, M. Pauline. *The Allegory of "The Faerie Queene."* Oxford: Clarendon Press, 1960.

Pearson, D'Orsay W. "*The Tempest* in Perspective." *Shakespeare Studies* 7 (1974):253–82.

Perkinson, Richard H. "Nature and the Tragic Hero in Chapman's Bussy Plays." *Modern Language Quarterly* 3 (1942):263–85.

Rabkin, Norman. *Shakespeare and the Common Understanding.* New York: Free Press, 1967.

Randall, Dale B. J. "Was the Green Knight a Fiend?" *Studies in Philology* 57 (1960):479–91.

Reed, Robert R., Jr. *The Occult on the Tudor and Stuart Stage.* Boston: Christopher, 1965.

Reinterpretations of Elizabethan Drama: Selected Papers from the English Institute. Edited by Norman Rabkin. New York: Columbia University Press, 1969.

Ribner, Irving. *Jacobean Tragedy: The Quest for Moral Order.* New York: Barnes and Noble, 1962.

Rice, Eugene. *The Renaissance Idea of Wisdom.* Cambridge: Harvard University Press, 1958.

Robinson, James E. "Time and *The Tempest*." *Journal of English and Germanic Philology* 63 (1964):255–67.

Roche, Thomas P., Jr. *The Kindly Flame.* Princeton: Princeton University Press, 1964.

Rossi, Paolo. *Francis Bacon: From Magic to Science.* Translated by Sacha Rabinovitch. Chicago: University of Chicago Press, 1968.

Rudwin, Maxmilian. *The Devil in Legend and Literature.* 1931; rpt. New York: AMS Press, 1970.

Ryken, Leland. "The Temptation Theme in *The Tempest* and the Question of Dramatic Suspense." *Tennessee Studies in Literature* 14 (1969):119–27.

Saccio, Peter. *The Court Comedies of John Lyly: A Study in Dramaturgical Allegory.* Princeton: Princeton University Press, 1969.

Sachs, Arieh. "The Religious Despair of Doctor Faustus." *Journal of English and Germanic Philology* 63 (1964):625–47.

Salingar, L. G. "Time and Art in Shakespeare's Romances." *Renaissance Drama* 9 (1966):3–35.

Samuel, Irene. *Plato and Milton.* 1947; rpt. Ithaca: Cornell University Press, 1969.

Sanders, Wilbur. *The Dramatist and the Received Idea: Studies in the Plays of Marlowe and Shakespeare.* Cambridge: Cambridge University Press, 1968.

Schrickx, W. *Shakespeare's Early Contemporaries: The Background of the Harvey-Nashe Polemic and "Love's Labour's Lost."* Antwerp: De Nederlandsche Boekhandel, 1956.

Science, Medicine and Society in the Renaissance: Essays to Honor Walter Pagel. Edited by Allen G. Debus. 2 vols. New York: Neale Watson Academic Publications, 1972.

Senn, Werner. "Robert Greene's Handling of Source Material in *Friar Bacon and Friar Bungay.*" *English Studies* 54 (1973):544–53.

Sensabaugh, G. F. "The Milieu of Comus." *Studies in Philology* 41 (1944):238–49.

Shapiro, I. A. "Shakespeare and Munday." *Shakespeare Survey* 14 (1961):25–33.

Shaw, Catherine M. *"Some Vanity of Mine Art": The Masque in Renaissance Drama.* Salzburg Studies in English Literature, Jacobean Drama Studies 81. 2 vols. Salzburg: Institut für Anglistik und Amerikanistik, 1979.

A Short-Title Catalogue of Books Printed in England, Scotland, & Ireland and of English Books Printed Abroad 1475–1640. Edited by A. W. Pollard and G. R. Redgrave. London: Bibliographical Society, 1926.

Shumaker, Wayne. *The Occult Sciences in the Renaissance: A Study in Intellectual Patterns.* Berkeley: University of California Press, 1972.

Sir Gawain and Pearl: Critical Essays. Edited by Robert J. Blanch. Bloomington: Indiana University Press, 1966.

Sisson, C. J. "The Magic of Prospero." *Shakespeare Survey* 11 (1959):70–77.

Snyder, Susan. "Marlowe's *Doctor Faustus* as an Inverted Saint's Life." *Studies in Philology* 63 (1966):565–77.

Steane, J. B. *Marlowe: A Critical Study.* Cambridge: Cambridge University Press, 1970.

Steele, Mary. *Plays and Masques at Court during the Reigns of Elizabeth, James and Charles.* New Haven: Yale University Press, 1926.

Sutherland, James. *A Preface to Eighteenth Century Poetry.* 1948; rpt. London: Oxford University Press, 1963.

Tait, Hugh. "The Devil's Looking-Glass: The Magical Speculum of Dr. John Dee." In *Horace Walpole: Writer, Politician, Connoisseur,* pp. 195–212. New Haven: Yale University Press, 1967.

Tetzeli von Rosador, Kurt. *Magie im elisabethanischen Drama.* Braunschweig: Georg Westermann, 1970.

Thomas, Keith. *Religion and the Decline of Magic: Studies in Popular Beliefs in Sixteenth and Seventeenth Century England.* London: Weidenfeld and Nicolson, 1971.

Thorndike, Lynn. *A History of Magic and Experimental Science.* 8 vols. New York: Macmillan, 1929–1934.

Towne, Frank. "White Magic in *Friar Bacon and Friar Bungay?*" *Modern Language Notes* 67 (1952):9–13.

Traversi, Derek. *Shakespeare: The Last Phase.* Stanford: Stanford University Press, 1965.

Tricomi, Albert H. "The Problem of Authorship in the Revised *Bussy D'Ambois.*" *English Language Notes* 17 (1979):22–29.

——. "The Revised Version of Chapman's *Bussy D'Ambois*: A Shift in Point of View." *Studies in Philology* 70 (1973):288–305.

Tuve, Rosemond. *Allegorical Imagery: Some Medieval Books and Their Posterity.* Princeton: Princeton University Press, 1966.

——. *Images and Themes in Five Poems by Milton.* Cambridge: Harvard University Press, 1957.

Twentieth Century Interpretation of "Doctor Faustus." Edited by Willard Farnham. Englewood Cliffs: Prentice Hall, 1969.

Waddington, Raymond B. *The Mind's Empire: Myth and Form in George Chapman's Poems.* Baltimore: Johns Hopkins University Press, 1974.

——. "Prometheus and Hercules: The Dialectic of *Bussy D'Ambois.*" *ELH* 34 (1967):21–48.

Waith, Eugene M. *The Herculean Hero in Marlowe, Chapman, Shakespeare and Dryden.* New York: Columbia University Press, 1962.

——. *Ideas of Greatness: Heroic Drama in England.* London: Routledge and Kegan Paul, 1971.

Walker, D. P. *Spiritual and Demonic Magic from Ficino to Campanella.* London: Warburg Institute, 1958.

Weiss, Roberto. *The Spread of Italian Humanism.* London: Hutchinson University Library, 1964.

Welsford, Enid. *The Court Masque: A Study in the Relationship between Poetry and the Revels.* 1927; rpt. New York: Russell and Russell, 1962.

Wertheim, Albert. "The Presentation of Sin in 'Friar Bacon and Friar Bungay,'" *Criticism* 16 (1974):273–86.

West, Robert H. "The Impatient Magic of *Doctor Faustus.*" *English Literary Renaissance* 4 (1974):218–40.

———. *The Invisible World: A Study of Pneumatology in Elizabethan Drama.* 1939; rpt. New York: Octagon, 1969.

———. *Shakespeare and the Outer Mystery.* Lexington: University of Kentucky Press, 1968.

———. "White Magic in *Friar Bacon.*" *Modern Language Notes* 67 (1952):499–500.

Westlund, Joseph. "The Orthodox Christian Framework of Marlowe's *Faustus.*" *Studies in English Literature* 3 (1963):191–205.

Williams, Kathleen. *Spenser's World of Glass: A Reading of "The Faerie Queene."* Berkeley: University of California Press, 1966.

Williams, Mary C. "Merlin and the Prince: *The Speeches at Prince Henry's Barriers.*" *Renaissance Drama*, n.s. 8 (1977):221–30.

Willson, David Harris. *King James VI and I.* 1956; rpt. London: Oxford University Press, 1967.

Wilson, F. P. *Marlowe and the Early Shakespeare.* The Clark Lectures, 1951. Oxford: Clarendon Press, 1953.

Wind, Edgar. *Pagan Mysteries in the Renaissance.* New Haven: Yale University Press, 1958.

Woodman, David. *White Magic and English Renaissance Drama.* Rutherford, N.J.: Fairleigh Dickinson University Press, 1973.

Wright, Louis. "Juggling Tricks and Conjury on the Stage before 1642." *Modern Philology* 24 (1927):269–84.

Yates, Frances A. *Giordano Bruno and the Hermetic Tradition.* London: Routledge and Kegan Paul, 1964.

———. *Theatre of the World.* Chicago: University of Chicago Press, 1969.

Zimansky, Curt A. "Marlowe's *Faustus*: The Date Again." *Philological Quarterly* 41 (1962):181–87.

Zimbardo, Rose Abdelnour. "Form and Disorder in *The Tempest.*" *Shakespeare Quarterly* 14 (1963):49–56.

Index

In Shakespeare Bib.